AMERICAN
IMPERIALISM AND
THE PHILIPPINE INSURRECTION

TESTIMONY OF THE TIMES:
SELECTIONS FROM CONGRESSIONAL HEARINGS

John A. Garraty, General Editor

AMERICAN IMPERIALISM AND THE PHILIPPINE INSURRECTION

Testimony taken from Hearings on Affairs in the Philippine Islands before the Senate Committee on the Philippines — 1902

Edited by
HENRY F. GRAFF
Columbia University

 LITTLE, BROWN AND COMPANY   *Boston*

Contents

v

INTRODUCTION

Imperialism — the raising of the flag on distant lands to signify dominion over them and their colored inhabitants — was a salient feature of international politics at the turn from the 1890's into the twentieth century. For white people living in Europe and America, the *fin de siècle* was a time of smug satisfaction that "civilization" was under their special stewardship, a condition that gave them license to acquire colonies as well as to brandish the sword. Modern technology, particularly military technology with an increasing power to devastate, was a notable instrument of the "Western" peoples in their self-assumed mission. The map of the world reflected their spectacular exploits. The color red usually denoted the British Empire, violet the empire of France, and beige Imperial Germany. For the United States, however, no color was firmly established — in part because its possessions were so few, and in part, no doubt, because its career in imperialism was begun so late that the choicest colors had already been assigned. Nevertheless, when the United States acquired the Philippine Islands by the treaty ending the Spanish-American War, Americans as a whole were pleased to find themselves among the leaders in the scramble for prestige among nations.

In the mid-1890's when the United States was exuberantly beginning to join the race for colonies, Senator Henry Cabot Lodge of Massachusetts, declared, in a sentence now famous: "As one of the great nations of the world, the United States must not fall out of the line of march." The martial beat of the jingos that can be heard in those words was the dominant sound in the rhetoric of imperialism. Albert J. Beveridge, the most expressive voice of expansionism in the Senate, delivered in 1900 a flaming address he called "The March of the Flag." To a degree that is practically inexplicable today, Beveridge captivated his audience with his unyielding tone and manner:

We will not renounce our part in the mission of our race, trustees under God, of the civilization of the world. And we will move forward to our work, not howling out regrets like slaves whipped to their burdens, but with gratitude for a task worthy of our strength and thanksgiving to Almighty God that He has marked us as his chosen people, henceforth to lead in the regeneration of the world.

When Beveridge uttered these peremptory words, he had just returned from a trip to the Philippine Islands where he had found "every foot of the way a revelation of vegetable and mineral riches." The United States, he declared, must remain steadfast in its determination to fasten

America's will on the recalcitrant Filipinos: "It is barely possible that a thousand men in all the archipelago are capable of self-government in the Anglo-Saxon sense. My own belief is that there are not a hundred men among them who comprehend what Anglo-Saxon self-government even means, and there are over five million people to be governed." Like other imperialists Beveridge heard also the insistent call to undertake the task of educating the Filipinos in the arcane art of self-government and, in the phrases of President McKinley, "to . . . uplift and civilize and Christianize them . . . as our fellow men for whom Christ also died."

The Filipinos were never able to feel as benighted as they were deemed by the Americans to be and, skillfully led, they battled fiercely against those they regarded as their new tormentors, the imperial Americans. How the United States had come to be imperialist is an often-told tale, but in the perspective of almost three-quarters of a century the process appears starker and more preceptive than ever. A generation ago interest centered on a war against Spain that was quick and full of the hoopla of the fighting itself. Now attention is focused on the cruel war against the Filipinos that it involved as well as on the breach in American isolation it brought.

* * * *

The Spanish-American War was the product, like many other wars, of accident and miscalculation. It began as a manifestation of American humanitarianism expressing itself in sympathy for the Cuban "insurrectos," who were eagerly seeking home-rule and social betterment from their Spanish rulers. Yet basic to the American war spirit was a deep desire to show off the national strength by flexing the muscle that modern armaments represented. The navy, long in the doldrums, had emerged in the 1880's as the freshest proof of the country's industrial might.

The new navy boasted an articulate theoreticist, whose views were all the more persuasive because he was a navy man himself. He was Captain Alfred Thayer Mahan, whose life-span, 1840 to 1914, embraced the very years of America's rise to world power. A close student of the influence of sea power upon history, he wrote extensively on the subject and its corollaries. A whole generation of thinking Americans who were also influential, including John Hay, Theodore Roosevelt, and Henry Adams, read Mahan and made him their oracle. In 1902 he was president of the American Historical Association, an honor no other man in uniform has received. Mahan's dominating idea was contained in these words of his:

The due use and control of the sea is but one link in the chain of exchange by which wealth accumulates; but it is the central link, which lays under contributions other nations for the benefit of the one holding it, and which history seems to assert, most surely of all gathers itself riches.

Mahan's argument seemed especially telling to a generation no longer "developing" its unused land. The United States, Mahan declared, was already pressing upon its natural frontiers:

. . . arrested on the South by the rights of a race wholly alien to us, and on the north by a body of states of like traditions to our men, whose freedom to choose their own affiliation we respect, we have come to the sea. In our infancy we bordered upon the Atlantic only, our youth carried our boundary to the Gulf of Mexico. Today maturity sees us upon the Pacific. Have we no right or no call to progress in any direction?

The answer was supplied by the success of American arms.

*   *   *   *

The arrival of the United States naval vessels in Philippine waters in 1898 was a signal event in United States history. And the swiftness and completeness of the ensuing victory over the Spanish navy — begun with the nation's best remembered command: "You may fire when you are ready, Gridley" — made that Fourth of July the most stirring since the first one. For Filipinos it had a different significance, because, unnoticed by most Americans, they also had aspirations. Thoroughly anti-Spanish, they viewed the outbreak of hostilities as a unique opportunity to overthrow their conquerors at last and enter the new century a free and independent nation. Nor were the Filipinos only pipe-dreaming: most Americans had never heard of the Philippine Islands and, therefore, surely did not covet them. Furthermore, the few Filipinos who were aware of events in the Caribbean knew that the United States had already pledged independence to Cuba; could the Philippines reasonably expect less?

Yet from the very start of the fighting against Spain American military and political leaders showed a stubborn unwillingness to say "yes" unequivocally to the plea of Filipino spokesmen for a promise of independence, and some of the potent shapers of opinion were calling for the annexation of the islands. *The New York Times*, for instance, insisted in an editorial on May 4 that under no circumstances could the United States take the islands. But only a few days later the same newspaper was speaking of "that paramount necessity," which forces America to take on "for a time" the task of owning and controlling them.

The American voice in the Pacific waters in the heady spring days of 1898 was Commodore George Dewey, only recently placed in command of the United States naval squadron in Asian waters. He had mobilized his vessels at the "neutral" port of Hong Kong and was under orders from the Navy Department to proceed to the Philippines in the event of war with Spain. Possibly he shared the pessimistic view of British naval officers at the Hong Kong Club that he would meet destruction. Dewey himself later said that among these navy men the common remark about the departing Americans was to the effect: "A fine set of fellows, but unhappily we shall never see them again." Under the mental pressure of such disagreeable prospects, it is not surprising that Dewey seems to have pondered the postwar future only cursorily, if at all. Patently he did not seem to measure accurately the strength and character of the Filipino insurgent leader, Emilio Aguinaldo.

Aguinaldo, who had been born on Cavite in 1869, was a self-educated man. Fired by the widespread patriotic fervor among his people in the 1890's, he had joined the anti-Spanish revolutionary group, the *Katipunan*, whose members, when caught by the Spanish authorities, could expect either the garrote or the firing squad. Aguinaldo became the head of the *Katipunan* in his home province and he and his followers soon discovered what modern insurgents invariably have learned — in his own words, "We were more ready spiritually than technologically." Furthermore he wrote: "Our men lacked training and experience. Our organization being secret, we could not put them through the usual military drills and manoeuvres. Most of them were unshoed and, for weapons, had only daggers and bolos."

Still the *Katipunan* gained in numbers despite their handicaps, and conducted increasingly daring forays against Spanish rule from their headquarters in the mountains of San Miguel north of Manila. To end the harassment, the Spanish authorities decided to make a deal. In delicate and hardheaded negotiations they "bought off" the *Katipunan* with 800,000 pesos and a promise to liberalize the Spanish control of the islands. The rebel leaders took the first installment of the money and went to Hong Kong, which by historical fortuity was about to witness the first stage of Dewey's adventure.

Aguinaldo and his cohorts were amazed by the arrival from Nagasaki of the American fleet. They seized the opportunity that presented itself when some of the Americans recognized the potential usefulness of the *Katipunan* leaders. Aguinaldo afterward said that the captain of the U.S. man-of-war "Petrel," Commander E. P. Wood, sought him out in the name of Dewey and held a series of secret conferences with him in March and April of 1898. The purport of the conversations was to urge the *Katipunan* leaders to return to the Philippines in order to mobilize their forces and commence all-out military operations against the Spanish, aimed at liberating the islands.

Aguinaldo, now no longer a novice in dealing with western military people, asked the central question of the day: What did the United States intend to do with the Philippines once the Spanish enemy had been defeated and driven from them? Wood responded, so Aguinaldo would recall: "The United States, my general, is a great and rich nation and neither needs nor desires colonies." Pleased beyond measure, Aguinaldo suggested that possibly this self-denying sentiment could be put in writing. Wood responded that he would refer the suggestion to Dewey, on the ground that Dewey had the authority to make such a formal pledge.

At this critical moment Aguinaldo had to leave Hong Kong. A dissident fellow-rebel was threatening a lawsuit in order to gain for himself half of the money the Spanish had paid the *Katipunan*. To avoid unpleasantness — and possibly the loss or the impounding of all the money, which the *Katipunan* called their "sinew of war" — Aguinaldo and the other rebel chiefs hurriedly took passage for Singapore.

The party had hardly arrived there when United States Consul General E. Spencer Pratt made contact with Aguinaldo. During a conversation held cheek-by-jowl, Pratt informed Aguinaldo that the United States and Spain were at war. "Ally yourself with America and you will surely defeat the Spaniards!" he exhorted him. Recovering from the startling news and prospect, Aguinaldo asked his question again: "What can we expect to gain from helping America?" "America," replied Pratt, "will give you much greater liberty and much more material benefits than the Spaniards ever promised you." Again as in Hong Kong, Aguinaldo requested that this openhanded offer be set on paper. And again he was told that such a commitment could only be made by Dewey. But this time, Pratt put the verbal pledge even more dramatically than Wood had:

You need not have any worry about America. The American Congress made a solemn declaration disclaiming any desire to possess Cuba and promising to leave the country to the Cubans after having driven away the Spaniards and pacified the country. As in Cuba, so in the Philippines. Even more so, if possible; Cuba is at our door while the Philippines are 10,000 miles away!

Aguinaldo was delighted, and he later said he told Pratt that if Dewey would make the invitation official and confirm the assurances, the Filipinos would regard the bargain as sealed and lay plans to fight alongside the Americans. Dewey never responded directly but Pratt told Aguinaldo the next day that the United States "would at least recognize the independence of the Philippines under the protection of the United States Navy. There was no necessity for entering into a formal written agreement because the word of the Commodore and the United States Consul were in fact equivalent to the most solemn pledge, that their verbal promises and assurances would be honored to the letter and were not to be classed with Spanish promises or Spanish ideas of a man's words of honor. . . ." It is not clear whether Dewey ever stood behind Pratt's allurements or even knew of them. And it is impossible to verify Aguinaldo's account recorded years later, because the handwritten note it was assertedly based upon no longer exists.

When the war broke out, the British, under the usual international procedure, gave Dewey twenty-four hours to move his vessels out of Hong Kong. And Dewey was on his way to war. The cable he had had from the Secretary of the Navy constituted orders that could crown an ordinary career in everlasting glory. The communication read:

Dewey, Hong Kong:
War has commenced between the United States and Spain. Proceed at once to Philippine Islands. Commence operations at once, particularly against the Spanish fleet. You must capture vessels or destroy. Use utmost endeavour.

[John D.] Long

The Americans and the Filipino rebels were fighting a common enemy but for different reasons. The Americans expected simply to vanquish the Spanish; the Filipinos' goal was to win independence. As Dewey steamed toward Manila, the insurgents sent word to supporters there and in its environs:

Compatriots:
Divine Providence is about to place independence within our reach. The Americans, not from mercenary motives, but for the sake of humanity and the lamentations of so many persecuted people have considered it opportune to extend their protecting mantle to our beloved country. . . . The Americans will attack by sea and prevent any reinforcements coming from Spain. . . . The insurgents must attack by land. . . . There where you see the American flag flying, assemble in numbers; they are our redeemers!

Aguinaldo soon afterward arrived in Manila, aboard the United States gunboat "McCulloch." Without delay he was piped aboard Dewey's flagship the "Olympia" and received — so Aguinaldo always insisted — the honors due a general. Dewey spurred Aguinaldo to action: "Go ashore and start your army." Aguinaldo later remembered also Dewey's suggestion to him that he have a Philippine flag made and hoist it when the Spanish power had been destroyed, in order to "catch the eyes of the world at the moment of victory."

The quick triumph Dewey gained is now embedded in history and legend. His ships successfully made their way past Spanish gun implacements on Corregidor, the rock-fortress guarding Manila Harbor. As daybreak came, the Americans encountered a Spanish squadron in the harbor. Shortly, the battle was joined and a fearful cannonading followed. Before eight o'clock the United States forces broke off the fighting in order to have breakfast. Before lunchtime the Americans had destroyed the Spanish fleet and battered into uselessness the Spanish shore guns. By dinnertime the scene in Manila Bay was calm again: Spanish power and authority in that part of the world, dating from Magellan's day, had vanished with the smoke of the exploding shells.

But how could Dewey follow up this titanic victory? He lacked the forces to make a landing and occupy the city of Manila. Aguinaldo, meanwhile, was ensconced at Cavite, drawing men like a magnet. As the rebels step-by-step formed themselves into a potent fighting force, the Americans were astounded. It seemed incredible that these undersized men lacking the technology and literacy modern armies require, should be making good their bid to be allies in fact as well as in spirit. Dewey observed: "I was waiting for troops to arrive, and I felt sure that Filipinos could not take Manila, and thought that the closer they invested the city the easier it would be when our troops arrived to march in. The Filipinos were our friends, assisting us; they were doing our work."

In this uncommon situation, the Secretary of the Navy had cabled Dewey to "exercise discretion most fully in all matters and be governed according to circumstances which you know and we cannot know." The same communication, however, contained the suggestion: "It is desirable as far as possible and consistent with your safety, not to have political alliances with insurgents or any faction in [the] islands that would incur liability [respecting] their cause in the future." Dewey himself was uninterested in the rebels or in the people at large: his operations had been a success and, like almost all of his professional contemporaries, he could comprehend no connection between military and political operations. With notable naivete and unanimity, the senior naval and military people were inclined to talk of "leaving politics to the politicians."

Unknowingly, however, Dewey was playing politics to the hilt. When Aguinaldo invited him to attend a ceremony at Filipino headquarters celebrating the Philippine Declaration of Independence, he declined to be present — giving the Filipinos thereby a clear message of American nonsupport. On the other hand, Dewey sent to Washington, through "channels," a copy of the Declaration accompanied by his explanatory letter stating: "In my opinion these people are superior in intelligence and more capable of self-government than the natives of Cuba, and I am familiar with both races."

In his public utterances Dewey was trimming his predilections, it must be assumed, in order to satisfy the requirements of political popularity at home. Dewey became a heroic name comparable with only a handful of others in American history. The thought of making him President of the United States did not seem beyond possibility.

*   *   *   *

The ease with which Spain's grip on Cuba and the Philippines had been broken had whetted imperialistic appetites. Men were seeing in the acquisition of the Philippines an opportunity for "true empire-building" — a completion of the work that the Founding Fathers had begun a century and a quarter earlier. Already the Washington *Post* had trumpeted on receiving the news of the victory in the Philippine waters: "The guns of Dewey at Manila have changed the destiny of the United States. We are face to face with a strange destiny and must accept its responsibilities. An imperial policy." Theodore Roosevelt was telling the diplomat Henry D. White in London that the Philippines "must be ours. . . . We hold the other side of the Pacific, and the value to this country is almost beyond imagination. . . ." And, as the drumbeats for colonies and dominion rose in America's high places, the larger public was being charmed by the giddy prospects, too. The call to empire for a time was so loud it almost drowned the utterances of those who described the Filipinos not as the beneficiaries of American ministrations but as the victims. America, for the first time in a position to implement for another people the right to self-government so proudly proclaimed in the American Declaration of Independence, chose to turn its back on the opportunity.

To invoke the Declaration of Independence in the face of such a shining possibility for territorial gain, wrote Senator Beveridge, was "like the reading of Job's lamentations would be at a wedding." Charles Francis Adams, Jr., whose great-grandfather John Adams had helped draft the Declaration, sounded a new note when he said that Americans far from being untrue to their Revolutionary tradition in seeking colonies were in fact "as wise now as Great Britain was then." And these strange sentiments echoed and reechoed in many forms across the country. But all were linked to the spirit of the ideas Josiah Strong, a Congregationalist minister, was uttering. Only a few years earlier, in a widely read book, *Our Country*, he had predicted that Americans as part of the Anglo-Saxon race were destined, "unless devitalized by alcohol and tobacco," to conduct a civilizing mission for the whole world.

Notwithstanding, the opposition to this prefigurement of America's future activities was also being heard. The counter argument focused on the tragic and lengthening struggle in the Philippines between the Americans and the Filipinos who in February, 1899, began a second war in the islands, one that goes by the name of the Philippine Insurrection. The United States had refused to grant independence to the islands, and under Aguinaldo's leadership the Filipinos ranged themselves against their American "enemy" in a guerrilla struggle that had many of the tactical problems and raised many of the moral questions that the war in Vietnam made familiar again in the 1960's. Before the struggle was over, 126,468 United States soldiers had participated. When it formally ended on July 4, 1902, over 4000 of them lay dead and almost 3000 had been wounded. By a "body-count," 16,000 Filipinos had been slain in combat — although 20,000 may be closer to the actual number. The suffering of the civilian population was intense and beyond measure. Possibly a quarter of a million noncombatants died as a result of the hostilities directly, and indirectly because pestilence and disease often raged uncontrolled. And the devastation of Filipino agriculture through the loss of so many *carabao* — indispensable in the raising of rice as well as for transportation — produced pitiable scenes of suffering.

No one put the anti-imperialist point of view more cogently than George S. Boutwell, the president of the American Anti-Imperialist League. A former Radical Republican who had served briefly as a Senator from Massachusetts in the 1870's, Boutwell pioneered in trying to build bridges between the different races. In an address in 1900 he made his case:

This question I put to the defenders of this war [in the Philippines]. What is the end that you seek? Is it the vassalage of these people? If so, then you are the enemies of the republic and the betrayers of the principles upon which the republic thus far has been made to rest.

Carl Schurz, the most prominent of the "reform" politicians in the post-Civil War era and who had participated in many a good crusade, angrily decried the fighting in the Philippines as "the President's War." Moreover, he used arguments that the present generation, which has debated the Vietnam involvement, will not find unfamiliar:

We are engaged in a war with the Filipinos. You may quibble about it as you will, call it by whatever name you will — it *is* a war; and a war of conquest on our part at that — a war of bare-faced, cynical conquest. Now, I ask any fair-minded man whether the President, before beginning that war, or while carrying it on, has ever taken any proper steps to get from the Congress, the representatives of the people, any proper authority for making that war.

The intensifying feeling of the anti-imperialists was reflected in the forthright planks of the platform offered by the Anti-Imperialist League:

We deny that the obligation of all citizens to support their government in time of grave national peril applies to the present situation. . . . We propose to contribute to the defeat of any person or party that stands for the forcible subjugation of any people. We shall oppose for reelection all who in the White House or in Congress betray American liberty in pursuit of un-American ends.

These far-reaching and passionate pronouncements were spoken on the floor of both houses of Congress no less clearly than on the outside. The Senate was the scene of especially acrimonious discussion, and in January, 1900, a Committee on the Philippines was established to deal with the most torrid issue now emerging from the war with Spain: What should be the fate of the Philippines? The chairman was Henry Cabot Lodge, an ardent imperialist, who explained that because the Filipinos are not "fit for self-government," to free them would only force them to turn into "a great group of Haitis and Santo Domingoes with . . . no Monroe Doctrine to prevent other nations from interfering" with them. He came to the conclusion that "their only hope of reaching the freedom which we desire them to have lies in our now holding, governing, and controlling the islands."

Lodge was not eager to investigate the war that developed in the Philippines. His position as a friend and supporter of President Theodore Roosevelt made him a powerful defender of administration policy. He was, however, goaded into holding hearings by the senior Senator from his own state, George Frisbie Hoar, a fellow alumnus of Harvard and an honored founder of the Republican party. A veteran of thirty-three years in Congress, the last twenty-five of them in the Senate, Hoar was almost seventy-six years old as the year 1902 began. On January 13 he introduced a resolution calling for the appointment of a committee of seven Senators to "examine and report into the conduct of the war in the Philippine Islands, the administration of the government there and the condition and character of the inhabitants." Suggesting to his colleagues that they postpone consideration of the resolution until the following day, Hoar was applying pressure on Lodge whose committee had been inactive. Almost in mock-apology to Lodge, Hoar on the following day attempted to justify his call for the proposed committee. He did not have, he said, "the smallest desire to interfere with the jurisdiction of the existing Committee on the Philippines. . . . Nothing would be more agreeable to me than to have the members of that Committee as now organized constitute this committee." He proceeded to enumerate the matters he regarded as deserving full-scale scrutiny. The first was the subject of Aguinaldo, his popularity, the degree to which he could be said to represent the aspirations of Filipinos, and the question of whether or not Dewey had promised him that the Philippines would have independence. The second was the issue of responsibility for the outbreak of hostilities between American and Filipino forces. The third was an explanation of how the policy of subjugation in the islands had been established. The fourth was an elucidation of the nature and character of the Philippine peoples with a view to finding out if they were fit to rule themselves. Lastly, Hoar was asking that Governor-General William Howard Taft be summoned home to report on the condition of government in the islands.

Lodge craftily responded to Hoar that if such an investigation were to be undertaken then the existing committee ought to do the job. The matters raised by Hoar, he said, were "questions of the past," already settled, "but if the Senate thinks we ought to investigate" then the Lodge committee would undertake the work. Hoar replied that he was satisfied with this response to his proposal — as long as the job was done by "somebody." On January 28 Lodge introduced a resolution for which he obtained unanimous consent, empowering his committee to "send for persons and papers and to administer oaths and to employ a stenographer in connection with any investigation which they may deem proper relating to affairs in the Philippine Islands. . . ."

*   *   *   *

The members of the committee were themselves significant actors in the drama that was about to be played. The following sketches of their careers show, among other things, that while some of the twelve men were seasoned and influential veterans of the Senate, six members were serving their first term.

Chairman Henry Cabot Lodge (Republican, Massachusetts) was the best-known. Born in Boston in 1850, he was a Harvard College alumnus of the class of 1871 and a graduate of the Harvard Law School three years later. A man of literary taste and ability, he possessed scholarly inclinations and gifts. In 1876 he received the first Ph.D. in political science ever awarded by Harvard. Although not an original thinker he wrote biographies of some notable Americans, including Alexander Hamilton and Daniel Webster, that won many admirers in spite of, and possibly because of, the Republican bias that dominated them. In 1887 he was elected to the House of Representatives and after serving three terms was elevated to the Senate in 1893. Although Lodge was in the forefront of the discussion of many issues, he regarded his domain of particular expertness to be foreign affairs.

William Boyd Allison (Republican, Iowa) was the senior Senator on the Committee in length of service in Congress. He was born in Perry Township, Ashland County, Ohio in 1829. After he took his bachelor's degree from Western Reserve College in 1849, he studied law, and in 1852 was admitted to the bar. Settling in Ashland County he threw himself into politics, becoming an early member of the emerging Republican party. Because of an unsuccessful campaign for district attorney he pulled up his stakes in disappointment, headed westward, and settled in Dubuque, Iowa. After brief service as a lieutenant colonel of volunteers in the Civil War, he was elected in 1862 to the House of Representatives and in 1872 he moved to the Senate, where he served six terms. For twenty-seven years he was the Chairman of the Senate Appropriations Committee, becoming one of the most powerful figures in the history of the Upper House. He declined cabinet posts, proffered by Presidents Garfield, Harrison, and McKinley, finding it more congenial to exercise from the Senate his influence on the growth of industrial America.

Albert Jeremiah Beveridge (Republican, Indiana) like Lodge was a practicing historian and, as such, much more distinguished. But his chief works — a classic biography of John Marshall and an uncompleted life of Lincoln — belong to his post-Senate career. Born in Highland County, Ohio in 1862, he was raised on a farm in Illinois. Before he was sixteen, he learned of the backbreak of hard work through labor as a plowhand, a railroad worker, a logger, and a teamster. In 1881 he entered Asbury College, now De Pauw University in Greencastle, Indiana. By the time of his graduation in 1885 he had demonstrated unique artistry as a college orator. This fact, as much as his early impoverishment, helped to set the pattern for his adult life. Becoming well-known and sought-after as a public speaker in the circles of the Republican party of Indiana, he was elected to the Senate in 1899 when he was only thirty-six, one of the youngest men ever to hold a seat there. With his wonted eloquence, Beveridge in his freshman year earned the applause and esteem of the supporters of imperialism.

Julius Caesar Burrows (Republican, Michigan) was born in North East, Pennsylvania in 1837. He was raised in Ohio where he went to school and studied law. In 1860 he moved to Richland, Michigan, and after working as a school principal for a year, began to practice law. During the Civil War he raised a company for the Seventeenth Regiment of the Michigan Volunteer Infantry. Serving as a captain, he participated in several decisive battles including Antietam, Fredericksburg, and Vicksburg. By 1864 he was back in Michigan and engaging in local politics. Between 1873 and 1895 he served on and off in the House of Representatives. In 1895 he was chosen to fill a Senate place made vacant by death, and was reelected in 1899.

Edward Ward Carmack (Democrat, Tennessee) was born in Sumner County, Tennessee in 1858. Admitted to the bar in 1871 he practiced law in Columbia, but only briefly because journalism began to have greater appeal for him. After a stint on the staff of the Nashville *Democrat* and service as the editor-in-chief of the Nashville *American*, he became the editor of the Memphis *Commercial* in 1892. Meanwhile, involved in Democratic-party politics, he was elected to the House of Representatives in 1896, and after a second term he entered the Senate in 1900.

Born in Dadeville, Alabama in 1855, Charles Allen Culberson (Democrat, Texas) was reared in Texas. He was educated at the Virginia Military Institute from which he was graduated in 1874. Returning to Texas he soon established a lucrative practice and a reputation as a man with a political future. In 1890 he became attorney-general of Texas and four years later was elected governor, his campaign manager being Colonel Edward M. House (afterward President Woodrow Wilson's confidant and alter ego). In 1898 Culberson was elected to the Senate.

Charles Henry Dietrich (Republican, Nebraska) was born in Aurora, Illinois in 1853. For a while as a youth he was a clerk in a hardware store in St. Joseph, Missouri; afterward he opened his own hardware business in Chicago. Restless, he moved to the town of Deadwood in what is now South Dakota and became a merchant, delivering his wares on pack animals through the Black Hills. A lucky strike in the mining rush there made him rich. Selling his mine property, he moved to Hastings, Nebraska in 1878. There, using his German background to advantage, he entered the banking field and formed the German National Bank in 1887. Three years later he was elected Governor of Nebraska, but he served only a few months, resigning in May, 1901 to fill a vacant seat in the United States Senate.

Fred Thomas Dubois (Republican and Democrat, Idaho) was born in Palestine, Illinois in 1851. In 1872 he was graduated from Yale College and shortly afterward moved to the Idaho Territory where he went into business. After being United States marshal of Idaho for a number of years, he was elected as a Republican Delegate from the Territory of

Idaho, serving from 1887 to 1890. At that time — in some measure through Dubois' efforts — Idaho entered the Union. Dubois was elected to the United States Senate in 1891 but was unsuccessful in 1896 when as a Silver Republican, in opposition to those of his party who defended a monetary standard based on gold, he sought reelection. In 1901, he was returned to the Senate as a Silver Republican but shortly afterward he switched parties, becoming a Democrat.

Born in Turner, Maine in 1836, Eugene Hale (Republican, Maine) was a graduate of Hebron Academy. He read law and was admitted to the Maine bar when he was twenty-one years old. He early became a Republican-party wheelhorse and was rewarded in 1869 by election to the House of Representatives. His party ties were strengthened by his marriage in 1871 to Mary Chandler, daughter of Senator Zachariah Chandler of Michigan who was one of the most influential men in the Reconstruction era. In 1881 Hale began the first of five terms in the Senate. Despite his party regularity and his growing importance based on seniority, he felt increasingly out of place in twentieth-century affairs as imperialism carried the day. He and Hoar were the only Republicans who voted against the Treaty of Paris in 1899, under which the Philippines had passed into American hands.

Louis Emery McComas (Republican, Maryland) was born near Hagerstown, Maryland in 1846. He received his bachelor's degree from Dickinson College in Pennsylvania in 1866. Returning to Hagerstown, he was admitted to the bar in 1868. Even before his practice began to flourish — as it did shortly — he was an active Republican-party worker. He was elected to three successive terms in the House of Representatives before going down to defeat in 1890. A scholar, he taught international law at the Georgetown University Law School. President Benjamin Harrison appointed him to the Supreme Court of the District of Columbia. There he served until, elected to the United States Senate, he assumed his new duties in 1899.

Thomas MacDonald Patterson (Democrat and Populist, Colorado) was born in County Carlow, Ireland in 1839 and was brought to New York City when he was ten years old. The Pattersons moved to Crawfordsville, Indiana in 1853 where the elder Patterson opened a jewelry store in which the boy worked. When the Civil War broke out, Patterson enlisted in the Eleventh Indiana Infantry. His military service was brief, and in 1862 he was a civilian again. Leaving Wabash College before graduation, he read law in the office of a local lawyer, and was admitted to the Indiana bar in 1867. Looking for greener fields, Patterson moved to Denver in 1872, when his arrival coincided with the Colorado silver-mining boom. He began to prosper both as a lawyer and as an investor in real estate. Politics also beckoned, and in 1874 he became Territorial Delegate to Congress, playing a central part in the admission of Colorado to the Union in 1876. Shortly afterward, Patterson, an ardent

Democrat, won a seat in the House of Representatives. An unsuccessful candidate for governor of his state in 1888, he became more and more at odds with the traditionalists of his party, and turned increasingly to the advocacy of free silver and the rights of labor. By 1892, although he was a millionaire, he was also a convinced Populist and he helped the Populist candidate for President, James B. Weaver, win the electoral vote of Colorado that year. Combined support from Democrats, Populists, and Silver-Republicans gained Patterson a Senate seat in 1901.

Redfield Proctor (Republican, Vermont) was sometimes called "the Marble King" in tribute to his role in promoting the marble industry in his home state. He was born in Proctorsville, Vermont in 1831 and he took his bachelor's degree at Dartmouth College in 1851. Trained in law at the Albany Law School, he entered practice in Boston in the eve of the Civil War. Soon after the war broke out he joined the Third Regiment of Vermont Volunteers. Mustered out in 1863 as a colonel, he returned to Vermont to resume his career as a lawyer and to play a part in politics. He held a number of state positions, including the governorship (1878–80). In 1889 President Benjamin Harrison made him Secretary of War in what was often characterized as "the Businessman's Cabinet." Two years later Proctor resigned to accept a vacant Senate seat. He remained in the Senate until the end of his life. When the trumpets of war were being heard in the late 1890's, he was among the ardent supporters of imperialism, and helped bring about the appointment of Dewey to the command of the Asiatic Squadron.

Joseph Lafayette Rawlins (Democrat, Utah) grew up among the first generation of Mormons. Born near Salt Lake City in 1850 he was educated at the University of Utah, and at Indiana University. For two years in the 1870's he was a professor at the University of Deseret in Salt Lake City. Switching from an interest in the classics to the law, he was admitted to the bar and began a practice in 1875. In 1892 he was elected to a term in the United States House of Representatives, and was defeated in his bid for reelection. He was elected to the United States Senate and took his seat there in 1897.

The hearings began on January 28, 1902. Continuing to resist the idea of holding them, Lodge participated in the proceedings only sporadically. The role of defending the Administration's course in the Philippines fell to Senator Beveridge, who accepted it gladly and played it with zeal. Senators Carmack, Culberson, and Patterson — Democrats — were no less vigilant and sharp-tongued on the other side. The intensity of feeling about the issues involved in the Philippines question is revealed not only in the testimony of the witnesses but in the exchanges between the Senators themselves.

1 WAS THERE A DEAL WITH AGUINALDO?

Testimony of George Dewey

Admiral George Dewey as Commodore commanded the Asiatic Squadron of the United States Navy from early January, 1898 until the middle of 1899. In this post he earned abiding fame as the exalted "Hero of Manila Bay." Born in Montpelier, Vermont in 1837, he was graduated from the United States Naval Academy in 1858. During the Civil War he saw action in the heavy fighting around the lower Mississippi River, and he profited from the tutelage of Admiral David G. Farragut under whom he served directly for a time. After the war he held the minor assignments that were typical for officers of the peacetime Navy. But in 1889 he became chief of the Bureau of Equipment for the Navy Department where he began to become intimately acquainted with the cruisers and the first battleships of the "new navy" that was being built. Soon afterward as head of the Board of Inspection and Survey he became expert in the performances and capabilities of these vessels, and when he was sent to the Asiatic Squadron, he seemed preeminently qualified to lead it. Almost immediately, assisted by the Navy Department, he started to study the Spanish defenses of the Philippines.

The Chairman: Admiral, the committee has asked you to be kind enough to come here because they were desirous . . . of hearing from you in regard to the early operations at Manila in which you were chiefly concerned, and especially as to our relations with the Filipinos in those days, in the beginning. The committee would be very glad to have you make any statement you care to make in your own way.

Adm. Dewey: I think it would be more satisfactory if the committee would ask me exactly what questions they like, because it would be a rather long narrative, which I have already reported upon — that is, the early operations.

The Chairman: When did you first hear from Aguinaldo and his friends?

Adm. Dewey: I should think about a month before leaving Hong Kong; that is, about the 1st of April, when it became pretty certain that

1

there was to be war with Spain, I heard that there were a number of Filipinos in the city of Hong Kong who were anxious to accompany the squadron to Manila in case we went over. I saw these men two or three times myself. They seemed to be all very young, earnest boys. I did not attach much importance to what they said or to themselves. Finally, the day before we left Mirs Bay for Hong Kong I received a telegram from Consul General Pratt at Singapore saying that Aguinaldo was there and was very anxious to see me. I said to him, "All right; tell him to come on"; but I attached so little importance to Aguinaldo that I did not wait for him. He did not arrive, and we sailed from Mirs Bay without any of the Filipinos, although I told these young men they could go if they wanted to. They did not go. I had been led to believe that there was a large number of Filipinos under arms in and about Manila, and our consul, Williams, had said: "At your first gun there will be 30,000 Filipinos rise." I joked him a good deal about it afterwards. I said: "Why don't they rise? I don't see anybody rising." As a matter of fact there was not a Filipino under arms the day I reached Manila.

I would like to say here that the governor-general of Manila virtually surrendered to me on the 1st day of May. During the engagement between the two squadrons they fired a number of rifle guns from batteries in front of the city at my squadron, and as soon as the Spaniards were sunk I took the squadron in front of the city and sent word to the governor-general that if he fired another shot at my ships I would destroy the town. He replied in writing that he would not fire if I did not. I anchored my ships in front of the city within easy range, and lay there twenty-four hours. That is not generally known. The city of Manila virtually surrendered to my squadron the 1st of May. If we had had 5,000 troops to have occupied the city that day we would have had no war; it would have been the end of it. I lay there twenty-four hours and then withdrew back to Cavite. I was afraid that someone might fire and I would have to keep my word. Then by the first steamer I sent over I received a letter from Consul General Wildman at Hong Kong saying that Aguinaldo was there, and a number of others, and they were very anxious to come over. So the next trip of the "McCulloch," my steamer (there was no other communication with Hong Kong except my vessel), I told the officer that went over that he might bring over about a dozen, still having no faith in them.

Sen. Burrows: Would it trouble you to explain a little more clearly that the governor-general virtually surrendered to you. What did that surrender consist of?

Adm. Dewey: He said, "I won't fire if you don't"; and I anchored my ships under his guns, within easy range, within less than 2,000 yards, and lay there twenty-four hours. Don't you see that that was virtually surrendering? He did not haul down the Spanish flag, and I may say that he sent word to me several times afterwards that he wanted to surrender to me; he wanted to surrender to the navy. I would not entertain any messages until enough troops came to occupy the city.

Sen. Burrows: Pardon me interrupting you. You may go on, if you please.

Adm. Dewey: I told this officer he could bring about a dozen on the "McCulloch," and the "McCulloch" came back with Aguinaldo and about a dozen young men. Aguinaldo came to see me. I said, "Well, now, go ashore there, we have got our force at the arsenal at Cavite, go ashore and start your army." He came back in the course of a few hours and said, "I want to leave here; I want to go to Japan." I said, "Don't give it up, Don Emilio." I wanted his help, you know. I said, "Don't give it up." He did not sleep ashore that night; he slept on board the ship. The next morning he went on shore, still inside my lines, and began recruiting men, and after a few days I went ashore to see him and said to him, "You had better go outside my lines. There is our enemy up there at Manila, and it would be better for you and better for me if we work independently; you go your way and I will go mine." He then went into the town of Cavite and began recruiting troops. We found in the arsenal 75 or 100 rifles which I had no use for. I gave him those. I told him also he could take any of the cannon at the arsenal. I gave him a lot of Mauser ammunition that we captured. We had a common enemy, and of course I wanted his help. Then when I heard our troops were coming I asked him to withdraw his troops from Cavite to make room for our men. He demurred at this, but finally withdrew and established headquarters across the bay at a place called Bacoor, from which place on the 15th of July he sent me a proclamation declaring the independence of the Philippines.

The Chairman: Was that the first?

Adm. Dewey: That was the first intimation; the first I had ever heard of independence of the Philippines.

The Chairman: He had said something to you ——

Adm. Dewey: Not a word. He had done what I told him. He was most obedient; whatever I told him to do he did. I attached so little importance to this proclamation that I did not even cable its contents to Washington, but forwarded it through the mails. I never dreamed that they wanted independence. Then he began operations toward Manila, and he did wonderfully well. He whipped the Spaniards battle after battle, and finally put one of those old smooth-bore guns on a barge, and he wanted to take this up — wanted me to tow it up so he could attack the city with it. I said, "Oh, no, no; we can do nothing until our troops come." I knew he could not take the city without the assistance of the navy, without my assistance, and I knew that what he was doing — driving the Spaniards in — was saving our own troops, because our own men perhaps would have had to do that same thing. He and I were always on the most friendly terms; we had never had any differences. He considered me as his liberator, as his friend. I think he had the highest admiration for us because we had whipped the Spaniards who had been riding them down for three hundred years.

The Chairman: Did you at any time, Admiral, recognize his government or his independence?

Adm. Dewey: Oh, never. I have seen it stated in print that I saluted his flag. Of course I never saluted it. The German admiral came to me and said, "These Filipino tugs that are running about here have hoisted the Filipino flag; are you going to permit it?" I said, "It is not a flag; they have no government; no government has recognized them; they have a little bit of bunting that anybody could hoist." I said, "That is not a Filipino flag." Well, that was the end of that. We know that any yacht, any vessel, any steamer, can hoist a bit of bunting, and they called this a Filipino flag, but I did not.

The Chairman: You, of course, never saluted the flag?

Adm. Dewey: Certainly not; and I do not think I ever called Aguinaldo anything but Don Emilio; I don't think I ever called him "general."

The Chairman: And when he came on board ship was he received with any special honors at the side?

Adm. Dewey: Never.

The Chairman: You remember the question of your recognizing his republic was a good deal discussed and you wrote me a letter, which I read in the Senate. Of course, I am only asking now about what you said in the letter. There was no recognition of the republic?

Adm. Dewey: Never. I did not think I had any authority to do it and it never occurred to me to do it. There was a sort of a reign of terror; there was no government. These people had got power for the first time in their lives and they were riding roughshod over the community. The acts of cruelty which were brought to my notice were hardly credible. I sent word to Aguinaldo that he must treat his prisoners kindly, and he said he would.

The Chairman: What, in your opinion, Admiral, would have been the effect of having allowed them to enter Manila when our troops did? They were not allowed to?

Adm. Dewey: That would be only an opinion. As you know, soldiers are generally given to looting.

The Chairman: However, they were not permitted to enter the city?

Adm. Dewey: No; they were not permitted by General Merritt and our troops; they were not permitted to enter. The Spanish authorities were very fearful about that. They surrendered the city to me. It was all arranged and we need not have lost a man there. The governor-general arranged with me that I was to go up and fire a few shots and then I was to make the signal, "Do you surrender?" and he would hoist the white flag and then the troops would march in; but he was fearful that the Filipinos would get in.

Sen. Burrows: Who was that arrangement with?

Adm. Dewey: The governor-general who commanded. I said, "If you are going to surrender, why must I fire any shots?" He said his honor demanded that. So I had to fire, to kill a few people.

Sen. Burrows: To preserve his honor?

Adm. Dewey: Yes. I said to his messenger, "Now make him understand that he must keep his word, because if he fires one shot down goes that city." They did not fire a shot; although they had probably 15,000 troops in the city and forty-seven rifled guns on the city front, they did not fire a shot at my squadron. I am glad for an opportunity to say this, because it has not been printed before. That is a part of the history which I was reserving to write myself.

The Chairman: Could the Filipino forces under Aguinaldo have taken Manila without your assistance? How large a force did he have?

Adm. Dewey: We never could tell exactly, they exaggerated so; but I suspect he had at that time 25,000 men. He had a large force.

Sen. Burrows: Armed?

Adm. Dewey: That I don't know. I did not, of course, see them. They were stretched right around the city, the back part of it, and I did not see them. The army officers would know better about that. Some were armed. They were getting arms; they captured a great many arms from the Spanish troops. In every battle they captured arms.

The Chairman: And there were 15,000 Spanish troops in Manila?

Adm. Dewey: Yes, probably that number.

The Chairman: Would they have fought if the Filipinos had tried to come in alone; would those 15,000 Spanish troops have fought them?

Adm. Dewey: They were pretty badly demoralized. You see, the navy controlled the situation there; we had cut off their supplies. Communication in the Philippines is principally by water, and we commanded that, controlling the situation, and they had gotten nothing in. They surrendered on August 13, and they had not gotten a thing in after the 1st of May. They were short of provisions and supplies of all kinds and were pretty well demoralized. They wanted to surrender, and were very anxious to surrender to the navy.

Sen. Burrows: The Spaniards?

Adm. Dewey: Yes.

The Chairman: How long were you there after that, Admiral; after the surrender of the city?

Adm. Dewey: I was there all winter, and until the following June.

The Chairman: You were there when the city was attacked?

Adm. Dewey: Yes.

The Chairman: Were you surprised at that attack?

Adm. Dewey: No. We had heard there had been threats; it had been in the air for a long time, and every now and then we would hear rumors that there was going to be a rising in the city — that there was going to be an attack. Of course I was in constant touch with General Otis and had my ships located so we could afford assistance in the event of such attack.

The Chairman: You did take part in the engagement when it came?

Adm. Dewey: Oh, yes; we protected the two flanks of the army, and rendered great assistance — the two flanks where they came down to the water on each side of the city.

Sen. Patterson: The first information that you received officially of Aguinaldo was about the 27th of April, was it?

Adm. Dewey: I should think so; it was a telegram from . . . Pratt.

Sen. Patterson: And he was the consul general at Singapore?

Adm. Dewey: Yes.

Sen. Patterson: This is a dispatch. Please see if you recognize it: "Aguinaldo, the insurgent leader here" — I will say that I am supplying the pronouns and conjunctions because they are omitted evidently in your telegraph cables — "will come to Hong Kong to arrange with the Commodore for general cooperation of insurgents at Manila if desired. Telegraph."

That was the first communication you had received from any American official upon the subject of Aguinaldo?

Adm. Dewey: I am not prepared to say that. Mr. Wildman in conversation may have said something about Aguinaldo; I don't remember.

Sen. Patterson: This is among the first?

Adm. Dewey: Among the first, yes.

Sen. Patterson: And your reply to that was: "Tell Aguinaldo to come as soon as possible."

Adm. Dewey: Yes.

Sen. Patterson: Did you receive any other communication from Consul General Pratt about that time with reference to Aguinaldo and his purposes in desiring to meet you, and in cooperating with the Americans in the Philippine Islands?

Adm. Dewey: No.

Sen. Patterson: Did you receive any communication from Mr. Pratt in which he stated what it was that Aguinaldo desired?

Adm. Dewey: I should say not. Of course this happened four years ago, and I remember Mr. Pratt wrote me a good many letters. I had a great deal on my mind; but if by that you mean to bring out that I in any way knew that Aguinaldo was to cooperate with me for the independence of the Filipinos I never received any letter of that kind. I don't remember when I first did hear from Pratt. He wrote me a number of letters, I remember.

Sen. Carmack: Admiral, did you see a publication in the *Singapore Free Press* about that time giving an account of the conference between Consul General Pratt and Aguinaldo?

Adm. Dewey: I have seen it; I don't remember when — written by a Mr. Bray?

Sen. Carmack: I don't remember.

The Chairman: Howard Bray.

Adm. Dewey: Howard Bray; a very unreliable person.

Sen. Carmack: That statement, however, was transmitted by Consul General Pratt himself to the State Department with a statement that it was substantially correct.

Adm. Dewey: I don't know that.

Sen. Patterson: Did considerable correspondence pass between you and Pratt?

Adm. Dewey: After I reached Manila, I should say yes. I think I had a number of letters from him.

Sen. Patterson: Were not Pratt's letters quite enthusiastic about Aguinaldo and his aims and purposes?

Adm. Dewey: I don't think so.

Sen. Patterson: Was there any communication between you and Pratt in which the matter of a written pledge or agreement with Aguinaldo was discussed with reference to the Philippine Islands?

Adm. Dewey: No.

Sen. Patterson: What became of the correspondence, Admiral, if you know?

Adm. Dewey: It is all in the Navy Department. When I turned over my command my official correspondence was all sent to the Navy Department. . . . [O]ur regulations require that. I may say that for my own information I kept copies of certain telegrams and cablegrams. I don't think I kept copies of Mr. Pratt's letters, as I did not consider them of much value. He seemed to be a sort of busybody there and interfering with other people's business and I don't think his letters impressed me.

Sen. Patterson: He was the consul general?

Adm. Dewey: Yes; but he had nothing to do with the attack on Manila, you know.

Sen. Patterson: I understand that.

Adm. Dewey: I received lots of advice, you understand, from many irresponsible people.

Sen. Patterson: But Pratt was the consul general of the government there?

Adm. Dewey: Yes; he was consul general.

Sen. Patterson: And he communicated with you, giving you such information as he thought you might be interested in, and among other information he gave you was this concerning Aguinaldo?

Adm. Dewey: I don't remember; no, I really don't remember his telling me anything about Aguinaldo more than that cablegram there, and I said he might come. And you see how much importance I attached to him; I did not wait for him.

Sen. Patterson: What you said was: "Tell Aguinaldo to come as soon as possible."

Adm. Dewey: Yes; but I did not wait a moment for him.

Sen. Patterson: Yes; but there was a reason for that.

Adm. Dewey: I think more to get rid of him than anything else.

Sen. Carmack: Rid of whom?

Adm. Dewey: Of Aguinaldo and the Filipinos. They were bothering me. I was very busy getting my squadron ready for battle, and these little men were coming on board my ship at Hong Kong and taking a good deal of my time, and I did not attach the slightest importance to anything that they could do, and they did nothing; that is, none of them went with me when I went to Mirs Bay. There had been a good deal of talk, but when the time came they did not go. One of them didn't go because he didn't have any toothbrush.

Sen. Burrows: Did he give that as a reason?

Adm. Dewey: Yes; he said, "I have no toothbrush."

Sen. Patterson: The question I was asking you was with relation to the reason for your leaving Hong Kong at the time you did. It was not simply because there were some young Filipino people talking to you on the subject of the Philippines; was there not a more important reason than that?

Adm. Dewey: That I left?

Sen. Patterson: Yes.

Adm. Dewey: Yes.

Sen. Patterson: Did any controversies or interviews you had with Filipinos have any effect upon your leaving Hong Kong at the time you did?

Adm. Dewey: Not the slightest.

Sen. Carmack: You did not mean a while ago that you left at the time you did to get rid of Aguinaldo?

Adm. Dewey: No; not of him alone, but of the Filipinos generally. They bothered me. They used to come aboard my ship and take my time, and finally I would not see them at all, but turned them over to my staff.

Sen. Patterson: You left on account of notice that was served on you by the British admiral?

Adm. Dewey: I left Hong Kong because of notice from the governor, but left Mirs Bay of my own volition.

Sen. Patterson: How far is Mirs Bay from Hong Kong?

Adm. Dewey: Twelve or fifteen miles. It is in Chinese territory. I had to get out of British territory. I left Mirs Bay the moment that our consul at Manila arrived. He was on his way over with information — the latest information. I waited for him. He came aboard, and, like a brave man, went back with us to Manila — took his life in his hands and went back. He gave me the very latest information.

Sen. Patterson: When you left Mirs Bay, you left because you were ready to go and you had a mission to perform?

Adm. Dewey: Yes.

Sen. Patterson: Aguinaldo or any of the Filipinos had no influence whatsoever on that action?

Adm. Dewey: No.

Sen. Patterson: Then came the battle; and how did it come that Aguinaldo came to the bay?

Adm. Dewey: I stated a little while ago that Consul General Wildman at Hong Kong wrote me that Aguinaldo and a number of Filipinos were in Hong Kong and were anxious to go to the Philippines, and I said they might bring twelve when the "McCulloch" came back.

Sen. Patterson: They brought fourteen, I think — Aguinaldo and what they called thirteen of his staff. What vessel did they come in?

Adm. Dewey: In the "McCulloch" — the revenue cutter "McCulloch."

Sen. Patterson: When the revenue cutter arrived, did you send your launch for Aguinaldo?

Adm. Dewey: I do not remember. Very likely I did, because they had the mail and they had provisions, and we sent boats over, probably many boats.

Sen. Patterson: In the talk with these little Filipino men you speak of before you started from Manila, had they said anything about the insurrection in the islands and what they desired?

Adm. Dewey: No.

Sen. Patterson: What was it they were bothering you about?

Adm. Dewey: God knows; I don't know. They were taking my time about frivolous things. I let them come over as an act of courtesy, just as you sometimes give money to a man to get rid of him; not that I expected anything from them. As I said in my direct testimony, I expected to find a large force of Filipinos under arms in insurrection to assist me. I was told that at my first gun there would be 25,000 or 30,000 Filipinos rise. But they did not rise. There was not one under arms, and when Aguinaldo came, the first information he received that they were beginning to assemble I gave him.

Sen. Patterson: Did you have any idea what Aguinaldo's hopes or desires were in connection with the Philippine Islands when he came to Manila Bay?

Adm. Dewey: I did not think much about it. Certainly it never entered my head that he wanted independence.

Sen. Patterson: You wrote to the Navy Department about the capacity of the Filipinos for self-government?

Adm. Dewey: Yes; I wrote that because I saw in the newspapers that Congress contemplated giving the Cubans independence, and I knew that our people did not know very much about the Filipinos at that time. I knew that because before going there I had great difficulty in finding out anything about them. Therefore I gave this information as something which was not generally known.

Sen. Carmack: What was the date of that telegram?

Adm. Dewey: I should think about the latter part of May. I had at that time several hundred of the Filipinos employed at the navy yard which we had captured. They were docile, amiable, intelligent, doing exactly the same kind of work that the men down at the navy yard here are doing, and they were most kindly disposed toward us. They looked on us as their liberators, and I say that in my opinion they are more capable of self-government than the Cubans.

Sen. Carmack: You repeated that subsequently in another dispatch?

Adm. Dewey: I think I did, and I still think so.

Sen. Carmack: When did you first begin to learn that they desired independence?

Adm. Dewey: I have already stated that Aguinaldo, on the middle of July, sent me a proclamation from Bacoor, across the bay, declaring the independence of the Filipinos, which I considered so unimportant and so trivial that I did not cable it to Washington but sent it by mail, "Respectfully forwarded for the information of the Navy Department."

Sen. Burrows: Did you make any response to Aguinaldo to that proclamation?

Adm. Dewey: No; none at all.

Sen. Carmack: What was the date of your dispatch, to the Navy Department I think it was, in which you said that these people expected independence?

Adm. Dewey: I don't remember that.

Sen. Carmack: I think you will find that language in one of your dispatches — "These people expect independence" — probably in the second dispatch, in which you reaffirm ——

Adm. Dewey: In which I said that they were more capable of self-government?

Sen. Carmack: Yes. I think where you reaffirmed that statement; I think probably it is in that.

Adm. Dewey: I don't remember that one. Perhaps if it were read ——

Sen. Carmack: "These people expect independence"; that was the language.

Adm. Dewey: Well, you may believe me, gentlemen, they did not at first; they did not.

Sen. Patterson: This is the dispatch referred to:

THE SECRETARY OF THE NAVY, *Washington:*
Receipt telegram June 14 is acknowledged; Aguinaldo, insurgent leader, with thirteen of his staff arrived May 19 by permission on "Nanshan."

Adm. Dewey: That was one of my steamers; but it ought to have been the "McCulloch."

Sen. Patterson (reading):

Established himself at Cavite outside the arsenal under the protection of our guns and organized his army. I have had several conferences with him, generally of a personal nature. Consistently I have refrained from assisting him in any way with the forces under my command, and on several occasions I have declined requests that I should do so, telling him the squadron could not act until the arrival of the United States troops. At the same time I have given him to understand that I consider the insurgents as friends, being opposed to a common enemy.

Adm. Dewey: That is pretty good.
Sen. Patterson (reading):

He has gone to attend a meeting of insurgent leaders for the purpose of forming a civil government.

Adm. Dewey: What is the date of that?
Sen. Patterson: June 27.

Aguinaldo has acted independent of the squadron, but has kept me advised of his progress, which has been wonderful. I have allowed to pass by water recruits, arms, and ammunition and to take such Spanish arms and ammunition from the arsenal as he needs. Have advised him frequently to conduct the war humanely, which he has done invariably. My relations with him are cordial, but I am not in his confidence. The United States has not been bound in any way to assist the insurgents by any act or promises, and he is not to my knowledge committed to assist us. I believe he expects to capture Manila without my assistance, but doubt his ability, they not having many guns ——

Adm. Dewey: And by that I meant cannon, you know.
Sen. Patterson (continuing):

In my opinion these people are far superior in intelligence and more capable of self-government than the natives of Cuba, and I am familiar with both races. Dewey.

Do you recall that dispatch?
Adm. Dewey: Yes.
Sen. Patterson: You say that the Spanish governor-general virtually surrendered to you on the 1st of May?
Adm. Dewey: Yes.
Sen. Patterson: And that you felt he would surrender to you at any time?
Adm. Dewey: Any time that I had the force to occupy the city.
Sen. Patterson: How did it come, Admiral, that you supplied Aguinaldo's men early in May with Mausers, allowed him to take possession of a lot of Spanish rifles or arms that had been sunk in the waters and commence the investment of Manila, if the Spanish governor-general was ready to surrender to you at any time you had forces to take possession of the city?
Adm. Dewey: How does it happen that I permitted that?

Sen. Patterson: Yes.

Adm. Dewey: Well, I permitted it as a good military act, a proper military act. The Filipinos were our friends, assisting us; they were doing our work. I believed then that they would be so thankful and delighted to get rid of the Spaniards that they would accept us with open arms, and Aguinaldo was advised by Vice Admiral Seymour when he was out there, when the former was at the summit of his power at Malolos (Admiral Seymour commanded the English squadron in the East), that the best thing for him (Aguinaldo) to do was to tie to the Americans. Admiral Seymour saw him at Malolos and advised him to tie to the Americans. He said to him, "They are your best friends."

Sen. Patterson: But, Admiral, why did you want to use Aguinaldo and the men that he could call to arms under him in connection with the city of Manila if it was true that the Spanish governor-general would surrender to your fleet any time that you had forces to occupy the city?

Adm. Dewey: Can't you see why I permitted him to do it? I was waiting for troops to arrive, and I felt sure that the Filipinos could not take Manila, and I thought that the closer they invested the city the easier it would be when our troops arrived to march in. It turned out as I expected, and we need not have lost a man.

Sen. Patterson: But there was no necessity for investing them.

Adm. Dewey: Yes; there was.

Sen. Patterson: No necessity for battle.

Adm. Dewey: Yes; there was. I was investing them by water. I cut off their supplies by water. I was in front blockading them closely, and my friends, the Filipinos, were assisting me in cutting off the supplies in the rear by investing the city.

Sen. Carmack: As I understand you, then, Admiral, the reason why they were willing to surrender was the fact they were invested on all sides.

Adm. Dewey: Oh, no; they were ready to surrender because the fleet commanded the water. The moment that that Spanish squadron was destroyed that was the end of the Spanish authority in the Philippines.

Sen. Carmack: Then the Filipino army might as well not have been there?

Adm. Dewey: Yes; as far as the capture of Manila is concerned.

Sen. Carmack: Did it serve any useful purpose whatever?

Adm. Dewey: Oh, yes; they were very friendly. They helped me. They were our friends helping us. I had no troops to land. If I had had troops I should not have needed them.

Sen. Carmack: The point I was getting at is this: If the Spaniards were ready and willing to surrender to the Americans, what need did you have of any forces, Americans or Filipinos?

Adm. Dewey: Well, there was a big city there. They had, I think, about 15,000 Spanish troops there, and I would have had to have some forces to hold the city — to police the city and to take care of the prisoners.

Sen. Carmack: You were not willing to intrust the Filipinos with the prisoners.

Adm. Dewey: Oh, no.

Sen. Carmack: Then what useful purpose did the Filipino army serve; why did you want the Filipino army at all?

Adm. Dewey: I did not want them.

Sen. Carmack: Did you not want the Filipino forces?

Adm. Dewey: No, not really. It was their own idea coming over there. We could have taken the city at any moment we had the troops to occupy it.

Sen. Carmack: Did you not encourage Aguinaldo organizing an army?

Adm. Dewey: Yes, to a certain extent; I let him take a few arms. We never turn away friends, do we?

Sen. Carmack: Did you not say that Aguinaldo was discouraged and ready to abandon it, and you encouraged him to make another effort to organize an army there?

Adm. Dewey: Yes. One's hindsight is a great deal better than his foresight. Looking back, I would not have had him there; I would not have had anything to do with any of them. I did not know as much then as I know now; none of us did.

Sen. Carmack: You thought, then, you would need them.

Adm. Dewey: I thought they would be friendly to us and would help us; and they were very ungrateful, I think, in turning against us after what we had done for them.

Sen. Carmack: That is a question of who turned.

Sen. Patterson: Admiral, in the statements that you made at first, were they with reference to your knowledge now or to your knowledge and feelings at the time you were in Manila Bay?

Adm. Dewey: What statements?

Sen. Patterson: About the immateriality of anything that Aguinaldo might do — the gathering of his forces, the assistance to you.

Adm. Dewey: That is what I thought then.

Sen. Patterson: Admiral, do I understand you to mean that, although you believed or knew that the Spanish governor-general would surrender to you at any time that you had forces to occupy the city, nevertheless you encouraged the formation of Aguinaldo's army, the investment of the city, the fighting of battles between the Spaniards and Aguinaldo, and matters of that kind?

Adm. Dewey: That was a matter — as I told Aguinaldo at the time — a matter entirely between the Filipinos and the Spaniards.

Sen. Patterson: Why, Admiral, did you allow Aguinaldo to act independently of you in the investment of a city, resulting in battles, in killing and wounding, and hardships incidental to actions in the field, when you knew that all you had to do was to await the arrival of enough forces to occupy the city and maintain peace there and that it would be surrendered to you?

Adm. Dewey: Oh, Aguinaldo had gotten beyond me at that time. He would not have listened to me; I could not have stopped him.

Sen. Patterson: What did you encourage the organization of his army for, Admiral, if you were expecting forces from the United States, and you knew the city would be surrendered as soon as you had those forces?

Adm. Dewey: I did not know what the action of our government would be; I did not know that they were going to send troops.

The Chairman: It was not decided for some weeks afterwards, was it?

Adm. Dewey: No. I was a long distance from home, with no cable communications, meeting these great questions, and acting as I thought best.

Sen. Patterson: I understand that. We all know how well you did it, too. . . .

Sen. Patterson: Then, Admiral, until you knew that they were going to send land forces to your assistance you thought there was a necessity to organize the Filipinos into land forces, did you?

Adm. Dewey: No; not a necessity.

Sen. Patterson: You thought it might prove of value to you?

Adm. Dewey: I testified here, I think, in a way that answers that. I said to Aguinaldo, "There is our enemy; now, you go your way and I will go mine; we had better act independently." That was the wisest thing I ever said.

Sen. Patterson: But you stated that you were using these people and they were permitted to organize, that you might use them.

Adm. Dewey: They were assisting us.

Sen. Patterson: Very well, they were to assist you. Did you not either permit them or encourage them — I do not care which term you use — to organize into an army, such as it was, that they might render you such assistance as you needed?

Adm. Dewey: They were assisting us, but incidentally they were fighting their enemy; they were fighting an enemy which had been their enemy for three hundred years.

Sen. Patterson: I understand that, Admiral.

Adm. Dewey: While assisting us they were fighting their own battles, too.

The Chairman: You were encouraging insurrection against a common enemy with which you were at war?

Adm. Dewey: I think so. I had in my mind an illustration furnished by the Civil War. I was in the South in the Civil War, and the only friends we had in the South were the negroes, and we made use of them; they assisted us on many occasions. I had that in mind; I said these people were our friends, and "we have come here and they will help us just exactly as the negroes helped us in the Civil War."

Sen. Patterson: The negroes were expecting their freedom ——

Adm. Dewey: The Filipinos were slaves, too.

Sen. Patterson: What were the Filipinos expecting?

Adm. Dewey: They wanted to get rid of the Spaniards; I do not think they looked much beyond that. I cannot recall, but I have in mind that the one thing they had in their minds was to get rid of the Spaniards and then to accept us, and that would have occurred — I have thought that many times — if we had had troops to occupy Manila on the 1st day of May before the insurrection got started; these people would have accepted us as their friends, and they would have been our loyal friends — I don't know for how long, but they would have been our friends then.

Sen. Patterson: You learned from Pratt, or Wildman, or Williams very early, did you not, that the Filipinos wanted their own country and to rule their own country; that that is what they were expecting?

Adm. Dewey: I heard from Williams that there was an insurrection there against the Spaniards. The Spaniards were very cruel to them, and I think they did not look much beyond getting rid of them. There was one, Dr. Rizal, who had the idea of independence, but I don't think that Aguinaldo had much idea of it.

Sen. Patterson: By the 1st of June, Admiral, how large an army did Aguinaldo have?

Adm. Dewey: I do not know that I ever knew.

Sen. Patterson: What would be your judgment about it?

Adm. Dewey: I could not tell how many they had. I never did know how many men they had under arms at any time. I don't believe they knew themselves.

Sen. Patterson: Well, but you can tell us whether there were in your judgment 3,000 or 10,000 or 20,000.

Adm. Dewey: It would be from memory, and I have no idea how many they had on the 1st of June. I could not tell — well, they did not have 100,000, but whether they had 1,000 or ——

Sen. Patterson: Did they have in the neighborhood of 20,000?

Adm. Dewey: I should think not.

Sen. Patterson: When was it they may have had 25,000?

Adm. Dewey: That was about the time they attacked us in February, when they made the attack on the lines around Manila.

Sen. Patterson: How many were there when you entered the city; how many Filipinos were under arms when you entered Manila?

Adm. Dewey: I don't know.

Sen. Patterson: About how many?

Adm. Dewey: I have no idea. Well, the largest army they had; I think they could have had any number of men; it was just a question of arming them. They could have had the whole population.

Sen. Patterson: Did they not gather to Aguinaldo with surprising rapidity?

Adm. Dewey: Yes; they did.

Sen. Patterson: When was it they captured the Spanish at Cavite? Where did they capture the first Spanish prisoners?

Adm. Dewey: Well, I should think it was sometime in the month of May. The Spaniards had small outposts — one company here and two companies there — and as soon as the Filipinos had gotten organized they went around the head of that big bay and attacked some of these outposts, and I should think it was the latter part of May that they began to make their first captures, and as fast as they would capture one of these posts that would give them so many more arms for their troops.

Sen. Patterson: How many arms did you supply them with besides the seventy-five Mausers?

Adm. Dewey: That is all.

Sen. Patterson: How many arms did they take from the bay that had been sunk by the Spaniards?

Adm. Dewey: That was not arms; that was ammunition. I had thrown a lot of Mauser ammunition into the bay. We captured it and we had no Mauser rifles, and so we threw tons of the ammunition into the bay, and they fished it out.

Sen. Patterson: Were there no arms taken out of the bay by the Filipinos?

Adm. Dewey: I do not think so. They may have taken something possibly from the sunken vessels.

Sen. Patterson: You knew of 2,000 stands of arms, did you not, coming from Hong Kong, that had been purchased by the Filipinos with their own money?

Adm. Dewey: Yes.

Sen. Patterson: When did those arrive?

Adm. Dewey: I captured the steamer that brought them there. She was owned by a renegade American.

Sen. Patterson: When was that?

Adm. Dewey: I should say in July, possibly. It was a little steamer; she landed at Batangas. I heard she was going to land. When I got there she had already landed the arms.

Sen. Patterson: When did the Filipinos first display a flag?

Adm. Dewey: They got some little launches that were hidden in the bayous about there, and I should think about midsummer, perhaps in June, they had a little blue flag on these tugs which they called the Filipino flag.

Sen. Patterson: And the German officials came there to you and explained to you about it?

Adm. Dewey: Yes; that is, they asked if I was going to permit it.

Sen. Patterson: And you put them off?

Adm. Dewey: I said, "That is no Filipino flag; there is no Filipino government." It was a little pennant that anybody could fly.

Sen. Patterson: You knew at that time, did you not, Admiral, that they were claiming the right to establish an independent government or a government of their own there?

Adm. Dewey: I am not sure whether that was before they issued that proclamation or after; I am not sure about that.

Sen. Patterson: At least after the proclamation was issued you knew that they were seeking to establish an independent government?

Adm. Dewey: Yes.

Sen. Patterson: You did not interfere in any way with the flying of the flag?

Adm. Dewey: No; until there got to be too many of them there, and then I captured about 20, all they had — just took them — and I said, "You don't need any" ——

Sen. Patterson: When was that?

Adm. Dewey: That was in the fall of 1898.

Sen. Patterson: That was after you took possession of the city; but I am talking about up to the time you took possession of the city on the 13th of August. You did not interfere — you knew at that time that they' were organized for the purpose of establishing a government of their own?

Adm. Dewey: I did not take that seriously, really.

Sen. Patterson: I know; but nevertheless you knew that there were many thousands under arms with Aguinaldo; they had formed a civil government of which you had knowledge, they were flying the flag of their own country, and you did not interfere with it?

Adm. Dewey: I knew that there was no government in the whole of the Philippines. Our fleet had destroyed the only government there was, and there was no other government; there was a reign of terror throughout the Philippines, looting, robbing, murdering; a reign of terror throughout the islands.

Sen. Patterson: We have no record of that, Admiral, up to the time you took possession of the city, that I know of, from the time you got there in May until you took possession of the city on the 13th of August.

Adm. Dewey: I think it is a fact, though; it is a fact that they were in possession, they had gotten pretty much the whole thing except Manila.

Sen. Patterson: Who?

Adm. Dewey: The natives.

Sen. Patterson: Yes. When was it they took Subig Bay, captured the Spanish land forces at Subig Bay?

Adm. Dewey: I took the land forces at Subig Bay.

Sen. Patterson: When was that, Admiral.

Adm. Dewey: That was long before the city was captured. There were about eight hundred Spaniards. I took them because there was a man-of-war of a foreign nation that was interfering in our affairs and preventing the Filipinos from going across to Isla Grande. Aguinaldo told me that, and I sent and took these prisoners and I told him (Aguinaldo) that I would turn them over to him; he could have the arms ——

Sen. Patterson: What interference was there with Aguinaldo by a foreign vessel?

Adm. Dewey: A German man-of-war was there and would not allow the Filipinos to pass from the mainland to Isla Grande.

Sen. Patterson: What did the Filipinos wish to pass to the islands for?

Adm. Dewey: To capture the Spanish garrison.

Sen. Patterson: And this German man-of-war would not permit them to do it?

Adm. Dewey: No.

Sen. Patterson: Aguinaldo complained of that to you?

Adm. Dewey: Yes.

Sen. Patterson: And you sent Captain Coghlan down with a couple of your vessels, which resulted in the German man-of-war ceasing to obstruct; and then did Aguinaldo go and take the prisoners?

Adm. Dewey: These Spaniards surrendered to Captain Coghlan, the garrison surrendered to him, and by my instructions he turned them over to the Filipinos.

Sen. Patterson: Admiral, why should you seek to get obstructions out of the way of the Filipino forces?

Adm. Dewey: I didn't want any other power to interfere in the Philippines.

Sen. Patterson: You wanted the Filipinos to go there and get the garrison?

Adm. Dewey: They were our friends; yes. . . .

Sen. Patterson: Admiral, when did you commence negotiations with the Spanish commander at Manila for capitulation or surrender — about how many days before the 13th of August?

Adm. Dewey: Of course I am speaking from memory; I should think within ten days or two weeks, through the Belgian consul. Understand, now, I have not posted myself as to dates.

Sen. Patterson: We only expect when it comes to the matter of dates that you will approximate it.

Adm. Dewey: And I am speaking of something that happened four years ago.

Sen. Patterson: When did you reach an understanding with the Spanish commander upon that subject — how long before the 12th or 13th of August?

Adm. Dewey: Several days before.

Sen. Patterson: To whom did you communicate the arrangement that you had?

Adm. Dewey: General Merritt and, of course, all of my own captains

— General Merritt, and I think a council of officers on board of one of the steamers. I think there were several army officers present when I told the General that; and I may say here that I do not think General Merritt took much stock in it.

Sen. Patterson: What statement did you make to them, Admiral, in substance?

Adm. Dewey: That the Spaniards were ready to surrender, but before doing so I must engage one of the outlying forts. I selected one at Malate, away from the city. They said I must engage that and fire for a while, and then I was to make signal by the international code, "Do you surrender?" Then they were to hoist a white flag at a certain bastion; and I may say now that I was the first one to discover the white flag. We had fifty people looking for that white flag, but I happened to be the first one who saw it. I fired for a while, and then made the signal according to the program. We could not see the white flag — it was rather a thick day — but finally I discovered it on the south bastion; I don't know how long it had been flying there when I first saw it. . . .

Sen. Carmack: Admiral, if I understood the nature of your testimony yesterday it was to the effect that all the trouble we have had in the Philippines has arisen largely, or chiefly, from the evil influence and evil motives of Aguinaldo. Was that substantially your statement?

Adm. Dewey: I do not remember making that statement; perhaps you could show it to me.

Sen. Carmack: I was not trying to quote your exact language, but I thought that was the substance of your statement.

Adm. Dewey: Will you repeat that?

Sen. Carmack: I gather that from the general testimony ——

Adm. Dewey: Will you state that again?

Sen. Carmack: The trouble we have had in the Philippines has been due chiefly to Aguinaldo — to his evil motives?

Adm. Dewey: I won't say that. I will repeat what I did say — that I believe if we had 5,000 troops with us on the 1st of May the city would have surrendered to us, we would have taken possession then, and we would have had no trouble with the natives. I do not know how soon we might have had trouble, but not then. They were our friends then. They were so grateful to us for liberating them that I think they would have accepted us. That is my judgment.

Sen. Carmack: That there was a feeling of friendship and gratitude among the natives?

Adm. Dewey: Yes. I don't know how long it would have continued; perhaps the insurrection was bound to break out, but there was no insurrection then, and I think they would have accepted us; I think so.

Sen. Carmack: You said yesterday — of course, I am not giving your exact language now, but I think this is the substance of it — that Aguinaldo's only object was loot and money.

Sen. Patterson: He said he believed that was his object.

Sen. Carmack: That that was your opinion of Aguinaldo's object in the insurrection — that his only object was loot and money?

Adm. Dewey: And that I did not believe he expected independence when he went there.

Sen. Carmack: Do you think, then, that he fomented the trouble we have had with the Philippines from mercenary motives? You said something about his having a desire to get money by selling out again, or something like that.

Adm. Dewey: We always say "Aguinaldo." I think, as a matter of fact, Aguinaldo played a very small part in the insurrection. I think he was a figurehead. He was surrounded by men of brains and ability who did the work. One of his ablest men, Luna, he had assassinated; at least it was reported that Aguinaldo had him killed. I think Mabini and a number of those men superior to Aguinaldo. . . .

Sen. Carmack: Reference was made yesterday to the alleged fact that Aguinaldo had before betrayed his people for money. Did you mean in your answer yesterday to endorse that accusation?

Adm. Dewey: It was generally reported that that was the fact. Of course all these matters are hearsay. Aguinaldo never told me anything about it, but that was the general report in the East. . . .

Sen. Patterson: This is in the statement prepared by General Greene at the request of the government for the Commission at Paris. We were then negotiating the treaty of peace in Paris. . . .

"In August, 1896, an insurrection broke out in Cavite under the leadership of Emilio Aguinaldo, and soon spread to other provinces on both sides of Manila. It continued with varying successes on both sides, and the trial and execution of numerous insurgents, until December, 1897, when the governor-general, Primo de Rivera, entered into written agreement with Aguinaldo, the substance of the document, which is in possession of Senor Felipe Agoncillo, who accompanies me to Washington, being attached hereto and marked 'A.' In brief, it required that Aguinaldo and the other insurgent leaders should leave the country, the government agreeing to pay them $800,000 in silver, and promising to introduce numerous reforms, including representation in the Spanish Cortes, freedom of the press, general amnesty for all insurgents, and the expulsion or secularization of the monastic orders.

"Aguinaldo and his associates went to Hong Kong and Singapore. A portion of the money, $400,000, was deposited in banks at Hong Kong, and a lawsuit soon arose between Aguinaldo and one of his subordinate chiefs named Artacho, which is interesting on account of the very honorable position taken by Aguinaldo. Artacho sued for a division of the money among the insurgents according to rank. Aguinaldo claimed that the money was a trust fund, and was to remain on deposit until it was seen whether the Spaniards would carry out their promised reforms, and if they failed to do so, it was to be used to defray the expenses of a new insurrection. The suit was settled out of court by paying Artacho $5,000.". . .

Sen. Carmack: Do you know that Aguinaldo's character was a matter of inquiry before the Paris Peace Commission and several witnesses were examined on that question?

Adm. Dewey: No; I do not. . . . I read the summing up, but not the proceedings.

Sen. Beveridge: I do not know how the other members of the committee feel, but I do not feel that it is competent or proper to examine Admiral Dewey as to what witnesses said before the Peace Commission. It is competent to ask him as to facts within his knowledge, or opinions he may have derived from those facts, concerning Aguinaldo ——

Sen. Carmack: Admiral Dewey is not testifying to his own knowledge, but ——

Adm. Dewey: Common report.

Sen. Patterson: I trust we will not get into this sort of a wrangle.

Sen. Beveridge (acting chairman): We will not get into any wrangle unless you bring it about.

Sen. Patterson: I hope you will not in.'erfere with the examination.

Sen. Beveridge: I will not interfere unless it is proper to interfere.

Sen. Carmack: I do not think the Chair means any harm by it.

Sen. Beveridge: No; I never mean any harm, but I do not think the committee would say that it is within the scope of the committee to examine Admiral Dewey as to what was testified by different people who appeared before the Peace Commission and testified about Aguinaldo. The Admiral has testified as to his own personal observations of Aguinaldo.

Sen. Carmack: My only idea was this: I questioned him in regard to the sources of his information in regard to Aguinaldo, and he said it was hearsay.

Adm. Dewey: You mean about his looting?

Sen. Carmack: No; about this particular transaction of his having betrayed his people for money.

Adm. Dewey: Yes.

Sen. Carmack: And he said that was hearsay, and that he had derived it from ——

Adm. Dewey: Common report.

Sen. Carmack: And I wanted to call his attention to the fact that other statements had been made by others to the contrary. I asked him if he had occasion to investigate the facts that they set forth.

Sen. Beveridge (acting chairman): I think it is proper for you to ask him what the current rumor was and then he can state it and let it stand on its own basis, and then of course if you have anything to refute that ——

Sen. Carmack: If I can show contrary statements from men of high authority, contradicting this, it may change the Admiral's opinion.

Sen. Beveridge: From that point of view, I do not know that I will make any objection, if you think you can change the Admiral's opinion.

Adm. Dewey: I do not think it makes any difference what my opinion is on these things.

Sen. Patterson: There is no man whose opinion goes further with the country than yours does, Admiral, and therefore I think you ought to be very prudent in expressing your view.

Sen. Beveridge (acting chairman): The chairman will not permit any member to lecture Admiral Dewey on his prudence or his imprudence.

Sen. Patterson: I was not lecturing him.

Sen. Beveridge: Yes; you said he ought to be prudent.

Sen. Patterson: And I think it was well enough to suggest those things.

Sen. Carmack: You said yesterday you suspected that Aguinaldo took the lion's share of the provisions that were gathered for the army. What was the ground upon which you made that accusation?

Adm. Dewey: Because he was living in Malolos like a prince, like a king, in a way that could only have come about by his taking the lion's share. Then, in regard to his looting, I repeat what I said yesterday. He began within forty-eight hours after he landed in Cavite to capture and take everything he wanted. I know these things of my own knowledge, because I saw the loot brought in; and I know that every dollar that was taken from the workingmen at the navy yard was taken at the threat of death.

Sen. Carmack: You say that began immediately?

Adm. Dewey: Yes; within forty-eight hours. Now, it seems a little ungrateful in me to say this; but you have asked me, and I consider that I am under honor to tell the truth. I know these things. For example, he would send me for my ships a herd of cattle that he captured. He did not have any money when he landed.

Sen. Beveridge: He captured these cattle from his own people?

Adm. Dewey: Indiscriminately. There was a reign of terror there. I know these things; it is not hearsay. . . .

Sen. Carmack: General Bell was commended to the Peace Commission by General Greene as a man who knew the Filipinos from Aguinaldo down. General Bell testified that Aguinaldo was honest, sincere, and poor. Do you think your opportunities for knowing him were better than those of General Bell?

Adm. Dewey: General Bell has a right to his opinion. I do not question ——

Sen. Carmack: I was asking you about your relative opportunities for forming a correct opinion.

Adm. Dewey: . . . I saw Aguinaldo in the beginning when he came there; I saw him almost daily; I don't know how many times, but many times, and I judged of the man. We were dealing with rather important subjects. I considered him then a man of no ability at all.

Sen. Carmack: General Greene and, I believe, General Whittier also, testified as to Aguinaldo's honesty. Do you think they had fair opportunities ——

Adm. Dewey: I would rather not answer these questions; these gentlemen are all friends of mine.

Sen. Carmack: I am asking of your knowledge and your opportunities to form a correct opinion.

Adm. Dewey: I would simply give my own opinion; I would rather not criticize their opinion.

Sen. Beveridge (acting chairman): You do not have to give any expression whatever which in your own mind would fall as a criticism of any brother officer in the army or navy.

Adm. Dewey: I am very glad. . . .

Sen. Carmack: I say is it a fact, do you think that the man you took to the Philippine Islands to be the leader of the people in an insurrectionary movement was a man who, as you believed, had but recently betrayed them for a bribe?

Adm. Dewey: I think that would not make any difference, whatever he did; it was a reign of terror during this time; it was a reign of terror absolutely.

Sen. Carmack: But you wanted a man there who could rally the people, call them to arms and accept his leadership, and the man you put forward was the very man who but a short time before had betrayed them for money?

Sen. Beveridge (acting chairman): Of course it is only proper to Admiral Dewey to say that in putting that question, "You wanted a man who could rally the people to his standard," and so on, you are putting in not what he expressed.

Sen. Carmack: He can answer the question in his own way.

Sen. Beveridge (acting chairman): But it is proper to call his attention to that.

Sen. Carmack: You did want a man there who could organize and rouse the people?

Adm. Dewey: I didn't want anybody. I would like to say now that Aguinaldo and his people were forced on me by Consul Pratt and Consul Wildman; I didn't do anything ——

Sen. Carmack: Did they have any power to force him upon you?

Adm. Dewey: Yes; they had in a way. They had not the official power, but one will yield after a while to constant pressure. I did not expect anything of them; I did not think they would do anything. I would not have taken them; I did not want them; I did not believe in them; because, when I left Hong Kong, I was led to suppose that the country was in a state of insurrection, and that at my first gun, as Mr. Williams put it, there would be a general uprising, and I thought these half dozen or dozen refugees at Hong Kong would play a very small part in it.

Sen. Carmack: Then by helping Aguinaldo arm and organize a force, knowing his character as you did, you placed the whole country and its people at the mercy of a man who had no higher object than to get rich by plundering them or betraying them, when, as a matter of fact, you had no need at all for their services?

Sen. McComas: That is an assumption and not a question.

Adm. Dewey: I am not a lawyer; I cannot debate with you, Senator.

Sen. Carmack: I want to get at your meaning. You said you had no need for Aguinaldo and his forces, but you did aid and assist him, did you not, in organizing an army, and when he grew despondent you urged him to continue his efforts to organize the army, and you assisted him and encouraged him to organize an army, knowing the character of the man?

Adm. Dewey: No, I did not know it then; I did not know his character. . . .

Sen. Carmack: You said you had no need of Aguinaldo or his army?

Adm. Dewey: Did I say that?

Sen. Carmack: You said you had no need of Aguinaldo or his army.

Adm. Dewey: That is quite different from did not need — that I did not want them.

Sen. Carmack: Could get along better without them?

Adm. Dewey: Yes; we know that now.

Sen. Carmack: Then you did not need them?

Adm. Dewey: Well; I did not want them.

Sen. Carmack: Then it is a fact, is it not, that you took a man to the Philippines, aided him and encouraged him to organize an army over which you were to have little or no control, a man who had no higher object than to get rich by plundering the people or by betraying them?

Adm. Dewey: I won't answer that; I am not going to answer that.

Sen. Carmack: Very well; you decline to answer the question. You say you did not know at the time that Aguinaldo was such a bad man?

Adm. Dewey: I did not know anything about him, really, at the time. I permitted him to come; I did not take him, but I permitted him to come; I did not know about him then.

Sen. Carmack: Did you encourage him to organize an army?

Adm. Dewey: Well, yes; I did to a certain extent; I gave him a few arms; I did encourage him. . . .

Sen. Patterson: And when Aguinaldo came there did he ever talk to you on the basis of selling out?

Adm. Dewey: No.

Sen. Patterson: Did he ever ask you for money?

Adm. Dewey: Yes.

Sen. Patterson: Give us that occurrence, whatever it was.

Adm. Dewey: He wanted a bill of exchange — let me correct that.

Sen. Patterson: Yes, sir.

Adm. Dewey: He wanted to exchange Mexican dollars for gold; he wanted me to give him gold for Mexican dollars.

Sen. Patterson: That was an exchange of funds.

Adm. Dewey: I was pretty sure in my own mind where he had gotten those Mexican dollars; he had not brought them in with him when he came, and I thought from the fact that he wanted to put that money into gold that he was getting ready to leave.

Sen. Beveridge: He could not use the gold for disbursements among the troops or purchase of supplies; the silver would answer that purpose better.

Adm. Dewey: That is correct; that is one thing which had escaped my mind, and that is one thing which made me believe that he was feathering his own nest.

Sen. Patterson: That was a suspicion on your part?

Adm. Dewey: Yes. He never told me so.

Sen. Patterson: Did he ever ask you, or any officer of the government that you know of, for compensation in any way for his services for you and in raising an army and in defeating the Spanish forces in Manila?

Adm. Dewey: No; he never asked it of me, or to my knowledge of anyone else.

Sen. Beveridge: He would not have been apt to have gotten it from you?

Adm. Dewey: No.

Sen. Beveridge: He probably knew he would not get it from you.

Sen. Patterson: But nevertheless ——

Adm. Dewey: He never asked it. The understanding between us was that we had a common enemy in Manila and that we were ——

Sen. Patterson: And you told him ——

Adm. Dewey: To go ahead.

Sen. Patterson: To gather his army?

Adm. Dewey: Yes.

Sen. Patterson: In the collection of his army, as the men came in, it became absolutely necessary to have commissary stores for them, did it not?

Adm. Dewey: Oh, they had to feed them.

Sen. Patterson: He had no treasury behind him?

Adm. Dewey: Not when he arrived.

Sen. Patterson: Nor was he furnished with any treasury by the government of the United States?

Adm. Dewey: No; not while I was in command.

Sen. Patterson: Not that you have any knowledge of?

Adm. Dewey: No.

Sen. Beveridge: Notwithstanding this, he lived in a state of magnificence, as you have described?

Adm. Dewey: Yes.

Sen. Patterson: I suggest you allow me to proceed.

Sen. Beveridge: I will; but I think it is pertinent to put that in there.

Sen. Patterson: I understand that. He established headquarters?

Adm. Dewey: First at Cavite.

Sen. Patterson: And when did he establish them at Malolos?

Adm. Dewey: After our troops came.

Sen. Patterson: Was it at Malolos that he lived in magnificence, as you have described?

Adm. Dewey: Yes. He had a chariot and four, and a band of a hundred pieces, and everything in the grandest style.

Sen. Patterson: That was very well calculated to inspire with respect the Filipinos he gathered to his standard, and to give them the feeling that there was something substantial behind their efforts?

Adm. Dewey: It inspired them more than it inspired those from whom he had taken the money to maintain this magnificence.

Sen. Patterson: Do you think those innuendos are just and proper?

Adm. Dewey: I do.

Sen. Beveridge (acting chairman): I do not know whether any Senator objects, but I will frankly say that such a question as that the Chair will rule is not proper and that it is discourteous.

Sen. Patterson: It is not.

Sen. Beveridge: The Chair thinks it is.

Sen. Patterson: I will let the record stand to show that the question is perfectly proper and perfectly justifiable.

Sen. Beveridge: And you will also let the record state what the opinion of the Chair is upon that subject.

Sen. Patterson: I don't care what the opinion of the Chair is.

Sen. Beveridge: And I will not permit the question to be put.

Sen. Patterson: Do you know that Aguinaldo has a dollar today?

Adm. Dewey: No; how should I know it? I have not been there for three years.

Sen. Patterson: Do you know, Admiral, from common experience that there was never a day when Aguinaldo might not, right from the government of the United States, have made himself very rich if he had not continued, or if he would have given up the effort he was making for the independence of his people?

Adm. Dewey: I won't answer that question. Of course I don't know. How could I know that? . . .

Sen. Patterson: Do you know, Admiral, that a number of those who were with Aguinaldo have been given good, fat offices by the United States over there?

Adm. Dewey: No; I do not know that.

Sen. McComas: You have not been there for three years?

Adm. Dewey: No. . . .

Testimony of Robert P. Hughes

Brigadier General Robert Patterson Hughes, a Pennsylvanian, was a career army officer. Born in 1839 and educated at Jefferson College at the town of Canonsburg in his home state, he enlisted as a private in the Twelfth Infantry of Pennsylvania immediately after the attack on Fort Sumter; by the end of the war he was a brevet colonel. In 1866 he entered the regular army and rose through the commissioned ranks to be a brigadier general at the time of the Spanish-American War. Arriving in Manila in August, 1898, he was appointed by General Ewell S. Otis to the post of Provost-Marshal-General of Manila and its environs. He commanded the First Military District of the Philippine Islands in 1899, and in 1900 the Department of the Visayan Islands.

Gen. Hughes: On the 9th of January I was appointed one of a commission . . . to meet the commissioners of General Aguinaldo to see if the difficulty between ourselves and the insurrectos could not be settled in some way. The order you will find in General Otis's report for 1899 at page 81. It reads as follows:

ORDER APPOINTING COMMISSION TO MEET AGUINALDO'S COMMISSIONERS

SPECIAL ORDERS, }   HEADQUARTERS DEPARTMENT PACIFIC,
No. 9.   }   *Eighth Army Corps,*
                                           Manila, P.I., January 9, 1899

[Extract]

8. Brig. Gen. R. P. Hughes, U.S. Volunteers, Col. James F. Smith, First California Volunteers, Lieut. Col. E. H. Crowder, judge advocate, U.S. Volunteers, are hereby appointed a commission to meet a commission of like number appointed by General Aguinaldo, and to confer with regard to the situation of affairs and to arrive at a mutual understanding of the intent, purposes, aim, and desires of the Filipino people and the people of the United States, that peace and harmonious relations between these respective peoples may be continued.

By command of Major General Otis:

THOMAS H. BARRY,
Assistant Adjutant General

This shows the desire of the governor to continue the peaceable relations that had nominally existed between the insurrecto forces and our own up to this time. We had gone to see them, and they had come to see us; but there are certain papers that indicate that while friendly relations seemed to exist, as a matter of fact it was not the case.

I should like to call your attention to a proclamation, or letter, you may call it, which Aguinaldo issued to the people of Manila who were in charge on the same day the Commission was appointed. . . .

PROCLAMATION OF AGUINALDO

MALOLOS, 9th of January, 1899

INSTRUCTIONS TO THE BRAVE SOLDIERS OF SANDATAHAN OF MANILA

ARTICLE 1. All Filipinos should observe our fellow-countrymen in order to see whether they are American sympathizers. They shall take care to work with them in order to inspire them with confidence of the strength of the holy cause of their country.

Whenever they are assured of the loyalty of the convert they shall instruct them to continue in the character of an American sympathizer in order that they may receive good pay, but without prejudicing the cause of our country. In this way they can serve themselves and at the same time serve the public by communicating to the committee of chiefs and officials of our army whatever news of importance they may have.

ARTICLE 2. All of the chiefs and Filipino brothers should be ready and courageous for the combat and should take advantage of the opportunity to study well the situation of the American outposts and headquarters. Observing especially secret places where they can approach and surprise the enemy.

ARTICLE 3. The chief of those who go to attack the barracks should send in first four men with a good present for the American commander. Immediately after will follow four others, who will make a pretense of looking for the same officer for some reason, and a larger group shall be concealed in the corners or houses in order to aid the other groups at the first signal. This wherever it is possible at the moment of attack.

ARTICLE 4. They should not prior to the attack look at the Americans in a threatening manner. To the contrary, the attack on the barracks by the Sandatahan should be a complete surprise and with decision and courage. One should go alone in advance in order to kill the sentinel. In order to deceive the sentinel the one should dress as a woman and must take great care that the sentinel is not able to discharge his piece, thus calling the attention of those in the barracks. This will enable his companions who are approaching to assist in the general attack.

ARTICLE 5. At the moment of the attack the Sandatahan should not attempt to secure rifles from their dead enemies, but shall pursue, slashing right and left with bolos, until the Americans surrender, and after there remains no enemy who can injure them they may take the rifles in one hand and the ammunition in the other.

ARTICLE 6. The officers shall take care that on the top of the houses along the streets where the American forces shall pass there will be placed four to six men, who shall be prepared with stones, timbers, red-hot iron, heavy furniture, as well as boiling water, oil, and molasses, rags soaked in coal oil ready to be lighted and thrown down, and any other hard and heavy objects that they can throw on the passing American troops. At the same time in the lower parts of the houses will be concealed the Sandatahan, who will attack immediately. Great care should be taken not to throw glass in the streets, as the greater part of our soldiers go barefooted. On these houses there will, if possible, be arranged, in addition to the objects to be thrown down, a number of the Sandatahan, in order to cover a retreat or to follow up a rout of the enemy's column, so that we may be sure of the destruction of all of the opposing forces.

ARTICLE 7. All Filipinos, real defenders of their country, should live on the alert to assist simultaneously the inside attack at the very moment that they note the first movement in whatever barrio or suburb, having assurance that all the troops that surround Manila will proceed without delay to force the enemy's line and unite themselves with their brothers in the city. With such a general movement, so firm and decided against the Americans, the combat is sure to be a short one, and I charge and order that the persons and goods of all foreigners shall be respected and that the American prisoners shall be treated well.

ARTICLE 8. All of our chiefs in the suburbs should prepare groups of the Sandatahan, who will attack with ferocity and decision the Americans within their lines, attempting to surround each group of Americans or to break through their lines. This must be done if the nature of the ground occupied by the Americans will permit and if the Sandatahan have the proper amount of courage and resolution, and the more courage and intelligence that they show in the moment of the attack, the surer will be the result and the fewer will be their own losses.

ARTICLE 9. In addition to the instructions given in paragraph 6 there shall be in the houses vessels filled with boiling water, tallow, molasses, and other liquids which shall be thrown as bombs on the Americans who pass in front of their houses, or they can make use of syringes or tubes of bamboo. In these houses shall be the Sandatahan who shall hurl the liquids that shall be passed to them by the women and children.

ARTICLE 10. In place of bolos or daggers, if they do not possess the same, the Sandatahan can provide themselves with lances and arrows with long and sharp heads, and these should be shot with great force in order that they may penetrate well into the bodies of the enemy. And these should be so made that in withdrawal from the body the head will remain in the flesh.

ARTICLE 11. It can be taken for granted that, if the above instructions are observed, the enemy will not be able to use firearms because of the confusion in his ranks, as they would shoot one another. For this reason I have always thought the rifle useless in this kind of combat, for experience has taught me, my dear brothers, that when the Sandatahan make their attack with courage and decision, taking advantage of the confusion in the ranks of the enemy, the victory is sure, and in that case the triumph is ours.

ARTICLE 12. At last, if, as I expect, the result shall favor us in the taking of Manila and the conquering of the enemy, the chiefs are charged with seeing that the officers and soldiers respect the consulates, the banks, and commercial houses, and even the Spanish banks and commercial houses, taking care that they be not seduced by the hope of plunder. As if God sees this, He will reward us and the foreign nations will note the order and justice of our conduct. I charge that in the moment of combat, the officers, soldiers, and whatever patriots take part in the struggle will not forget our noble, sacred, and holy ideals, liberty and independence. Neither will you forget your sacred oath and immaculate banner; nor will you forget the promises made by me to the civilized nations, whom I have assured that we Filipinos are not savages, nor thieves, nor assassins, nor are we cruel; but, on the contrary, that we are men of culture and patriotism, honorable and very humane.

Above all I expect that you will respect the persons and goods of private persons of all nationalities, including the Chinese; that you will treat well the prisoners and grant life to those of the enemy who surrender. And that you be on the sharp lookout for those traitors and enemies who, by robbery, will seek to mar our victory.

Emilio Aguinaldo

Gen. Hughes: I will read this part of it:

"All Filipinos should observe our fellow-countrymen in order to see whether they are American sympathizers. They shall take care to work with them in order to inspire them with confidence of the strength of the holy cause of their country.

"Whenever they are assured of the loyalty of the convert they shall instruct them to continue in the character of an American sympathizer in order that they may receive good pay, but without prejudicing the cause of our country. In this way they can serve themselves and at the same time serve the public by communicating to the committee of chiefs and officials of our army whatever news of importance they may have."

Then he goes on and defines how they shall prepare for action.

Sen. Hale: Where was Aguinaldo at that time?

Gen. Hughes: He was at Malolos. This is on the same date that the order was issued appointing a committee to see if some peace arrangements could not be made.

Sen. Beveridge: This commission might be called the first peace commission?

Gen. Hughes: Really we were no commission at all. We were a committee appointed by General Otis to meet a like committee appointed by General Aguinaldo.

Sen. Hale: What did you do?

Gen. Hughes: That is what I am coming to. We met on the 9th of January.

The Malolos committee consisted of Judge Torres, General Flores, and Colonel Arguelles, Arguelles being especially Aguinaldo's representative, as he was one of his staff officers.

At the first meeting this committee was unprepared to act. It had no instructions. We met on the 14th, giving them time to consult Aguinaldo and get their data. They came back, as I recall it now, although I have not a single paper of those meetings, with a letter from Mabini, who was the brains of Aguinaldo's establishment, stating that the first requisite was absolute independence; that after we had conceded that, they could discuss some kind of protection, or something of that kind.

. . . [W]e met from time to time and spent hours in trying to arrive at just what these men really wanted. For instance, we asked them: "What are we to understand by your absolute independence? Do you mean that you wish the Americans to go out and take their transports and sail out of this harbor?" "Oh, no; for God's sake, no. No; we will make the laws and you will stay here and see that outsiders do not disturb us." And we never, from the day we began until the day we quit, could get the definition of what they really wanted. They did not know themselves.

Sen. Allison: They seemed to be clear on this business.

Gen. Hughes: Yes; on this business, but beyond that there was nothing else — absolute independence and somebody to take care of them.

They recognized the fact that they could not stand on their own feet. They recognized the fact that they would fall into someone's hands unless they were protected, but they wanted first absolute independence and then a dicker with the world as to what they could do.

Arguelles was a very honest sort of man. He was honest enough to go back after his numerous talks with us and tell Aguinaldo that the best thing he could do was to make terms and quit. For this he got a trial by court, and just escaped with his life, but was incarcerated, the order being that it should last twelve years. But our people were fortunate enough to get him out later on. He is now in Manila in the employ of the civil government, I think. . . .

Testimony of Ewell S. Otis

Major General Ewell Stephen Otis had been in command of all the United States troops in the Philippines when, in the late summer of 1898, he was designated military governor of the islands. As such he was responsible for the complicated work of relieving the Spanish officials and replacing them with Americans in the takeover of authority. Serving until May, 1900, he was forced to deal with the Filipino insurrection which broke out in Manila on February 4, 1898. Born in Frederick, Maryland in 1838, Otis was a graduate of the University of Rochester (1858) and of the Harvard Law School (1861). Performing gallantly with the Army of the Potomac during the Civil War, he became an Indian-fighting career officer in the postwar years. His work in creating the army school (now the Command and General Staff School) at Fort Leavenworth, Kansas — of which he was commandant in the 1880's — is his most lasting achievement.

Sen. Patterson: Did Aguinaldo, any of his cabinet, any of his high officials, ever state to you that the reason they wanted to drive the Spaniards out was so that the United States might come in and run their government?

Gen. Otis: A number of the cabinet stated to me that they desired United States supremacy early.

Sen. Patterson: Did Aguinaldo, or the officers under Aguinaldo, or his troops, give it or make it known their purpose was, in assembling together, to resist the Spaniards if they returned, in order that the United States might take possession of the islands and exercise dominion over them?

Gen. Otis: Aguinaldo expressed himself in his proclamation.

Sen. Patterson: Do you understand my question, General?

Gen. Otis: Why, certainly.

Sen. Patterson: Would you kindly answer it?

Gen. Otis: I never met Aguinaldo ——

Sen. Patterson: Cannot you answer that in a soldierly way? It is a plain, ordinary question.

Gen. Otis: Just ask it again.

Sen. Patterson: The question is this ——

Gen. Otis: It is a hypothetical question, is it not?

Sen. Patterson: No, sir; it is not.

Gen. Otis: Do you not wish an expression of opinion?

Sen. Patterson: No, sir; I want your knowledge and experience.

Gen. Otis: You want me to state what they were there for, why they were there. I don't know.

Sen. Patterson: Did you have any doubt that that army was gathered for the purpose of asserting and maintaining the independence of the Philippine Islands?

Gen. Otis: Independence of the Philippine Islands?

Sen. Patterson: The independence of the Philippine Islands. For the purpose of enabling the Philippine people to establish a government of their own by which they would control that island as against both the United States and Spain and any other country.

Gen. Otis: I had an idea, very often expressed, for two months before hostilities broke out that the insurgents intended to drive us out if they could.

Sen. Carmack: For what purpose?

Gen. Otis: I do not know for what purpose.

Sen. Patterson: Now, General Otis, have you ever had any single, serious doubt in your mind, from the time you went there until hostilities commenced, that what the Filipino army was there for was to gain, if possible, the independence of the Philippine Islands?

Gen. Otis: The army was there to overawe the people, which it did in northern Luzon, which it did in Dagupan, where it had difficulty, and in other portions of the islands. It surrounded us to be prepared, as they said, for Spain, in case they attempted to take the islands again, professing all the time the most friendly sentiments toward the Americans.

Sen. Patterson: Assuming that they were there to overawe the people of northern Luzon and were there to overawe the people in other portions, I ask you again did you have any doubt in your mind but what the object of that army was to secure the independence of the islands?

Gen. Otis: They never intended to secure their independence; they proposed to set up a government under Aguinaldo, possibly.

Sen. Patterson: Very well; to secure a government of their own under somebody that they would be willing to have govern them; independence of some kind. I am not talking about a republic now, but a government of their own. Was not that the purpose for which that army was assembled?

Gen. Otis: Not according to their own protestations.

Sen. Patterson: Was it there for the purpose of plunder?

Gen. Otis: Yes.

Sen. Patterson: Was it there for the purpose of driving the Americans into the sea? . . .

Gen. Otis: They wanted to drive the Americans into the sea and kill every white man in Manila.

Sen. Patterson: Simply to convert themselves into your robbers? Is that your statement as a soldier's [*sic*] — that that was the purpose of the army?

Gen. Otis: It was made up largely of robbers.

Sen. Patterson: I know; made up of bad people; no good in them?

Gen. Otis: Yes; there was some good ——

Sen. Patterson: But I want to know the purpose which you as a soldier know they were there for.

Gen. Otis: I don't know.

Sen. Patterson: Is that the reason you impute everything bad to them — because you don't know?

Gen. Otis: No, sir.

Sen. Patterson: What is the reason?

Gen. Otis: I do not impute everything bad to them. There were some very good men.

Sen. Patterson: I read your correspondence with Aguinaldo, and I have read it with pleasure — and also Aguinaldo's letters to you — in which time and time again you ascribed the highest motives, the most sincere desire for peace, the most sincere desire upon the part of Aguinaldo for friendship and fellowship between the United States troops and his troops.

Gen. Otis: Which I do.

Sen. Patterson: Your own letters; yes. I can refer you to them. Did you mean what you said when you said those things?

Gen. Otis: Certainly I did.

Sen. Patterson: Then, do you want this committee to understand when you were communicating with Aguinaldo, as the general in command of the Filipino forces, and commending his efforts for peace, that you at heart believed that he was a robber and a looter, and was at the head of 20,000 or 30,000 men ——

Gen. Otis: I do not say that Aguinaldo was a robber or a looter. Aguinaldo is very much better than a great majority of them. In many matters I believe that Aguinaldo is strictly honest. In duplicity he has few equals.

Sen. Patterson: Well, he has a good many illustrious colleagues, so far as that is concerned, in the world. . . .

Sen. Patterson: Speaking of Aguinaldo, I believe you say you do not regard him as pecuniarily a dishonest man?

Gen. Otis: No; I never have.

Sen. Carmack: He is said to be, I believe, a man of dignity and a very reserved man?

Gen. Otis: He knows how to keep his counsel if he has any.

Sen. Carmack: He is not a man disposed to divulge anything?

Gen. Otis: No; in that lies his strength.

Sen. McComas: What about his ability?

Gen. Otis: In his secrecy lies his strength.

Sen. McComas: Is he an able man or not?

Gen. Otis: I never regarded him as an able man. I never saw but two or three of his productions, and I have seen some of his letters written to his friends; but I saw one or two proclamations written to his people, which they said he wrote himself, which they suppressed very shortly. . . .

2   INDEPENDENCE OR WHAT?

Testimony of William Howard Taft

William Howard Taft, who in a few years would be President of the United States (1909–13) and afterwards Chief Justice (1921–30), had been appointed civil governor of the Philippine Islands in 1901. Born in Cincinnati in 1857, he had ancestral roots deep in New England. These connections he reinforced by attending Yale College from which he was graduated in 1878. Returning to the Middle West he took a law degree from the Cincinnati Law School, and after being admitted to the bar in Ohio, he entered Republican-party politics. His faithful regularity was rewarded early: an appointment in 1887 to be a judge of the superior court of his state. He became a national figure for the first time in 1889 when President Benjamin Harrison named him to be Solicitor General of the United States. Taft's main vocation was the judiciary and he eagerly accepted a federal circuit court seat in 1892. A legal scholar, he was offered the presidency of Yale in 1899 but could not be tempted to leave the bench. In early 1900, however, President William McKinley persuaded him to become the president of the Philippine Commission, charged with effecting the transfer of the Philippines from military to civilian rule. He showed himself a determined administrator, and skillfully managed the delicate transition in the islands from military to civil rule.

Sen. Carmack: You made a close and careful study of the conditions in the islands and the character of the people. I wish to ask you what is your opinion of the proposal that the Philippine Islands shall be made an integral part of the United States — leaving out for the present the question of statehood — giving them equal constitutional rights, and full rights of citizenship to the people. What is your opinion of that proposal?

Gov. Taft: . . . The condition of the people of the Philippine Islands today is such that the extension of the constitutional restrictions which apply in a state would very much interfere with the establishment of a stable and successful government.

A government ought to be established under American guidance which shall form a stable government, by which and under which the Filipinos shall gradually improve their knowledge of what is individual liberty and what is a constitutional government, and subsequently the time will come when the United States and the Filipino people together can agree upon what their relations shall be.

Whether a colony — I mean a quasi-independent colony as Australia and Canada are to England — an independent state, or a state of the Union, is a question so far in the future, dependent upon the success of the operation of the stable government, and that I have not myself reached a conclusion on the subject.

Sen. Carmack: You think, then, it is an open question whether the people of the Philippine Islands — islands populated with eight or ten million Asiatics — should be admitted to the full rights of American citizenship or whether or not an archipelago so populated should be admitted to statehood in the Union? You think it is an open question?

Gov. Taft: I think it is a question that I would not answer two or three generations before it will arise. I think the great evil today is the discussion of something that is utterly impossible of settlement today. The thing the Filipino people need today is a stable government under the guidance of American control, teaching them what individual liberty is and training them to a knowledge of self-government, and when they have that, the question of what relations shall then exist between the islands and this country may be settled between them and the citizens of the United States.

But to attempt to decide in advance something that is utterly impossible wisely to decide now, it seems to me, with deference to those who differ with me, very unreasonable.

Sen. Carmack: I was speaking of it from the standpoint of the people of the United States, as to whether you thought it was a question of possibility ——

Gov. Taft: What the people of the United States may think, or what they ought to think, fifty or a hundred years from now I do not venture to say.

Sen. Patterson: It is a century problem?

Gov. Taft: It is quite possible, as we say in our report, that it may take a generation, or two generations, but no matter how long it is, it is in my judgment the duty of the United States to continue a government there which shall teach those people individual liberty, which shall lift them up to a point of civilization of which I believe they are capable, and which shall make them rise to call the name of the United States blessed. . . .

Sen. Carmack: You say the great trouble in all this matter has been that we are thinking about what may happen a generation or two generations from now. If the possession of the Philippine Islands by the United States involves the possibility of an archipelago 7,000 miles away, inhabited by people of an Asiatic race, becoming a state of the Union fifty or a hundred years from now, do you not think it is a question which deserves consideration now? Do you not think we ought to consider what may happen fifty years from now?

Gov. Taft: No, sir; and I will say why. Nothing that can today be said to the Filipino people in the nature of a promise as to the form of government which may take place after an established stable government shall be formed could be otherwise than misleading to them and confusing in establishing that government.

It would at once begin the agitation among those who desire that separation to have that separation, because, in their opinion, they are fitted for it at once. It would drive away from the support of the stable government that conservative element who are strongly in favor of American guidance and control, because they would anticipate an early change.

They would think they would early be left without the support which the presence of the American government necessarily gives, and the promise of something in the future, instead of helping to establish, would render unstable any government which was attempted to be established.

Sen. Patterson: Then this statement by the Federal party [in the Philippines], of which three members of the United States Commission are active members, is false?

"To make of the Philippines a colony of the United States or to grant independence to the Philippines would be to hand the islands over to disorder and to anarchy, to destruction and to chaos.". . .

Gov. Taft: . . . It is just as true as gospel.

Sen. Patterson: It is just as true as gospel that to make the Philippines a colony of the United States is to hand the islands over to disorder and anarchy ——

Gov. Taft: No.

Sen. Patterson: To destruction and chaos?

Gov. Taft: No.

Sen. Patterson: That is exactly what this party states to the Congress of the United States.

Gov. Taft: To give them independence now, it is true.

Sen. Patterson: But, Governor ——

Gov. Taft: So far as a colony is concerned I object to that course just the same as I do to establishing what the permanent relation between these islands and the United States shall be.

All that I think is necessary and all that ought to be done is (to do more, it seems to me, would interfere with that which everyone — I will not say everyone, because there are so many differing opinions — but that which most people think is essential) the establishment of a stable government before anything is done. It would make that impossible.

Sen. Patterson: Is it not the distinction between a territory, with the

Constitution of the United States extended over it, such as our Territories in the United States, and a colony clear and distinct?

Gov. Taft: I do not think it is.

Sen. Patterson: You do not?

Gov. Taft: No, sir; the idea which the Federal party have with respect to colonial government is the government that prevailed under Spain.

Sen. Patterson: The Federal party have no idea that the United States would treat them in that way?

Gov. Taft: The treatment of these islands for exploitation, with complete government in Spain, is just what they have in mind in that statement.

Sen. Patterson: Let me ask you a question.

Sen. McComas: Let him answer the last. I should like to hear his answer.

The Chairman: Let him answer one question at a time.

Gov. Taft: I thought I had answered it.

Sen. Patterson: I thought so, too. Would you be in favor of the Congress of the United States making the following declaration?

"That the Philippine Islands, as they are described in the treaty of Paris and subsequent conventions with Spain, are an integral part of the Republic of the United States of North America, the said Philippine Islands constituting a Territory with the rights and privileges which the Constitution of the United States grants to the other Territories, such as that of becoming eventually a State of the Union."

Would you favor Congress making a declaration of that kind?

Gov. Taft: To begin with, the Constitution does not grant any such rights to the Territories.

Sen. Patterson: The question I ask you is, whether you would favor a declaration of that kind?

Gov. Taft: I do not wish to be involved in a misstatement ——

Sen. Carmack: Where the Constitution is extended by Congressional action.

Gov. Taft: I would not be in favor of making any such statement.

Sen. Patterson: That is exactly what the Federal party demands at the hands of Congress.

Gov. Taft: It asks. It does not demand.

Sen. Patterson: Well, asks. This is its language:

"In behalf, then, of the Federal party, this convention has the honor to very respectfully present to the Congress the following petition, praying a declaration by the Congress of the United States" ——

Then follows what I have heretofore read.

Gov. Taft: I am opposed to any declaration now with respect to the Philippine Islands other than a declaration in favor of the formation of a stable government, in which the voice of the Filipino people shall grow more and more powerful in the control of that government.

Sen. Beveridge: As they come to know its operations?

Gov. Taft: Yes, sir.

Sen. Culberson: Is not your proposition, then, in substance, that the Government of the United States shall govern the islands as a colony in the broad and best sense of the term —

Sen. Carmack: Or as a province?

Sen. Culberson: For fifty or a hundred years, it may be necessary, after which it shall then consider whether that territory shall become a colony such as Canada or Australia or an independent state or a state of the Union? Is not that the substance to what you have testified to?

Gov. Taft: My proposition is this: You can call it a colonial form of government; you can call it a territorial form of government; I do not quarrel with names.

My proposition is that it is the duty of the United States to establish there a government suited to the present possibilities of the people, which shall gradually change, conferring more and more right upon the people to govern themselves, thus educating them in self-government, until their knowledge of government, their knowledge of individual liberty shall be such that further action may be taken either by giving them statehood or by making them a quasi-independent government like Canada and Australia, or if they desire it by independence.

My point, and the point I insist upon, if I may be pardoned for using that expression, is that the discussion today of independence, of statehood, of a colonial form of government, in the sense of a permanent relation of colony to mother country, is altogether aside from the questions which are now presented.

Those are, and those concern, the establishment of a firm and stable government in which the Filipino people shall learn self-government by exercising it partially.

Sen. Culberson: In consenting to be the medium of presenting this petition of the Federal party to Congress, have you not yourself presented that very question for discussion to Congress and to the American people?

Gov. Taft: I have consented to present it as I should consent to present any respectful petition that was turned over to me. I stated to the Federal party at the time that the discussion of the future relations of the United States was not such as the Commission indulged in; that the Commission had made a recommendation in their report not unlike, though differing in details, the form of government now proposed for the Philippine Islands; but that in the discussion of what should happen as to statehood, independence, or anything else, the Commission took no part.

Sen. Culberson: Notwithstanding the fact that you have presented this petition from the Federal party, you do not believe that the issue which you present ought to be discussed by Congress or the American people.

Gov. Taft: I think Congress ought not to act upon it. Undoubtedly, I do.

Sen. Culberson: You are, then, opposed to granting the request made by the Federal party?

Gov. Taft: I am opposed to granting certain of the requests, and I am in favor substantially of granting others.

Sen. Culberson: I mean the broad request that Congress shall at this time declare its policy of creating a Territory under the Constitution of the United States?

Gov. Taft: And a promise of statehood.

Sen. Culberson: And a promise of statehood?

Gov. Taft: Yes, sir; I do.

Sen. Patterson: Eliminating from the controversy for the time being the question of statehood, are you in favor of Congress declaring "that the said Philippine Islands constitute a Territory, with the rights and privileges which the Constitution of the United States grants to the other Territories."

Gov. Taft: No, sir; I am not in favor of it. I am not in favor of granting the right of jury there, for instance, for I do not think they are fitted for it, or a jury in all common-law cases involving $20. There are other constitutional restrictions which would very much interfere, for instance the uniformity of taxation, with the prosperity of those islands or the possibility of conducting a government. Therefore, I am opposed to the extension of the Constitution to those islands. . . .

The Chairman: Do you think . . . we having withdrawn and a state of anarchy having arisen, it would probably lead to the partition of the islands among other powers? . . .

Gov. Taft: It is a question of opinion as to the interest which foreigners take in the islands. They are called among foreigners whom I know in Manila the gems of the orient. The interest that Japan has taken in the islands the records of the military department will show. The interest that other governments would take in the islands may be judged of by reference to the foreign capital invested there. The Germans have a great deal of capital. The English have a good deal.

Sen. McComas: You have comprehended in your answer other questions which I had contemplated asking. Could we in any way, at any time, in your opinion, obtain sufficient guaranties for the safety of the inhabitants who have adhered to the United States? . . . What would happen to them if we withdrew . . . ?

Gov. Taft: The personal hostility between leading Filipinos at times has been so great as to lead to bloody measures. How far they would be carried here I have no idea. That is conjectural.

I should like to say, if I may, although I had not expected to come to this part of the discussion now, that it is a very logical and reasonable proposition on its face to say: Will not the insurrection come to an end;

will not there be general peace and tranquillity if you promise to give these people independence when they shall be fitted for it? That proposition, put in that way, seems to have a great deal of force.

Practically, the effect of such a promise would be exactly the opposite from that which the argument presupposes. The promise to give them independence when they are fit for it would be accepted by them as a promise to give them independence certainly during the lifetime of the present generation. It would at once bring into a discussion of every issue the question whether now were not the people ready for independence. It would drive out capital; prevent capital from coming there; and upon the investment of capital, the building of railroads, the enlargement of vision of the Filipino people much of our hope of progress must depend.

In addition to that, by reason of the constant agitation as to the granting of this independence in a year or two years or three years or a decade, it would at once discourage the sincere efforts of the educated Filipinos who are with us today in building up a stable government. For these reasons I think such a promise as that would be a great mistake.

Sen. McComas: If we later, according to the proposition you have in your hand, leave the control and sovereignty to the inhabitants, to which tribes could we safely intrust it, and would not we for many years necessarily continue a de facto sovereignty as does England over Egypt or Austria over Bosnia? Could you, in deciding the question of leaving the sovereignty of the islands, determine now, from your several years' experience there, to which inhabitants you would leave it, with their rivalries and confusions of tongues?

Gov. Taft: Of course, if you left the islands to anybody you would leave them, I assume, to some sort of a committee or parliament, appointed or selected, who would be dominated probably by those whose violent methods have continued the guerrilla warfare; and that such a body could be created by proclamation within a reasonable time I have no doubt. But that it would not constitute a stable government, that it would give rise to anarchy and division between the tribes and between individuals of power and force, I have no doubt.

Sen. McComas: What would be the effect of such a government of the Tagalogs over the other tribes and people there in respect of the inhabitants themselves?

Gov. Taft: It would probably lead to a division between the Visayans and the Tagalogs, as disappointed officeholders or persons disappointed in the policy agreed upon by Manila might lead them on.

The Chairman: Would the Moros submit to such government?

Gov. Taft: So far as the Moros are concerned they are entirely out of this question. It is utterly impossible for the Filipinos to govern the Moros.

Sen. Carmack: Would it be possible for us to govern them?

Gov. Taft: It is possible for us to govern them as we govern the Indian tribes. They are nowhere near so amenable to education, to complete self-government by way of partial self-government, as are the Christian Filipinos. The Moros have no desire for popular government. . . .

I ought to say that the effect of giving the people independence now would be, in my judgment, to consign the 90 percent of uneducated people largely to the same condition that they occupied under Spanish rule. They would never learn individual liberty or the power of asserting it, and I am afraid they would continue separated from each other, shut out from the light of civilization by a continuance of the knowledge of the dialects only and knowledge of no common language, which would prevent their taking in modern ideas of popular government and individual liberty.

One of our great hopes in elevating those people is to give them a common language and that language English, because through the English language certainly, by reading its literature, by becoming aware of the history of the English race, they will breathe in the spirit of Anglo-Saxon individualism. . . .

Sen. Carmack: On the line suggested by Senator Beveridge, I saw in the Associated Press, attributed to General Funston, a statement to the effect that any sort of popular assembly would give an opportunity to agitators and demagogues to stir up the people and arouse again the spirit of independence. Do you think there is any danger of that?

Gov. Taft: I have no doubt that demagogues would be present there. That they are in the islands is undoubtedly true.

Sen. Carmack: We sometimes find them even in popular assemblies in this country.

Gov. Taft: It does not become me to say that.

Sen. Culberson: To whom, in the islands, would you apply the term "demagogue"? Do you mean those who agitate independence?

Sen. Beveridge: Men who would be demagogues anywhere.

Sen. Culberson: I am asking the governor.

Gov. Taft: The literal meaning of the word "demagogue" is a leader of the people, if I recollect my Greek correctly, but the term "demagogue" has come to mean, I believe, a man who uses those arguments with the people which are likely to arouse their passions and not their reason to accomplish some purpose that is neither for the benefit of the people nor of the country. Now I may give too severe a definition of the term "demagogue."

Sen. Rawlins: All politicians are demagogues, according to that definition.

Sen. Culberson: My question was to whom in the Philippine Islands you would apply the term.

Gov. Taft: For instance, I should regard as a demagogue a man who would go among the people and misrepresent what the laws are, and misrepresent what our purposes are as expressed, and misrepresent the conditions of the country in other provinces, and upon those misrepresentations would seek to arouse the passions of the people.

Sen. Culberson: Then you regard as a demagogue a man in the Philippine Islands who is opposed to the government of the Philippines by the United States?

Gov. Taft: Do you think that is the logical inference from what I say?

Sen. Culberson: I am trying to ascertain your opinion.

Gov. Taft: Oh, no. A man who is conscientiously in favor of the independence of the islands and uses no false statement in advocacy of it could not very well be a demagogue.

There are a number of those in the city of Manila. But "demagogue," as I understand it, is a term which points rather to the methods used in influencing the people than to the ends, though the ends sometimes add to the reason for calling him a demagogue.

Sen. Carmack: A man may have a patriotic end in view and pursue demagogic methods?

Gov. Taft: Yes, sir. . . .

Sen. Rawlins: The Filipinos, desiring some definitive policy declared with reference to them, if we fail to do that and proceed to deal with them and legislate for them as if they were a dependent colony, to be treated like other subject colonies, would it not be a constant source of trouble?

Gov. Taft: I think not, if you show by your legislation, as I hope you may, that you are really extending to them the means of self-government. What they desire definitively, as I understand it, is a declaration that Congress expects to establish a civil government, and to say what kind of a civil government it is. They also point out that they would like to know where the Filipinos stand with reference to the rights under the Constitution and with reference to the United States in the relation of the islands to the United States.

I think it would be well to reiterate, in a law like this, the rights set forth in the President's instructions to the Commission, which include everything secured by the bill of rights except the right to bear arms and the right to a trial by jury. I see no objection — although, of course, it follows without such a statement, because of the relation that the treaty establishes — to a declaration that the citizens or residents of those islands, owing allegiance to the United States, shall have the same protection with respect to foreign countries that a citizen of the United States has.

My objection to extending those personal rights contained in the Constitution is chiefly based on the fact that I do not think they are ready for trial by jury. I do not think that, educated in an entirely different system of law and having the defects which I have already pointed out, they are ready for trial by jury, and then I do not think that the Filipinos themselves would ask to have the right to bear arms. The right to bear arms conferred upon a people in which ladronism [thievery] is so chronic would lead to oppression of the Filipinos, and the Filipinos would be the last to desire to have it. If there is in the law a declaration of the rights I have mentioned, I should think it would help us. . . .

Sen. Beveridge: What would be the effect upon the people and conditions there if agitation here upon this question should cease, or any encouragement to those in insurrection should cease, and the people of the islands should be given to understand that just such a government as you describe, and just such a course of action as you have indicated, will be firmly and unalterably pursued?

Gov. Taft: It would be of great advantage to us. There is this to be said: Congress has made very few declarations at all with respect to the islands. What is known as the Spooner amendment is perhaps the only one, and the people there would welcome an expression by Congress in a law like this.

The Chairman: To give the expression in law rather than by promises of any kind?

Gov. Taft: Yes, sir.

Sen. Allison: There are Filipino people, and I suppose very intelligent people, from what I hear, who want independence. Do they mean by "independence" that they shall establish there a government of their own, which shall be responsible for domestic tranquillity and also take care of all their relations with the governments of the world, and that they shall be cut loose entirely from the friendship and protection of the United States? Is that the kind of independence they are talking about, or is it an independence that shall rest upon some stronger power to help them maintain themselves? I should like to know just what is the idea of the intelligent people and also of the other 90 percent when they talk about independence.

Gov. Taft: It is very difficult to answer that question with exactness. The term "independence," when used by the insurgents, was supposed to indicate something very good, without any definition of what it was; so that many of the troops, as Professor Worcester tells me, for I am not myself an authority on that question, in cheering said *dependencia* instead of *independencia*. On the other hand, there are intelligent people who use the expression "independence" in an oratorical way without having thought out what the giving of it involves. . . .

I wish to impress the fact, that were the government turned over to those who profess to be the leaders in the insurrection today, among the irreconcilables or *intransigentes*, though not in arms, the idea of civil liberty would be the last idea which would be practically carried into effect.

Sen. Allison: That is, liberty regulated by law? . . .

Gov. Taft: Yes, sir. The tendency of all governments under them would be toward absolutism, an oligarchy which would mean that the *presi-*

dente * of the village would control absolutely the village; the governor would control the province, and the head of the government would control the governors. The idea of elevation and protection to that indifferent mass of 90 percent would be possibly professed, but would fall far short of actual realization; and, therefore, offering to them independence now is offering to them — that is, to 90 percent of the people to whom I have referred — a condition of things which would be as far from enjoyment of free institutions as it is possible to imagine. . . .

Sen. Rawlins: The difficulties in regard to self-government are the diversity of dialects, or at least that is one difficulty.

Gov. Taft: Yes, sir.

Sen. Rawlins: Of course, there is always a certain percentage in all the provinces or districts who can communicate with one another, having a common tongue.

Gov. Taft: In the country over which the dialect is spoken.

Sen. Rawlins: Yes.

Gov. Taft: And then the intercommunication between tribes is made through that small percentage who speak Spanish.

Sen. Rawlins: There are many countries entirely capable of government; for instance, Great Britain, where in the different counties they have dialects which are scarcely intelligible to the inhabitants of other counties.

Gov. Taft: That analogy would hardly apply to the archipelago.

Sen. Rawlins: I do not want to go off into that question, particularly. This race of people, like other Asiatic races, as far as we are advised, in all history have never established and perhaps never will establish a civil republican form of self-government and maintain it. That being true, are we not attempting to fly in the face of human nature, as displayed in the characteristics of that race? Will not, after all, our efforts in the way of uplifting and civilizing them end, if we turn over the government, in a government that will result in absolutism?

Gov. Taft: After we have educated them?

Sen. Rawlins: After our efforts.

Gov. Taft: . . . We feel this way about the people: They are unlike other Malay races, first, in that for three hundred years they have been educated in the Christian religion. That is one bond of sympathy which we have with them. They tend — where they are very ignorant and where the priesthood is also ignorant — and that, I think, is the danger which the Catholic Church fears — toward fetishism. But, nevertheless, they have churches all over the islands, and the doctrines of the Christian religion have been taught there for three hundred years.

The problem of government, the problem of the development of the people in the Philippine Islands, is not at all to be compared with the development of the people in India. The difficulties in India far surpassed

---

* *Presidente* refers to the leader of the local political jurisdiction.

those in the Philippines, because of the diversity of religion and an actual diversity of tribes.

Now, India has never attempted a popular government. I do not think any popular government has even been attempted in the Orient, except possibly in Japan. If I am wrong about that I can be corrected, but that is my impression. . . .

We have a hope that with the imitative character of the people, with their real desire for improvement, shown especially by their anxiety to learn English and to be educated, we can carry out an experiment and justify our course, even though history has heretofore offered no example of the establishment of a popular government by a Malay race.

Sen. Rawlins: Another condition. These people are in a tropical climate.

Gov. Taft: Yes, sir; and that is another difficulty.

Sen. Rawlins: You will find that zone of course circumscribing the globe; and the people are indolent.

Gov. Taft: Yes, sir.

Sen. Rawlins: However energetic men and women may be, when they go into the tropics they degenerate as respects indolence.

Gov. Taft: Certainly; the tropical sun induces leisurely habits.

Sen. Rawlins: It is said that eternal vigilance is the price of liberty.

Gov. Taft: So it is said.

Sen. Rawlins: With such indolent people there is no possibility of such vigilance as against the aggression of aspiring men. Do you not think that in our attempts there for these two reasons — all former experience seems to have demonstrated it to be true — we are flying in the face not only of human nature but of the climate in our efforts to mold those people into a republican self-governing community?

Sen. Carmack: An Anglo-Saxon republic.

Gov. Taft: I agree to the statement of the difficulties, and I am not blind to them. I am very hopeful, however, that we can overcome them.

Sen. Rawlins: Now, another suggestion. When you say that these people cannot be fitted for self-government, I think we are all disposed to agree with you, if I understand your meaning of that term. Is it not true also that that condition cannot be changed by a process of education (which seems to me entirely probable), and that if we leave the islands and accord them independence, as we understand it, some strong character or combination of the most intelligent and educated men of the islands will assume the reins of government and administer the government as practically absolute rulers, just as we find in Mexico and throughout the South American republics? That would probably be the result, would it not?

Gov. Taft: It possibly might be the result if you could have the certainty of securing a man like President Diaz in Mexico after they had gone through the bitter experience that Mexico had to go through for a great number of years. My own impression is that at present there is not sufficient solidarity among the people of the various islands, not sufficient identification of interest, and too much personal ambition on the part of educated persons, and too great power in the hands of a little coterie at the head of each tribe to call out that tribe and to arouse them to resist the government of the other tribes, to make possible such a strong government, as you characterize it — an absolute government under one man or . . . a few men — without a series of conflicts between the tribes, which of course would be injurious to the people.

Sen. Rawlins: It seems to me probable, too, that there will be conflicts, civil discord, and acts of injustice and oppression. Of course now we find the people practically united by a bond of fellow-feeling and sympathy, deeming that they are subject to a common misfortune or oppression, and they are resisting it. That at present would unite them.

Sen. McComas: I did not so understand Governor Taft.

Sen. Rawlins: I am not stating that as Governor Taft's opinion.

Gov. Taft: You are stating the probable hypothesis of the people over there.

Sen. Rawlins: I am not suggesting that as his opinion or mine, but the probable hypothesis of the people over there — assuming that they have that fellow-feeling.

Sen. Beveridge: It is your view of their hypothesis.

Sen. Rawlins: My understanding; that they have that national feeling that was described here the other day.

Gov. Taft: I said they were growing to have a racial or national feeling for the Filipino people.

Sen. Rawlins: That would enable them for a short while to hold together, and then there will be insurrection and discord. Is it not equally probable or more probable that if our rule is obtruded there, using that word in the sense of being sent there against their wishes, we also will have insurrection and discord as we have had to a certain degree within the last three years?

Gov. Taft: I think not. I think what we are doing in the islands and what we would do under the law I have suggested would be so surprising to them, in view of their experience in the past with respect to promises and with the policy such as I have defined, that the people would become exceedingly friendly to their association with the United States. I think the educated Filipino, unless he is intoxicated with the oratorical use of the term "independence," is quite conscious of the defects of his own people and quite capable of seeing that the assistance of a government in which civil liberty does prevail would be of the utmost use to them, not only in securing aid in capital for investment in the islands, but also in leading and guiding them into a government which shall respect the rights of the minority as well as accord the privilege of control to the majority.

Sen. Rawlins: In describing the extent to which we have pacified the islands, you have referred to the fact that in northern Luzon, where foreign agents and representatives of governments had not penetrated, there is comparative peace; that the seat of insurrection was near Manila, and among that class of people who had come most in contact with foreigners — I mean Americans and others — and that, so far as we have had actually experience, the contact of our soldiers and these foreigners has been a disturbing element among the people and aroused them to resistance. That is true, is it not?

Gov. Taft: That the foreigners aroused them to resist?

Sen. Rawlins: Yes; to a certain extent.

Gov. Taft: I think I said, with respect to foreigners dealing in hemp, that they had made contributions to the insurgent cause. They are Englishmen and Germans.

Sen. Rawlins: Not to be diverted from the purpose of the question I want to ask upon this line, in order that you may answer it ——

Gov. Taft: Very well, sir.

Sen. Rawlins: You spoke of the temptations and dangers [to] officials and agents of the government of the United States in that remote territory?

Gov. Taft: Yes, sir.

Sen. Rawlins: Of course we who have long lived in Territories know something about that. You know there will grow up of necessity a feeling of hostility among the local people against those people, sometimes without just cause, on account of the misconduct of certain classes of the people. That is true, is it not?

Gov. Taft: It is possible. I would not attempt to deny that that is one of the possible difficulties we shall encounter.

Sen. Rawlins: You are aware, also, that it is the purpose of a good many speculators to go there for the purpose of making money, and who would have no other interest or desire?

Gov. Taft: Yes, sir.

Sen. Rawlins: And they will gain control of certain kinds of property in the islands and use it to that end?

Gov. Taft: Yes, sir. That there are men who would do that, and that there are men who are likely to come there who would attempt to do that, I do not intend to deny. . . .

Sen. Rawlins: . . . Now, as a result of all that, which we can see is certain to come if we retain the islands and carry out the program suggested, do you not think we will have constant trouble in the islands in the future?

Gov. Taft: . . . If I may say it, personally I did not favor going into the Philippine Islands. I was sorry at the time that we got into it. But we are there. I see no other possible means of discharging that duty which chance has put upon us than to carry out the plan I suggest, for any other plan, Senator, would lead us back to the same place where we now are or were two years ago. That is one thing.

Then I am not disposed to concede as yet that because there are dangers of corruption in an American government, because there are possibilities of danger in some of the agents that are to be sent out there, and great temptations to them, we are not equal to the task.

I believe that the American government and the American people are exceedingly adaptable; that they have had the advantage of the experiments of other nations in dealing with people like these, and with no other course before us that I can see that is practicable and with a possibility, I may even say a probability, of success, we would not be justified in throwing those people back into an absolutism and into a condition where they would enjoy no civil liberty and very little prospect of improvement because of the mere possibility of failure and the formidable character of the obstacles which you have so well stated. . . .

The answer to the question is really an answer to the question, Do you think what you propose to do out there will be successful or otherwise? Now, I have been called an optimist, I think, the Mark Tapley of this business. It is true. I am an optimist. If I did not believe in the success of what we are attempting to do out there I would resign and come home. Certainly no man ever succeeded who did not believe in the success of what he was doing. We think we can help these people; we think we can elevate them to an appreciation of popular government; and we think that because the experiment has not really ever been tried before is not reason for saying that the trial of the experiment may not be a success in this instance. . . .

Sen. Allison: Chance having taken us there, do you think that what we are doing there is wise for us and for the Filipinos as well?

Gov. Taft: I do. I think it is the only course open to us, Senator Allison. Of course I made some study of the question of what we could do. It is a matter of opinion. My own opinion is that it was utterly impossible to do anything but what we did do, and that, with deference to the opinion of gentlemen on the other side of the table, if they had been in the same position, they could not have done anything else.

I ought to add, if I may, what I said to my friend Judge De Armond and Senator Bacon, that they ought to be preparing themselves not only on the general principles involved in political discussion, but also to the details of government, because in the mutations of politics it is quite likely they will come into power, and I venture to prophesy that they cannot do anything but carry on the work we have done there.

Sen. Allison: You mean by that suggestion that they should refrain from rash promises?

Gov. Taft: Yes, sir.

Sen. Culberson: There is just one question on that line. Being opposed to the acquisition of the Philippine Islands, and we having gone there, as you think, by chance, do you not think it would be best for the people of the United States, if any safe and honorable method can be devised, to withdraw?

Gov. Taft: Of course, that assumes that a safe and honorable method can be devised.

Sen. Culberson: That is my question.

Gov. Taft: I do not think it can be devised. . . .

Testimony of Ewell S. Otis *

Sen. Beveridge: I will ask you, General, what your opinion is as to the conditions that would result if the American authority were withdrawn and the islands were turned over to the natives?

Gen. Otis: It would be anarchy or a military despotism, and they all understand it. There is not a Filipino or anybody else over there who desires self-government.

When [Apolinario] Mabini [an insurrection leader] came in I said to him, "You know the United States is essential to the welfare and integrity of the island." He said, "I know it." I said, "What are you fighting for?" He replied, "We are fighting in order to make the best terms possible."

Aguinaldo himself never wanted self-government without outside protection. You understand that they know very well that other nations would divide up those islands if we let them go. We had long conferences before the war broke out. General Torres, a very able man, who was at the head of Aguinaldo's commission, was one of those with whom we were in conference; but all they said was this: They wanted the protection of the United States, and they wanted to control the internal affairs of the island, and they would turn over to us the customhouses in payment for the protection which we would give them on the outside.

Sen. Proctor: I suppose, General, that there are very able men there?

Gen. Otis: Very able men; yes, sir.

Sen. Proctor: And men of patriotic sentiment ——

Gen. Otis: And without their experience I do not know what I should have done.

Sen. Proctor: But you are referring to the general mass of the people in the statement you have just made?

Gen. Otis: I am referring to the general mass of the people; yes, sir.

Sen. Proctor: And you think it is not safe to judge the whole mass of the people by these exceptional cases of intelligent men from whom we have heard expressions of opinion?

* See above, page 31.

Gen. Otis: Well, the able men have correct ideas of government.

Sen. Dietrich: You mean when they say they do not want self-government that they do not want absolute independence?

Gen. Otis: Yes; that is the idea. They want to control the internal affairs of the island.

Sen. Beveridge: You do not mean the people themselves?

Gen. Otis: No; I am speaking of Aguinaldo and his cabinet.

Sen. Beveridge: The people themselves, as I understand it, want peace as you say.

Gen. Otis: I do not think the people themselves care very much what they have, so that they have peace and plenty of subsistence. They are tired of war.

Sen. Culberson: Did any of these leaders propose to you an American protectorate; do I understand you to answer the question of Senator Beveridge ——

Gen. Otis: You will find in my report, the first report, that I reported the results of a commission appointed by Aguinaldo and myself.

Sen. Culberson: That is the reason I am asking you; I understand your report to be different, somewhat, from your answer to the Senator's question.

Gen. Otis: I do not understand that it is. They wanted control of the internal affairs of the island, but protection outside. . . .

We asked the question how they were going to compensate the United States for this protection they demanded from the United States, and they said they would turn over the customhouses and balance the debt in that way.

Sen. Beveridge: To put the question I asked a little while ago, as to what would result if we were to withdraw our authority, in a different form, what in your opinion would occur if this expressed desire of the commission who surrounded Aguinaldo, to be left in control of the internal affairs of the archipelago, and we to maintain a fleet to protect them from outside interference — what would be the effect of such a condition as that upon the people and industries of the islands themselves? We not to have, you understand, any interference at all or management of their internal affairs, but to leave that entirely to themselves. That is merely my first question in another form.

Gen. Otis: It might result in military control with very harsh features, but, in my opinion, it would mean anarchy.

Sen. Rawlins: When you went to the Philippines, and before you left the United States to go there, what, if any, instructions did you receive as to the policy you were to pursue?

Gen. Otis: I did not receive any instructions. General Merritt had received all the instructions. I went on to San Francisco quite early, I think about the 12th of May, and I think I arrived there on the 15th or the 16th of May. I received the troops there. General Merritt reported at

San Francisco on the 29th of May, and he had been in Washington, and he received the instructions; I never received them.

Sen. Rawlins: Did he communicate to you the instructions which he received?

Gen. Otis: The written instructions, yes.

Sen. Rawlins: Have those been published?

Gen. Otis: General Merritt published a number of orders.

Sen. Rawlins: What I would like to get are the instructions received by General Merritt which he communicated to you.

Gen. Otis: There were no instructions except those contained in the orders and correspondence.

Sen. Rawlins: Will you tell me where those can be found?

Gen. Otis: I suppose in General Merritt's report.

Sen. Rawlins: You make that a matter of supposition. I have not seen them, and that is the reason I make inquiry about them. . . .

Sen. Patterson: General, what is your standard of qualifications for self-government, applying it to a people?

Gen. Otis: That is not a fair question to ask me. I am a soldier, and not a statesman.

Sen. Patterson: But you stated that these people were not capable of self-government. I want to know the standard by which you test it. You did not have to make the statement if you did not feel called upon by reason of being a soldier and not a statesman ——

Gen. Otis: I should not be called upon to answer that.

Sen. Patterson: No?

Gen. Otis: I have been answering every possible question, but I do not think a great many of your questions are fair. I have been trying to answer them.

Sen. Patterson: That, perhaps, is something upon which there is a difference of opinion between you and me. But you have stated you did not think the Filipinos were capable of self-government. Now I ask you what is your standard by which you measure the capacity of the Filipinos for self-government?

Gen. Otis: They have no correct idea of liberty.

Sen. Patterson: But now you are speaking of the Filipinos ——

Gen. Otis: Liberty with them means license.

Sen. Patterson: Yes, I know ——

Gen. Otis: For each man to have freedom to do about as he pleases without any restraining influences. That is their idea of liberty.

Sen. Patterson: But, General, what is your standard of qualification for self-government as applied to the whole people?

Gen. Otis: What kind of a government do you mean — a despotic government?

Sen. Patterson: Self-government.

Gen. Otis: Oh, I think they are qualified for a despotic military government.

Sen. Patterson: Do you consider the people, say, of Mexico qualified for self-government?

Sen. Beveridge: Mr. Chairman, I submit to you whether or not the examination of General Otis upon the capacity of various peoples for self-government is relevant.

Sen. Patterson: I insist that it is perfectly proper.

Sen. Beveridge: It has not been shown ——

Gen. Otis: I do not believe they understand self-government. They do not understand the republican form of government which prevails in the United States. I do not believe that they have the slightest conception of it.

Sen. Patterson: Whom do you refer to?

Gen. Otis: The Filipinos.

Sen. Patterson: I asked you about the people of Mexico.

Gen. Otis: I decline to answer that.

Sen. Beveridge: It has not been shown that General Otis has any particular knowledge of the people of Mexico.

Sen. Allison: I suppose he does not know about the people of Mexico.

Sen. Patterson: I have no means of forcing you, General, at present. Do you measure the capacity of the people of the Philippines by the capacity of the American people; do you take that as your standard?

Gen. Otis: No, sir.

Sen. Patterson: Then what do you take as your standard; what people, if any?

Sen. Beveridge: Did you understand Senator Patterson's first question?

Gen. Otis: He wanted to know if I took the American people as a standard.

Sen. Beveridge: For self-government ——

Gen. Otis: As the proper standard of self-government.

Sen. Patterson: He said he understood it. Now, I want to know what people, if any, you do take as the proper standard to judge of the qualifications of a people for self-government.

Gen. Otis: Why, I do not think that is a fair question. Ask me why I do not consider those people capable of self-government.

Sen. Patterson: The question I ask you is an expert question and I am trying to find out whether you are capable of answering that question.

Gen. Otis: I am not an expert upon any question of politics ——

Sen. Patterson: I see. Then, did you measure the capacity of the people of the Philippine Islands for self-government by any known standard?

Gen. Otis: By my own standard, of what I believed they should possess.

Sen. Patterson: Now, would you answer my question?

Gen. Otis: What is your question?

Sen. Patterson: Let the stenographer read it.

The stenographer read as follows: "Then, did you measure the capacity of the people of the Philippine Islands for self-government by any known standard?"

The Chairman: He answered that question.

Gen. Otis: I applied my own views as to what knowledge a people should possess, which was this: That they should have some idea of the meaning of liberty as divorced entirely from license. . . .

Testimony of Arthur MacArthur

Major General Arthur MacArthur was appointed military governor of the Philippines and given command of the troops there when General Otis departed for home in 1900. Born in Springfield, Massachusetts in 1845, he was raised in Wisconsin; his father became governor of that state in 1855. In 1862 young Arthur was promised an appointment to West Point for the following year by President Lincoln. Impatient to be a soldier, however, MacArthur enlisted as a first lieutenant of the 24th Wisconsin Volunteers, commanded by General Philip Sheridan. For bravery at Murfreesboro in November, 1863, he was awarded the Congressional Medal of Honor; he was a colonel at the Civil War's end. After studying law for a year he returned to the army and became an infantry officer on the Western frontier, engaged in the sporadic but bloody Indian struggles of that era. (While he was serving at Arsenal Barracks in Little Rock, in 1880 his son Douglas was born.) Shortly after war with Spain broke out in 1898, Arthur MacArthur was assigned to the Philippines as a brigadier general of volunteers.

Sen. Culberson: I believe you said in your opening statement that you believed we ought to hold the Philippine Islands upon two broad principles: first, those of a mercantile or commercial character; and second, because of the opportunity it had afforded us of planting the principles of republican institutions in the archipelago. Am I correct?

Gen. MacArthur: Yes; you are correct in that general idea, without exactly representing the fine shades that I tried to throw in my statement.

Sen. Culberson: I have not got the fine shades yet.

Sen. Patterson: Not many can throw them in.

Sen. Culberson: We will find the fundamental principles of republican institutions in the Declaration of Independence and the Constitution of the United States, will we not?

Gen. MacArthur: I should say in the constitutional history of the United States. The Declaration of Independence and the document of the Constitution itself would of course be the starting points.

Sen. Culberson: They are the groundwork of republican institutions in the United States, you think — the Declaration of Independence and the Constitution of the United States?

Gen. MacArthur: Yes; and the preceding constitutional history of England has got to be considered in that connection.

Sen. Culberson: Was not one of the principles of the Revolution of 1776 embodied in the Declaration of Independence — that there should be no taxation without representation?

Gen. MacArthur: I believe there was a reference to it; yes.

Sen. Culberson: That doctrine had something to do with the Revolution, did it not?

Gen. MacArthur: That was one of the pretexts put forward by the people to make a vehicle for the expression of their psychological feelings.

Sen. Culberson: We have not yet planted that idea in the Philippines — that idea of representation before taxation — have we?

Gen. MacArthur: That will come in due time, I think.

Sen. Culberson: Up to the present time, however, that has not been embodied or planted, as you would term it, in the Philippines?

Gen. MacArthur: They are represented in a way in the legislative body. There are three native commissioners that are managing the finances of the islands now. The taxes are collected under the legislation of that Commission and disbursed under its action. So in a broad sense they are represented in a legislative body. The only legislative body there has native representatives on it, and the questions that arise are discussed by those three men as well as the American representatives.

Sen. Culberson: Care is taken, however, to have the Americans in the majority?

Gen. MacArthur: That would be necessary at present, of course.

Sen. Culberson: Those Filipinos, of course, are not selected by the Filipino people, but by the American authorities?

Gen. MacArthur: They have been selected with all the considerations possible to get the best representative men; not by a public expression through a vote or a ballot, however.

Sen. Culberson: They are selected by the American authorities?

Gen. MacArthur: Precisely so.

Sen. Culberson: And not by the Filipinos?

Gen. MacArthur: But not by any eccentric or capricious method. With a view of satisfying the feelings of the Filipinos themselves.

Sen. Beveridge: The governors of the provinces are elected, are they not?

Gen. MacArthur: Yes; under the operation of the organic law passed, from the 1st of February this year the people of the provinces elect their own governors. That is my recollection of the instrument.

Sen. Culberson: That refers to provincial taxes. That is the matter which I wanted and have called your attention to. With reference to provincial taxation, that is levied now in a large degree by the Congress of the United States.

Sen. Allison: Provincial taxes?

Sen. Culberson: Yes.

Sen. Beveridge: That is something within the records here. What is the use of asking General MacArthur about that?

Gen. MacArthur: I do not know about that.

Sen. Culberson: Tariff taxes are levied by Congress, are they not?

Sen. Beveridge: I submit that is a subject more within the Senator's own knowledge, since the Senator is one who voted upon that bill. So I do not see the fairness, the expediency, or the pertinency of asking the General what we are doing in Congress.

Sen. Culberson: I want to ask him what he means by planting republican institutions in the Philippine Islands, and that is what I am trying to get at, and whether the Filipinos are not being taxed without representation, contrary to the Declaration of Independence?

Gen. MacArthur: I could answer that in this way, perhaps, to clear the situation, by saying that as far as those taxes are imposed by our Congress they are being taxed without representation.

Sen. Allison: One word there. I understand that these tariff taxes levied in the Philippine Islands are levied by this Commission and not by Congress. We have approved them by an act passed some time ago; but they are levied by the Philippine Commission, as I understand it.

Sen. Patterson: Is not that the same thing? The Commission are not the agents of the Filipino people?

Sen. Allison: The Commission?

Sen. Patterson: No; the Commission is appointed by the President.

Sen. Allison: I supposed they were acting for the Filipino people.

Sen. Patterson: They are; but they are appointed without a reference to the wishes of the Filipino people by the people by the United States.

Sen. Allison: I think General MacArthur just now stated that they were appointed taking in the wishes and desires, and so forth, of the Filipino people there.

Sen. Patterson: They are appointed by the President.

Sen. Allison: I understand that perfectly well. We are all familiar with these matters.

Sen. Culberson: The Senator from Iowa is of course aware of the fact, as stated by General MacArthur, that tariff taxes in the Philippine Islands are now levied by act of Congress.

Sen. Allison: As I understand it, these tariff taxes are not levied by Congress; they are levied by the Philippine Commission. Still that is a matter that we could ascertain by a little further reference to the record.

Sen. Culberson: Your recollection is, as you have stated, that the tariff taxes in the Philippines are levied by Congress and to that extent the Filipinos are taxed without representation.

Gen. MacArthur: I should answer as I did before; that as far as any tax is imposed by the Congress of the United States directly on the Filipino people that that tax is imposed without any representation of the Filipinos.

Sen. Culberson: I will ask you whether one of the other fundamental principles of the Revolution was not self-government?

Gen. MacArthur: Of our own Revolution?

Sen. Culberson: Yes.

Gen. MacArthur: Unmistakably so.

Sen. Culberson: And the Filipinos have not that yet, have they?

Gen. MacArthur: No; and I tried to make one of my shades right there.

Sen. Culberson: I would like you to shade it again, if you please.

Gen. MacArthur: That they are after personal rights, essentially so, and not forms of government.

Sen. Carmack: Do you think personal rights can be secure without political rights?

Gen. MacArthur: I think they can under the American flag, most decidedly.

Sen. Culberson: We have taxation over there without representation and we have a lack of self-government in the Philippine Islands, have we not, in the sense to which you have referred?

Gen. MacArthur: How is that? That there is an absence of self-government?

Sen. Culberson: Yes; and foreign people are conducting the government for the Filipinos.

Gen. MacArthur: I do not regard the United States as a foreign people in the Philippines. They are trying at the present to suppress an insurrection.

Sen. Culberson: And people, who, at the beginning of the insurrection, were foreign to the Filipinos are now governing the Filipinos.

Gen. MacArthur: How is that?

Sen. Culberson: A people foreign to the Filipinos at the time of the opening of the insurrection, or at the beginning of the Spanish war, are now governing the Filipino people?

Gen. MacArthur: The people of the United States are governing themselves, and, as I said before, I regard the Philippine Islands as a tuitionary annex of the United States, and they are being governed accordingly in that respect.

Sen. Culberson: What kind of an annex?

Gen. MacArthur: A tuitionary annex.

Sen. Culberson: What I meant by foreigners is this: I am not attempting to argue the question as to the rights of the United States in the Philippine Islands, from the legal or the international law standpoint; but I wanted to ask if at the beginning of our trouble with Spain the people of the United States were not in the ordinary sense of the term foreign to the Filipinos?

Gen. MacArthur: Most unquestionably.

Sen. Culberson: And we are now undertaking to govern those people?

Gen. MacArthur: But in the intervening period there has been the treaty of Paris, by which we acquired absolute sovereignty over everything Spain owned in the Philippine Archipelago.

Sen. Culberson: Certainly, I understand that. Now, coming to the essential principles of freedom which you say we are trying to plant in the Philippines, I will ask you if the Filipinos have freedom of speech.

Gen. MacArthur: In the Philippines?

Sen. Culberson: Yes.

Gen. MacArthur: They did during my administration. I told them if they would give me their guns they could have a mass meeting on every corner in Manila whenever they wanted to, where they could utter any sentiments they wished.

Sen. Culberson: How is it since you left?

Gen. MacArthur: That I do not know, except from the same sources of information that you have.

Sen. Culberson: Under the sedition law, passed since you left there, has not their freedom of speech been practically taken away from them?

Gen. MacArthur: The operation of that law would limit the licentiousness of riotous argument, of course, and I would like to make my position clear on that head. I do not object to the Filipinos talking; on the other hand, I rather encouraged it; and I made the condition only that they would give me their guns.

Sen. Culberson: I infer from what you say that you probably would not have approved the sedition law.

Gen. MacArthur: I certainly should not if I had had any control of the premises.

Sen. Culberson: Have they freedom of the press in the Philippines?

Gen. MacArthur: During my time there I should say yes, absolutely.

Sen. Culberson: Have they now?

Gen. MacArthur: Well, I should answer the same as before. It is restricted to the extent those laws apply.

Sen. Culberson: It is restricted by the sedition law?

Gen. MacArthur: It is restricted, as I understand, to the ordinary common-law restrictions. They have imposed penalties for attacks on individuals, and upon the government generally. I have not read the sedition laws carefully. I do not know precisely how they apply. That is a matter of record, I presume, that everybody could learn about by simply reading the papers.

Sen. Culberson: But you are from the Philippine Islands, and have an intimate knowledge of the matters in that country, and I wanted to ask you this question, and now I want to ask you if you do not know that under the sedition law the press of the Philippines is forbidden to advocate political independence.

Gen. MacArthur: I believe that has been so stated in the newspapers. I have not read the law itself, and I am willing to say again that I deplore, in that, the passage of that law.

Sen. Culberson: Are people of the Philippine Islands entitled under the present régime to keep and bear arms?

Gen. MacArthur: I should say not, and hope not most sincerely.

Sen. Culberson: Are they entitled to trial by jury?

Gen. MacArthur: No; and I may say right there that the right to bear arms and the right to trial by jury were about the only things during my time that they did not enjoy as a part of their daily life in the city of Manila, and wherever there were not actual military operations. They are the only two constitutional privileges those people did not enjoy to almost the full extent — the right to bear arms and the right to trial by jury. . . .

Sen. Carmack: I asked you a question yesterday. I asked you if you thought personal rights could be secure without political rights, and you said you thought they could under the American flag. Do you think the personal rights of American citizens could be secure without political rights? What is the object of giving the people political rights except for the protection of their personal rights?

Gen. MacArthur: You mean the right of self-government as it exists here?

Sen. Carmack: Yes.

Gen. MacArthur: There are a good many answers to that. I will say, in the first instance, that our war for independence was entirely for political rights. We were enjoying the personal rights that the people living in Great Britain were enjoying. The effort in the islands has been for personal rights entirely, and it was resentment against Spain because she would not give personal rights that brought about revolution.

Sen. Carmack: Was not the origin of the American Revolution due to the invasion of what we considered our personal rights, and did not we desire further political rights because that was the only way to preserve our personal rights? Taxation without representation, taking our property without our consent — was not that an invasion of our personal rights, and did we not demand independence and the government of our own country?

The Chairman: I am sorry to interrupt this examination, but it is after 12 o'clock and I must be on the floor, and I have something to lay before the committee in executive session before we adjourn. If Senators wish to examine General MacArthur further the general will come tomorrow.

Sen. Carmack: I have nothing further.

Gen. MacArthur: I am discharged?

The Chairman: You are discharged.

Gen. MacArthur: Thank you very much. . . .

Testimony of Robert P. Hughes *

The Chairman: What is the attitude of the Visayans toward us now? I mean when you first went there as compared with when you came away.

Gen. Hughes: When I came away there was no trouble in going anywhere you pleased in Panay, in Negros, and in Cebu. Bohol had not yet turned in their arms, although a day for doing so had been arranged. In Leyte there were still some rifles out as I have previously said. While they did not attack at all, there would probably have been some risk in going about that island.

The Chairman: I mean what was the general attitude of the people?

Gen. Hughes: They were very friendly. They worked for us willingly and were always ready to do anything we wished.

The Chairman: What do you think of their capacity for civil government?

Gen. Hughes: My personal opinion is that it will be a long time before they are qualified to run a civil government of their own. I understand your question to relate purely to the Visayans?

The Chairman: That is what I mean.

Gen. Hughes: I should say not inside of two generations. The people have no earthly idea of equity. They simply know their own wishes, and they have no regard for the wishes of others.

The Chairman: If left to themselves what sort of government, in your opinion, would they establish?

Gen. Hughes: They would try, undoubtedly, to establish a republic of some kind, and they would do it. The ordinary Tao of the Visayans is one of the most gullible creatures the world contains. He will believe anything he is told by his acknowledged superior, no difference how absurd the statement is, and there is the great strength that their leaders have over them — the enormous lies that are published to them as to their plans and what is going to take place. They gull them right along.

The latest I got hold of from Lukban to his people was that a German fleet would be in those waters at such a date to blow the Americans out,

* See above, page 27.

and that they would then secure their independence. That was the last one I heard.

Sen. Culberson: Do you mean by that to suggest that the Visayans desire independence?

Gen. Hughes: These people of whom I speak, the Taos, do not know what independence means. They probably think it is something to eat. They have no more idea what it means than a shepherd dog.

Sen. Culberson: How could this proclamation have such a wonderful effect on them as you describe if they do not know what it means?

Gen. Hughes: Simply because they want to get rid of the Americans.

Sen. Culberson: They do?

Gen. Hughes: Yes, sir.

Sen. Culberson: They want independence so far as the Americans are concerned?

Gen. Hughes: They want us driven out, so that they can have this independence, but they do not know what it is.

The Chairman: Are they pretty generally hostile, or are there among them many friendly to us?

Gen. Hughes: You will find a very great deal of good will in all the provinces where absolute peace has been established.

The Chairman: Do you think if they were left to themselves they would submit to a Tagalo government in Luzon?

Gen. Hughes: I think probably they would submit for a while, until some of their leaders did not get what they wanted. Then they would probably take the course as to which one of their great advocates remarked on one occasion. They were discussing what could be done as a republic, and he and his friends had their ideas, and they said they would do so and so. A man who was discussing the matter with them suggested that there might be a good deal of opposition to that. "No," said he, "if anybody opposes it we will take off his head. That is all."

The Chairman: You think the tendency would be to break up into separate republics?

Gen. Hughes: I do not think it would live long enough to break up into different republics. I think the islands would be taken possession of by somebody else.

The Chairman: You think the islands would be taken possession of by some other power?

Gen. Hughes: Yes, sir. . . .

Sen. Beveridge: In your former testimony you stated that when they asked you for independence, you asked them what they meant by it; whether or not we should withdraw our troops and ships and leave them; and they said, "For God's sake, no, no"; they did not want that kind of independence.

Gen. Hughes: Yes. . . .

Sen. Patterson: One moment. Do you want the committee to understand that these commissioners, representing the Philippine army, did not want independence if it was accompanied by the withdrawal of the American fleet and the American Army? Do you want the committee to understand that?

Gen. Hughes: I want you to understand that they wished protection ——

Sen. Patterson (to the reporter): Will you read the question to the witness to see if I can get an answer?

Gen. Hughes: It is totally unnecessary. I know it.

Sen. Patterson: Read the question.

The reporter read as follows: "*Sen. Patterson:* One moment. Do you want the committee to understand that these commissioners, representing the Philippine army, did not want independence if it was accompanied by the withdrawal of the American fleet and the American Army? Do you want the committee to understand that?"

Gen. Hughes: I understood that they felt themselves totally unable to stand alone, and that some protection must be furnished from the beginning; and in the further discussion . . . of that idea . . . it developed that they did not want to commit themselves, so far as we could understand the committee of Aguinaldo, to a protectorate of the United States. But after they got their independence they would negotiate their protectorate with any power they saw fit.

Sen. Patterson: General, I will ask you if you can answer my question yes or no. (To the reporter.) Kindly repeat the question to the General.

The reporter read the question, as follows: "*Sen. Patterson:* One moment. Do you want the committee to understand that these commissioners, representing the Philippine army, did not want independence if it was accompanied by the withdrawal of the American fleet and the American Army? Do you want the committee to understand that?"

Gen. Hughes: Am I bound, Mr. Chairman, to answer according to the gentleman's dictation?

The Chairman: You can answer every question in your own way.

Sen. Patterson: I want to know whether he will answer it "yes" or "no."

The Chairman: The witness can answer in his own way.

Sen. Patterson: I want to know whether he will answer it "yes" or "no." If he will not, that is the end of it. He has already taken the liberty of attempting to answer it in a very lengthy way, but he has not answered the question.

Sen. Beveridge: I submit that putting to the General the question whether he will answer it "yes" or "no" is not proper under any circumstances.

Sen. Patterson: I believe it is.

The Chairman: The witness can answer the question as he pleases.

Sen. Patterson: I have a right to reask the question, and I want to know whether you will answer that question more directly and specifically than you have done.

The Chairman: I do not think that it is a proper course of examination.

Sen. Beveridge: I do not, either.

Sen. Patterson: I press the question.

The Chairman: I don't think we have any right to dictate to the witness how he shall answer a question.

Sen. Patterson: Do I understand from the chairman that after the witness has made an evasive reply we have no right to ask him for a more direct answer to a question?

The Chairman: You can not dictate the form of his answer.

Sen. Patterson: I have a right to ask him for a more direct answer.

The Chairman: I think his answer was direct.

Sen. Patterson: I do not think it was.

The Chairman: Very well; that is a difference of opinion.

Sen. Beveridge: And it can not be called evasive.

Sen. Patterson: I differ with you.

Sen. Beveridge: Of course that does not settle it.

The Chairman: The committee can not undertake to dictate in what form the witness shall answer.

Sen. Patterson: Do you want the committee to understand by these answers that at that conference the representatives of the Filipinos would not have accepted independence if it was accompanied by the withdrawal of the American troops and the American fleet?

Gen. Hughes: My understanding of the matter at the time was that they fully appreciated their utter inability to stand alone; but there was Mabini's letter stating that they must first have absolute independence and then talk of protectorate afterwards.

Sen. Patterson: Now, that is as definite an answer as you will give me, General, is it?

Gen. Hughes: If it does not answer your question, will you show me in what way it has failed?

Sen. Patterson: Let the reporter read the question, and I will leave it to the General's own knowledge of language.

The reporter read as follows: "*Sen. Patterson:* Do you want the committee to understand by these answers that at that conference the representatives of the Filipinos would not have accepted independence if it was accompanied by the withdrawal of the American troops and the American fleet?"

Sen. Beveridge: Do you feel that you have answered the question, General?

Gen. Hughes: I have answered it three times, I believe.

Sen. Patterson: There are answers and there are answers. . . .

3   COUNTER-INSURGENCY

Testimony of Robert P. Hughes *

Sen. Rawlins: . . . [I]n burning towns, what would you do? Would the entire town be destroyed by fire or would only offending portions of the town be burned?

Gen. Hughes: I do not know that we ever had a case of burning what you would call a town in this country, but probably a barrio or a sitio; probably a half a dozen houses, native shacks, where the insurrectos would go in and be concealed, and if they caught a detachment passing they would kill some of them.

Sen. Rawlins: What did I understand you to say would be the consequences of that?

Gen. Hughes: They usually burned the village.

Sen. Rawlins: All of the houses in the village?

Gen. Hughes: Yes; every one of them.

Sen. Rawlins: What would become of the inhabitants?

Gen. Hughes: That was their lookout.

Sen. Dietrich: About what does one of these houses or shacks cost and about how long does it take to build one?

Gen. Hughes: The cost as sworn to by women on courts-martial and courts of inquiry, etc., is given as ranging between three and eight dollars.

Sen. Dietrich: Mexican?

Gen. Hughes: Mexican pesos.

Sen. Dietrich: That would be from a $1.50 to $4.00 of our money.

Gen. Hughes: Yes, sir. I should not like to be certain as to the length of time it takes to build them. They probably could build them in about three days, but there is a question as to how long it takes to put on the nipa. About that I am not absolutely certain. I have had a good deal of nipa put on, but I never noticed the time it required.

Sen. Rawlins: If these shacks were of no consequence what was the utility of their destruction?

Gen. Hughes: The destruction was as a punishment. They permitted these people to come in there and conceal themselves and they gave no sign. It is always ——

Sen. Rawlins: The punishment in that case would fall, not upon the men, who could go elsewhere, but mainly upon the women and little children.

* See above, page 27.

Gen. Hughes: The women and children are part of the family, and where you wish to inflict a punishment you can punish the man probably worse in that way than in any other.

Sen. Rawlins: But is that within the ordinary rules of civilized warfare? Of course you could exterminate the family, which would be still worse punishment.

Gen. Hughes: These people are not civilized.

Sen. Rawlins: But is that within the ordinary rules of civilized warfare?

Gen. Hughes: No; I think it is not.

Sen. Rawlins: You think it is not?

Sen. Dietrich: In order to carry on civilized warfare both sides have to engage in such warfare.

Gen. Hughes: Yes, sir; certainly. That is the point.

I think if I am allowed to go on I will come to a place where I shall have something to say that will bear directly on this subject.

Sen. Hale: You made a very interesting statement some time ago that from year to year, or from summer to summer, the conduct of the war was sterner, stiffer, as you called it. You are describing what took place the second summer, not the first?

Gen. Hughes: Yes.

In the first campaign the rules of civilized warfare were rigidly enforced. The fact is there was a building burned the first two or three days I was out, and I issued an order that any man caught setting fire to a building should be promptly arrested, and if he ran and could not be stopped in any other way, shoot him. I could not tell whether these fires were started by some of our own men or by Chinamen with our command, who were there for the purpose of transporting the wounded and the sick, etc., but anyway in nearly every encampment up to that time there was some little fire somewhere. That stopped it, and from that time on I do not think there were any fires or anything of that kind, and there was none, so far as I can recall, in that year's operations. But the next year we found it necessary to adopt more stringent methods in order to reach these people. . . .

Sen. Rawlins: Is it not true that operations in the islands became progressively more severe within the past year and a half in dealing with districts which were disturbed?

Gen. Hughes: I think that is true. I would not say it is entirely so. The severities depend upon the man immediately in command of the force that he has with him. In the department I suppose I had at times as many as a hundred and twenty commands in the field. Each commander, under general restrictions, had authority to act for himself. These commanders were changed from time to time. The new commanders coming in would probably start in very much easier than the old ones.

Sen. Hale: Very much what?

Gen. Hughes: Easier. They would come from this country with their ideas of civilized warfare, and they were allowed to get their lesson.

Sen. Rawlins: As soon as it was recognized by those in command in the islands that a departure from civilized warfare might be made, and it was left largely to the discretion of the local commanders as to what should be done, did not that leave them practically without limit as to the severity of the methods to which they might resort?

Gen. Hughes: No.

Sen. Rawlins: If not, what rules restricted them?

Gen. Hughes: There is one rule that is generally pretty safe, and that is that the army officer is an educated man, a man educated in civil society ——

Sen. Rawlins: Apart from the personal equation and the disposition of the individual in command, I ask what limitations or restrictions were there upon what he might do? . . .

Gen. Hughes: Everyone is governed by the laws of war. They all have them. They are laid down in the books to govern, and attention of the whole division to that order was called more than once by the division commander, which of course extended throughout my department as well as the others. His order was good throughout the archipelago.

Sen. Rawlins: Of course some men would be disposed to be lenient and humane in carrying on the war, so far as that quality can be exercised, and other men would be harsh and cruel in many cases under provocation, and in the latter instance of course the inhabitants against whom the war was waged would correspondingly suffer. Would not that be the case?

Gen. Hughes: I think I would refer you for a precedent as to what should be done, or might be done, in such cases as those of which I speak, men attacking couriers, interfering with your lines of communication, attacking in unauthorized commands, etc. — that is, commands that had no organization with them, to the action of the Germans in France.

Sen. Hale: You have been diverted from what I thought you were going on to say. You have stated what the general conditions were; that as the summers succeeded one another you resorted to sterner or stiffer processes.

Gen. Hughes: Yes, sir.

Sen. Hale: You were going on to state how that was exemplified under your different local commanders. I wish you would go on and state that, so that we may have the situation as it actually was there from year to year under your local commanders. I refer to this closing, this tightening of the iron hand.

Sen. Allison: And why?

Sen. Hale: And of course the whole conditions.

Gen. Hughes: The first year, as I have said, we adhered strictly to the rules. We did not arrest anyone and confine him unless he was actually caught with arms in his hands. In such cases he was, of course, kept as a prisoner of war.

The next year we found that we had to arrest a great many people who were not in uniform, the evidence being that they were in the habit of assisting the enemy in different ways. They would assist them by sending food to them. They were collectors, collecting money. They were possibly getting cartridges from our men, making collections of them, and sending them out. There were all these things of that sort. Those people were arrested, and in some instances probably tried. Of course, I cannot fix this positively by dates. . . .

The third year we arrested a great many more, and as to those who were caught red-handed, I think the local commander was very apt to burn them out.

Sen. Hale: What did he do with the individual?

Gen. Hughes: He was very apt to burn his shack.

Sen. Hale: What did they do with the individual?

Gen. Hughes: They probably carried him off.

Sen. Hale: Where?

Gen. Hughes: To one of their prisons. You will understand that there were a hundred and twenty posts probably in the department. I do not know by actual count how many there were. They changed.

Sen. Rawlins: You used the term "red-handed." What do you mean by that?

Gen. Hughes: Caught in the act, whatsoever the interference, or whatsoever the act was he was committing, where there could be no question whatever of the charge against him. In those cases as a summary punishment, as I say, possibly, his establishment was burned. That was occasionally done. If there was simply strong evidence, but the man was not self-convicted, nothing would be done without a trial.

Sen. Patterson: When you went there did you expect to find the inhabitants of the country sympathizing with the insurrectos?

Gen. Hughes: I expected, rather, to find the Visayans somewhat friendly to us. I had tried to inform myself in Manila of the disposition, of the character, of the general situation of those people, and the general impression I got was that the Visayans did not want any war, would not have made any war had they not been interfered with and dominated by the Tagalogs; that they were a very gentle, docile, polite sort of people.

I went down hoping that getting rid of the Tagalogs would avoid all war with the Visayans, and, as I have previously told you, I succeeded, or at least it was effected that the Tagalogs should leave Iloilo, which was the strongest province in the whole group. And yet the Visayans kept me in siege until the dry season came, when I could move. Then I had to break their lines with our own troops.

Sen. Patterson: You found yourself disappointed ——

Gen. Hughes: Very much disappointed.

Sen. Patterson: In the disposition of the Visayans?

Gen. Hughes: I hoped to get the thing settled without any struggle whatever with the Visayans, and my information was such that I believed it practicable when I went down there. . . .

Sen. Patterson: Was it this expectation which led you the first year to observe strictly the rules of civilized warfare?

Gen. Hughes: No. I believed when I started out that the people were sufficiently informed of what civilized war was, and that they would follow civilized methods, but I did not have such a high opinion of them by the time that campaign ended.

Sen. Patterson: Was not this in your mind: If their disposition was such as you had been led to expect it was, observing the rules of civilized warfare would be more likely to increase their friendship or transform indifference into friendship or induce them the more willingly to submit to the force of government?

Gen. Hughes: My theory of war is that it should be made entirely civilized and just as light as possible to succeed in getting the result your government expects. I went there supposing these people to be sufficiently civilized to follow the ordinary rules of civilized warfare. I became convinced, greatly to my sorrow, that they would not follow the rules of war. . . .

Sen. Rawlins: Were there many engagements around in the vicinity of Iloilo after its capture originally by the American troops?

Gen. Hughes: As to actual engagements, there were very few. It was very hard to get an engagement of any kind. You could get what we would call a little skirmish, and probably there would be ten or twelve killed. . . .

Sen. Rawlins: You speak about the mutilation of this soldier. It was committed by a mob of some two hundred people?

Gen. Hughes: That I do not know. I simply know it took place in a village community where there seemed to be quite a number present; how many, I do not think I ever inquired.

Sen. Rawlins: It was in the nature of a mob of people who happened to get hold of him?

Gen. Hughes: It was the people of that mountain village, right on the edge of the mountain, near Leon.

Sen. Rawlins: It followed after some difficulty; some fighting?

Gen. Hughes: The fight had been with the insurrecto soldiers. As I understand it, they were not the people who caught this one man who refused to surrender.

Sen. Rawlins: Of course you give it, as I understand you, as an illustration of the character of the Visayan people?

Gen. Hughes: Yes.

Sen. Rawlins: Would you think that the frenzied action of a mob would give any indication of what the people would do ordinarily?

Gen. Hughes: I am not sure.

Sen. Rawlins: I will ask you to answer that question if you can.

Gen. Hughes: I have not said that it was a mob. . . .

Sen. Rawlins: This case of mutilation was the subject of investigation by court-martial, was it not?

Gen. Hughes: I have been trying to recall whether the murderer who finally killed him was tried or not. I cannot recall reviewing the case, which I would have done had the man been tried.

About the time that these investigations were made there was an escape of some prisoners from Leon, where this man was held during the investigation of the judge advocate. I rather think that the man either escaped or was killed in trying to get away, for I cannot recall that he was tried or that I reviewed the case, but I know we were trying to prepare the case and get the evidence ready for the purpose of trying him. But I cannot determine whether or not I actually reviewed the case; I had to review a great many.

Sen. Rawlins: You were not present, of course, and you do not remember the details of the transaction?

Gen. Hughes: I only remember them as they were told me in a general way by the judge advocate who was making the investigation and who came to me to have the body exhumed and all that sort of thing.

Sen. Rawlins: And the precise circumstances under which this mutilation occurred or the number of persons by whom it was inflicted you are not prepared to state, I understand?

Gen. Hughes: No, sir; except that it was done by the people of a certain neighborhood.

Sen. Rawlins: Only that it was done by the people of a certain neighborhood, but whether by insurrectos or whether by persons in the community suddenly frenzied, you are not prepared to say?

Gen. Hughes: No, sir.

Sen. Culberson: You are certain it was not done by insurrecto soldiers?

Gen. Hughes: So far as I know, it was not, because the insurrecto soldiers with whom this affair occurred delivered their prisoners to our garrison and sent the Young Men's Christian Association man in without —

Sen. Culberson: They saved him?

Gen. Hughes: Yes, sir.

Sen. Rawlins: Within your jurisdiction do you know of other instances of mutilation by the Visayans of American troops falling into their hands?

Gen. Hughes: I have some other cases here. Do you mean of natives against natives?

Sen. Rawlins: No; I mean the mutilation of American soldiers falling into the hands of native people.

Gen. Hughes: I do not know of any other mutilation unless you would call killing a man by crushing in his head with a stone mutilation.

Sen. Rawlins: That would be the act of killing, I suppose?

Gen. Hughes: Some were killed, but we do not know exactly how.

Sen. Rawlins: I suppose there were a number of American soldiers who fell into the hands of insurgents or insurrectos among the Visayans, were there not?

Gen. Hughes: Yes, sir.

Sen. Rawlins: Will you tell us, so far as you have knowledge upon the subject, how they were treated.

Gen. Hughes: That is what I was going on to do.

In Cabatuan, under the direction of the *presidente* and chief of police, a soldier of the Eighteenth Infantry was induced to go out to meet a woman of loose character. He did go out. They gave him tuba * and proceeded to kill him with bolos and sent his gun to the insurrectos.

At Calinog the Twenty-sixth Infantry Volunteers, Captain Tutherly's company, had four men missing on taking up the march. I had left that battalion to escort the train while I moved with two battalions to Passi. They would make it a two days' march and I would make but one. Captain Tutherly, I think, sent back a corporal to find these men and bring them on. He found the people. He brought in one, but the others refused to come and he abandoned them.

I heard nothing of this until possibly five days later, but it was too late then to do anything. But we pursued the matter with the idea of bringing the criminals to trial until after the establishment of the civil government.

The facts, when they finally came out, showed that these men had been full of tuba, and two of their guns had been taken from them, while the third one had kept his gun. They were just in such condition as to go back into Calinog, where they had camped, and demand these two guns of the people. I think the padre was one of the people to whom they spoke on the subject. The result of it was that they were all three killed by the people of that town.

Captain Tutherly was sent to Calinog when it became practicable to do so, and tried to find out the individuals who did it. They were people of that community, but he never was able to make a case. He is a lawyer of good repute in New Hampshire or Vermont — Vermont, I think — and he did his best to make a case, but all he could find was that they had been killed by the people of Calinog, the padre being present, I think.

From Pototan three men of the Eighteenth United States Infantry

* Tuba is an alcoholic drink of the Philippines. It can be made from the fermented sap of various palms.

went to Barotac Nueva, some five or six miles distant, on a tuba hunting expedition. The information came from an old man of Spanish blood, I should imagine, from what they told me. I did not see him, although I was at Pototan at the time, but I did not know anything about the missing men at that time. I was preparing the command for crossing the mountain. This old man came in and notified those concerned that there was danger that these men would be gotten away with if they were not looked after. The captain of the company immediately sent a detachment. The men could not be found, and never have been found. The old man who brought in the evidence that they were there and would get into trouble had his head taken off.

The three soldiers, by common report, were taken down into the *manglares* [mangrove] between Barotac Nueva and Dumangas and boloed in the mud of this mangle, and of course the bodies would sink and disappear, and we have never been able to locate where they were killed. Some of the natives would show the spot where it occurred, but there was no longer any evidence on the surface.

One man of the Twenty-sixth United States Volunteers left his companions while across the Jalaur River from their camp one evening near Dingle. Diligent search was made for him the next morning, but he could not then be found and he never has been found.

In Cebu Captain Smith went on an expedition in the northern end of that island, and had five men either get lost or stray from his command. I have forgotten just the details of it. Two of them, we learned on good authority afterwards — because these cases were carefully looked into — were killed at a convent, I think, in Sogod. The other three were heard of as prisoners.

When the insurrectos came in in Cebu in October I asked Maxilom, the commanding officer of their forces in that island, before accepting his submission to the United States, for these three prisoners that his people had taken. He said he had no further information than the fact that when he heard of the capture he sent an order that these three men should be sent to him; that an officer was started to take them to his camp, and the men had never arrived there, and the officer was dead. So he knew nothing about it. That is all I could get. . . .

Sen. Patterson: You told us about the increasing severity of your campaigns, covering, I think, a period of three years. Please state, generally, whether you learned anything about the water cure during that period of time.

Gen. Hughes: I never have learned anything about it. The water cure may mean anything.

Sen. Patterson: I refer to the water cure as it is popularly understood here.

Gen. Hughes: If you will tell me what that is, I will tell you.

Sen. Patterson: The holding of a person, usually a native, the pouring of water into his mouth and into his stomach until he is distended, and thereby forcing him, through the pain, to give information such as you desire to secure from him, as, for illustration, the location of arms or anything of that kind.

Gen. Hughes: I heard of but one case of that character. That case was tried by the police — by what you might call a police force — and they said they would not do it again.

Sen. Patterson: Do you mean by the Macabebes?

Gen. Hughes: No; it was done by Americans, and they said they would never resort to that measure. They had heard of it, I presume, or somebody had come down from Luzon and given them the method, and they tried it, and my information was they never would try it again.

Sen. Patterson: Have you any knowledge of any court-martial for or of the punishment of any person alleged to have been guilty of that conduct?

Gen. Hughes: I do not know that I have. I should like to explain that.

Sen. Patterson: Anything you please, General.

Gen. Hughes: The water cure with us out there may mean a great many things. As one of my friends remarked to me the other day, "You are getting the water cure down there."

Sen. Patterson: The only knowledge we have here is that it is used in the way of torture.

Gen. Hughes: I have read a paper since I came home, emanating from Boston, describing it, and I can assure you, Mr. Senator, that the thing was not practiced under my command, or at least I think I am sufficiently well advised as to what was being done to say that that never was practiced in the Department of Visayas. The best information I have is that they tried it in one case and rejected it.

Sen. Patterson: There was no punishment given in that case, but they promised to reform?

Gen. Hughes: I did not know of it until long afterwards; then they confessed that they had tried it.

Sen. Patterson: That is all. . . .

Testimony of Charles S. Riley *

The Chairman: Are you now in the Army of the United States? — A. No, sir; I am not.

Q. You have been in the Army? — A. Yes.

Q. What regiment? — A. I was in the First Connecticut in 1898 for

* Biographical details are contained in the testimony.

six months, and afterwards in the Twenty-sixth Infantry Volunteers for twenty-two months.

Q. While you were in the Twenty-sixth Volunteer Infantry were you in the Philippine Islands? — A. Yes, sir.

Q. During the whole period of your service? — A. For eighteen months. . . .

Sen. Rawlins: You have given your place of residence, I believe. — A. Northampton, Mass.

Q. When did you arrive in the Philippine Islands? — A. October 30, 1899. That is, we arrived in the harbor of Manila on the 25th and we arrived at outstation October 30.

Q. When did you leave? — A. I went aboard the vessel March 4, 1901, and we sailed the next day.

Q. And when did you arrive in San Francisco? — A. April 20, 1901.

Q. During your service in the Philippine Islands what position in the Army did you hold? — A. I held all the positions from private to first sergeant. I was discharged as the first sergeant of the company.

Q. During your service there did you witness what is generally known as the water cure? — A. I did.

Q. When and where? — A. On November 27, 1900, in the town of Igbaras, Iloilo Province, Panay Island.

Q. You may state, Mr. Riley, what you saw in that regard. — A. The first thing I saw that I thought was anything out of the ordinary, in going into the quarters from downstairs ——

Q. Let me premise that, perhaps. Was your company stationed at Igbaras? — A. One detachment of fifteen men garrisoned the town.

Q. And what building did you occupy? — A. It was known as the convent, the convent in connection with the church. It was a convent or a school.

Q. Did you occupy the first floor or the second floor? — A. We occupied the entire building.

Q. The entire building? — A. The entire building.

Q. You may state whether there was an upper floor. — A. There was. Downstairs it was a stone building, with stone floors, and then there was a second story; it was two stories, and we occupied the upstairs with our quarters.

Q. How was the second story reached? — A. By stone steps.

Q. You may state whether or not there was a corridor at the head of the stairway. — A. There was a corridor on the right, and then we went through another corridor into the room we called our squad room, known as the quarters of the soldiers.

Q. Did you arrive there the morning of the 27th? — A. Yes, sir; at daylight.

Q. Who [sic] were with you at the time you arrived there? — A. There were from twelve to fourteen men of Company M, Twenty-sixth Infantry, and about forty men of the Eighteenth United States Infantry, a mounted detachment, known as the Gordon Scouts.

Q. Did you pass into the upper story of this building? — *A.* What is that, sir?

Q. Did you pass that morning into the upper floor of this building? — *A.* Yes, sir.

Q. What soldiers and officers were there? — *A.* Taking all the men, there must have been about forty of the Twenty-sixth and about an equal number of the Eighteenth Infantry, regulars, about forty of each.

Q. About eighty men in all? — *A.* Yes.

Q. Who commanded your company? — *A.* Captain McDonald, of the Twenty-sixth Infantry — Captain Fred McDonald.

Q. What other officers connected with the regulars? — *A.* Captain Glenn, captain, Twenty-fifth United States Infantry, judge-advocate Department Visayas, commanded the forces, consisting of detachments of Eighteenth United States Infantry, and the Twenty-sixth United States Infantry Volunteers.

Q. Was he judge-advocate under General Hughes? — *A.* Yes; that was General Hughes's department. Then there was Lieutenant Conger, commanding the scouts, and the contract surgeon, Lyons.

Q. Did you pass up the stairway into the corridor above that morning, into the main hall? — *A.* Yes.

Q. And as you passed up, you may state what you saw. — *A.* I saw the *presidente* standing in the ——

Q. Whom do you mean by the *presidente*? — *A.* The head official of the town.

Q. The town of Igbaras? — *A.* Yes, sir.

Q. A Filipino? — *A.* Yes, sir.

Q. How old was he? — *A.* I should judge that he was a man of about forty or forty-five years.

Q. When you saw him, what was his condition? — *A.* He was stripped to the waist; he had nothing on but a pair of white trousers, and his hands were tied behind him.

Q. Do you remember who had charge of him? — *A.* Captain Glenn stood there beside him and one or two men were tying him.

Q. You may state whether or not there was a water tank in the upper corridor. — *A.* Just at the head of the stairs on the right there was a large galvanized-iron tank, holding probably one hundred gallons, about two barrels. That was on a raised platform, about ten or twelve inches, I should think, and there was a faucet on the tank. It was the tank we used for catching rainwater for drinking purposes.

Q. As you passed up, did you pass through the corridor into the hall? — *A.* Yes; directly through the hall into the squad room.

Q. Into the squad room? — *A.* Yes, sir.

Q. And you may state whether or not soldiers were passing up and down. — A. Yes, sir; men were congregated around the door, and they were passing back and forth from downstairs upstairs and from upstairs downstairs.

Q. You first saw the *presidente* under the condition you describe, with his hands being tied behind him? — A. Yes.

Q. What else did you observe being done with him? — A. He was then taken and placed under the tank, and the faucet was opened and a stream of water was forced down or allowed to run down his throat; his throat was held so he could not prevent swallowing the water, so that he had to allow the water to run into his stomach.

Q. What connection was there between the faucet and his mouth? — A. There was no connection; he was directly under the faucet.

Q. Directly under the faucet? — A. Directly under the faucet and with his mouth held wide open.

Q. Was anything done besides forcing his mouth open and allowing the water to run down? — A. When he was filled with water it was forced out of him by pressing a foot on his stomach or else with their hands.

Q. How long was his mouth held open? — A. That I could not state exactly, whether it was by pressing the cheek or throat. Some say that it was the throat, but I could not state positively as to that, as to exactly how they held his mouth open.

Q. About how long was that continued? — A. I should say from five to fifteen minutes.

Q. During the process what officers were present, if anybody? — A. Lieutenant Conger was present practically all the time. Captain Glenn walked back and forth from one room to the other, and went in there two or three times. Lieutenant Conger was in command of water detail; it was under his supervision.

Q. You may state whether or not there was any Filipino interpreter present. — A. There was a native interpreter that stood directly over this man — the *presidente* — as he lay on the floor.

Q. Did you observe whether the interpreter communicated with this *presidente?* — A. He did at different times. He practically kept talking to him all the time, kept saying some one word which I should judge meant "confess" or "answer."

Q. Could you understand what was said? — A. No, sir; I could not understand the native tongue at all.

Q. At the conclusion, what then was done? — A. After he was willing to answer he was allowed to partly sit up, and kind of rolled on his side, and then he answered the questions put to him by the officer through the interpreter.

Q. You say they pushed the water out of him. How was that done — what was the process? — A. I did not see the water forced from him. Some said it was forced by the hand, and others by placing the foot on the stomach; I didn't see the water forced from him.

Q. You did not see that? — A. No, sir.

Q. After he got up what did you next see? — A. It was after he gave all the desired information. He was then untied and allowed to dress, and taken downstairs in front of the quarters.

Q. Where did they take him? — A. They took him downstairs outside the building, and he stood in front of the building, waiting for his horse. He was to guide the expedition up into the mountains.

Q. While standing on the sidewalk what took place? — A. More information was sought for; and as he refused to answer, a second treatment was ordered.

Q. Where were you at that time? — A. I was in front of the building at the time, on the sidewalk.

Q. In front? — A. Yes; on the stone walk. They started to take him inside the building and Captain Glenn said, "Don't take him inside. Right here is good enough." One of the men of the Eighteenth Infantry went to his saddle and took a syringe from the saddlebag, and another man was sent for a can of water, what we call a kerosene can, holding about five gallons. He brought this can of water down from upstairs, and then a syringe was inserted, one end in the water and the other end in his mouth. This time he was not bound, but he was held by four or five men and the water was forced into his mouth from the can, through the syringe.

Sen. Burrows: Was this another party? — A. No; this was the same man. The syringe did not seem to have the desired effect, and the doctor ordered a second one. The man got a second syringe, and that was inserted in his nose. Then the doctor ordered some salt, and a handful of salt was procured and thrown into the water. Two syringes were then in operation. The interpreter stood over him in the meantime asking for this second information that was desired. Finally he gave in and gave the information that they sought, and then he was allowed to rise.

Q. May I ask the name of the doctor? — A. Dr. Lyons, the contract surgeon.

Q. An American? — A. Yes, sir.

Sen. Rawlins: Was it Captain Glenn who said not to take him in? — A. Captain Glenn.

Q. Did he make any other command before that at that time? — A. Not that I know of.

Q. Not that you recall? — A. No.

Q. How long did the second infliction of this torture continue? — A. About the same as the first; from about five to fifteen minutes. I could not tell you the exact time.

Q. How many men held this Filipino down when the first torture was inflicted? — A. About four men; one to each arm and one to each leg.

Q. Was this same interpreter present at the second infliction of the torture? — A. Yes; he was.

Q. What did he do? — A. He stood over him asking him — the same language used before until he was willing to confess, and then they stopped the water. As soon as he made a sign, or as soon as he answered that he would confess, he was allowed to get up.

Q. Do you know what information they obtained from him? — A. The question asked, the information they sought for, was as to whether runners or messengers had been sent out notifying the insurgents of our arrival; and not giving a satisfactory answer, or he refusing to answer, he was given this treatment and then he acknowledged that he had done so, and as we entered the lower gate one of his police went out at the upper gate notifying the insurgents that reinforcements were in town, to be on the watch.

Q. First Lieutenant Conger and Captain Glenn were of the Regular Army? — A. Captain Glenn and Lieutenant Conger, yes, sir. . . .

The Chairman: What was the conduct of the men of your regiment — those whom you saw — toward natives? — A. I did not see anything out of the ordinary. I did not see any inhuman treatment; anything more than there naturally would be. Any ill treatment against natives at all was by soldiers under the influence of liquor. As a rule, soldiers in their sober senses treated the natives all right.

Sen. Carmack: When they were sober they treated them all right? — A. Yes, sir.

Q. Do you mean that when they were drunk it was sometimes otherwise? — A. There were reports at different times of trouble with natives on account of men drinking outside in the towns around among the natives.

Q. What was the nature of such trouble? — A. Usually a fight; a free hand fight, or something to that effect.

The Chairman: In the case of these fights and attacks on natives that you speak of, were they punished for that conduct?

Sen. Beveridge: Put in the guardhouse?

The Witness: Sometimes they were, sometimes they were not; it all depended. If a native reported it to the officers, it was invariably investigated. Sometimes the natives were found to be in fault, and if a man was found to be in fault he was usually punished.

Sen. Beveridge: When he was in fault, he was punished? — A. Yes, sir.

Q. Our own men? — A. Yes, sir.

Q. I notice that you said that this treatment was continued from five to fifteen minutes. Did you time it? — A. No, sir; I did not.

Q. It might have been only five minutes instead of fifteen; that would make a good deal of difference.

Sen. Culberson: That is what he has already said.

The Witness: I could not state the time. It seemed longer than five minutes.

Sen. Beveridge: Did he suffer any ill effects from that treatment? — A. His eyes were bloodshot; otherwise he seemed to be ——

Q. Did you see him the next day? — A. Yes, sir.

Q. Did he seem all right then? — A. Yes; he was taken prisoner and was confined after that. . . .

Sen. Burrows: I understand you to say that American soldiers were present when this water cure was administered? — A. Yes, sir.

Q. How many? — A. About eighty.

Q. Did any of them take part in it? — A. Yes, sir.

Q. How many of them? — A. I could not tell you the exact number of different ones. There were usually five or six employed. Whether they were the same five or six employed the time the treatment was given the second time, I could not state.

The Chairman: Were they the men of the Eighteenth?

The Witness: Yes, sir.

Sen. Burrows: By whose orders —— — A. Captain Glenn.

Q. Who is Captain Glenn? — A. Judge-advocate of the Department of Visayas. He was captain of the Twenty-fifth Infantry.

Q. Were those eighty men intoxicated, or were any of them intoxicated? — A. No, sir.

Q. All sober and in their right minds? — A. Yes, sir.

Q. When they filled this man up with water they were sober? — A. Yes, sir.

Q. What had been his crime? — A. Information had been obtained from a native source as to his being an insurgent officer. After the treatment he admitted that he held the rank of captain in the insurgent army — an active captain. His police force, numbering twenty-five, were sworn insurgent soldiers. He was the *presidente* of the town and had been for a year, and he always showed himself to be friendly on the outside to the officers, and the men the same way.

Sen. Beveridge: But in reality ——

The Witness: He was an insurgent officer and his men were insurgent soldiers. He acknowledged that, and his police acknowledged the same thing. When they took the oath as police they took the oath of an insurgent soldier.

The Chairman: Were they supposed to be friendly to the United States?

The Witness: They were; yes, sir.

Sen. Beveridge: That was a pretense? — A. Yes, sir.

Q. And this was during the time of active warfare? — A. Yes, sir; during the entire time he held the place as the *presidente* in that town.

Sen. Burrows: His offense was treachery to the American cause? — A. Yes, sir.

Q. And for that the water cure was given? — *A*. No; the water cure was given to find out this information. The information had been obtained from another source.

Q. This water cure was given to find out whether he would admit it? — *A*. Yes, sir; to find out whether it was true.

Sen. Beveridge: No; you said it was given to find out whether warnings had been given to the insurgents of your arrival.

The Witness: No; that was the second treatment.

Sen. Burrows: I am talking about the first treatment. — *A*. That was given to corroborate the information that had been obtained.

Q. And so he was put to this torture for the purpose of finding that out? — *A*. Yes, sir.

Sen. Culberson: Do I understand you to say that he was put to this torture to compel him to give evidence against himself?

The Witness: Yes, sir.

Sen. Burrows: You never had the water cure administered to you? — *A*. No, sir.

Q. Should you judge from the actions of the person to whom it was administered that it was a pleasant operation? — *A*. No, sir.

Q. Painful? — *A*. Yes, sir.

Q. What makes you think so? — *A*. From the way he would struggle and try to get up, and of course he could not holler or make any noise, any loud noise.

Q. Why not? — *A*. On account of the water being in his mouth. He could gurgle, and he would struggle and try to get up. Being held by main strength he was practically helpless.

Sen. Culberson: When the foot was applied to his stomach with what force did the water come out of his mouth? — *A*. I did not see that.

Q. Do you know whether the water came out of his nose? — *A*. I could not state as to that, any more than what the men who were there said that it would squirt up two or three feet in the air.

Sen. Culberson: Like an artesian well?

Sen. Beveridge: What man stated that?

The Witness: Sergeant Davis stated that.

The Chairman: Of the Eighteenth?

The Witness: Of the Twenty-sixth Infantry.

Sen. Burrows: Then the infliction of this water cure on this person was not for the various outrages that had been committed in the various parts of the islands? — *A*. No, sir; it had no connection with them.

Q. Simply to make him disclose —— — *A*. Simply to make him corroborate what they had heard.

Q. Whether he was loyal to the American cause or a traitor? — *A*. Yes, sir.

Q. Who did you say this officer was that ordered the salt? — *A*. Doctor Lyons, the contract surgeon.

Q. Of what regiment? — A. He was a contract surgeon and did not belong to any regular command.

Q. Where does he live? — A. He did not have any regular command.

Q. Is he an American? — Yes, sir. He was there in connection with the Department of Visayas, either connected with the hospital or he was connected with the Eighteenth Infantry, detailed for that purpose.

Q. At the second performance water was injected into the mouth and into the nose? — A. Yes, sir.

Sen. Beveridge: Did you see that?

The Witness: Yes, sir.

Sen. Burrows: Who suggested putting tubes in the nose? — A. Dr. Lyons.

Q. Did anybody kill him? — A. Kill who, the Doctor?

Q. Yes. — A. No, sir. . . .

Testimony of Daniel J. Evans *

The Chairman: Give your full name. — A. Daniel J. Evans.

Q. And you have been in the Army? — A. Six years.

Q. In the regulars? — A. Yes, sir.

Q. In what regiment? — A. My first enlistment was in the First Cavalry, for three years; my second enlistment, two years and seven months in the Twelfth Infantry, and transferred to the artillery stationed at Honolulu.

Q. Are you a resident of Kansas? — A. Yes, sir.

Q. Concordia, Kans., I believe? — A. Yes, sir.

Q. Were you born in Canada? — A. Yes, sir.

Q. And Concordia is your home? — A. Yes, sir.

Q. And did you serve in the Philippines? — A. Yes, sir; for two years.

Q. From when; when did you go there? — A. I got there in April, 1899, and left about the 1st of February, 1901.

Q. Where did you serve during that time; what part of the islands? — A. The Island of Luzon.

Q. What was your rank? — A. Private, at the time of enlistment.

Q. And your rank at the time of your discharge? — A. Corporal.

Q. You received an honorable discharge, did you? — A. Yes, sir.

Q. The committee would like to hear from you in regard to the conduct of the war, and whether you were the witness of any cruelties inflicted upon the natives in the Philippine Islands; and if so, under what circumstances. — A. The case I had reference to was where they gave the water cure to a native in the Ilicano Province at Ilocos Norte.

* Biographical details are contained in the testimony.

Q. That is in the extreme northern part of Luzon? — A. Yes, sir. There were two native scouts that were with the American forces. They went out and brought in a couple of insurgents. They were known to be insurgents by their own confession, and, besides that, they had the mark that most insurgents in that part of the country carry; it is a little brand on the left breast, generally inflicted with a nail or head of a cartridge, heated. They tried to find out from this native ——

Q. What kind of a brand did you say it was? — A. A small brand put on with a nail head or cartridge.

Sen. Beveridge: A scar on the flesh?

The Witness: Yes, sir.

They tried to get him to tell where the rest of the insurgents were at that time. We knew about where they were, but we did not know how to get at them. They were in the hills, and it happened that there was only one path that could get to them, and we did not get to them that time. They refused to tell this one path and they commenced this so-called "water cure." The first thing one of the Americans — I mean one of the scouts for the Americans — grabbed one of the men by the head and jerked his head back, and then they took a tomato can and poured water down his throat until he could hold no more, and during this time one of the natives had a rattan whip, about as large as my finger, and he struck him on the face and on the bare back, and every time they would strike him it would raise a large welt, and some blood would come. And when this native could hold no more water, then they forced a gag into his mouth; they stood him up and tied his hands behind him; they stood him up against a post and fastened him so he could not move. Then one man, an American soldier, who was over six feet tall, and who was very strong, too, struck this native in the pit of the stomach as hard as he could strike him, just as rapidly as he could. It seemed as if he didn't get tired of striking him.

Sen. Allison: With his hand? — A. With his clenched fist. He struck him right in the pit of the stomach and it made the native very sick. They kept that operation up for quite a time, and finally I thought the fellow was about to die, but I don't believe he was as bad as that, because finally he told them he would tell, and from that on he was taken away, and I saw no more of him.

Q. Did he tell? — A. I believe he did, because I didn't hear of any more water cure inflicted on him.

Sen. Rawlins: How many were present then? — A. This was an expedition. There were thirty, I think, of our company. We were not at our station at that time: we were on a little expedition down south, and I should think out of the thirty — I should judge that there were about fifteen of our men present, maybe twenty; and out of G Company, of our own regiment, that is the town they were stationed at — there were a greater number of them present.

Q. How many American soldiers altogether were there present? — A. I can safely say there were fifty.

Q. Who was in command of them? — A. Capt. Robert K. Evans.

Q. Was he present at the time the water cure was inflicted? — A. He did not see it; no, sir.

Q. What, if any, officer was present? — A. This is a subject that I have debated on and I can not arrive at a conclusion. It was either Lieutenant Drum or Lieutenant Aloe; and I prefer to think it was Lieutenant Aloe, for the simple reason that our lieutenants were transferred about that time. Lieutenant Drum was promoted from second lieutenant to first lieutenant, and transferred to the Twenty-fourth Infantry, and about that time we got Lieutenant Aloe; and which of those two was on that expedition I cannot say for certain.

Q. Where was the commander? How far distant from where this business was performed? — A. The captain in charge?

Q. Yes. — A. He was not over 200 yards away.

Sen. Burrows: Captain Evans, you mean?

The Witness: Yes, sir.

Sen. Rawlins: Not over 200 yards away? — A. Yes, sir.

Q. Was there any effort to conceal it? — A. Not in the least.

Q. Was it a matter of common knowledge? — A. Yes, sir; it has been the talk of almost the whole army. They do not try to conceal it.

Q. How long has that been the case? — A. Well, it has been practiced, to my knowledge, from along in July, 1900, until the time I left the islands; and, of course, after that time I know nothing about it. I left the islands about February, 1901.

Q. When did this particular case occur? — A. It was about the month of August, 1900. I have not the dates accurate, but it was about that time.

The Chairman: Did you witness any other cases? — A. No, sir; I could have witnessed others, but I did not.

Q. Was this man taken by the native scouts? — A. Yes, sir; he was taken by a couple of native scouts.

Sen. Allison: What do you mean by native scouts?

The Witness: They were scouts — they reconnoitered through the country and gained information for the American soldiers.

Sen. Beveridge: What was this date? — A. 1900; about August.

Q. About two years ago? — A. Yes, sir.

Q. How long did you serve altogether in the Philippine Islands? — A. Very nearly two years.

Q. During that time you were in what part of the archipelago? — A. I was in the island of Luzon, from Manila to — do you want ——

Q. Just generally. And during this time what is the fact as to your having observed any number of prisoners taken by our troops? — A. I have seen a great number of prisoners; yes, sir.

Q. Tell the committee what the fact is as to the treatment of those prisoners by American officers and men, as to kindness and consideration, or the reverse. — A. The majority of the prisoners until the time I went north, if they were taken and had arms they would be kept a few days and their arms would be taken away, and then, probably, they would be paroled or released.

Q. During the time they were in your custody what is the fact as to the food given them? — A. They were fed, and if there was any work to be done they had to do it, but they were treated, up to this time the water cure commenced, as well as they could be. Some of the Filipino prisoners actually preferred to remain in the American lines, prisoners, than to be among their own people.

Q. And the sick and wounded among them? — A. They were given hospital treatment.

Q. The same as our men? — A. Yes, sir. In the front of their hospital, I believe, there were two wards.

Q. You speak of their hospital. Do you refer to the hospital in Manila? — A. Yes, sir.

Q. That was given up entirely to the Filipino sick and wounded? — A. Yes, sir.

Q. And what physicians attended them? — A. Our physicians and our nurses.

Q. Our nurses also? — A. Yes, sir.

Q. What is the fact as to the treatment of these prisoners, and sick and wounded being given the same as to our sick and wounded? — A. I could not see any difference, except probably the rations would not be the same. The Filipinos themselves would prefer rice.

Q. They would prefer rice? — A. Yes, sir.

Q. They were given what they preferred? — A. Yes, sir.

Q. Do you understand that to be the reason why there was any difference in the rations given to our own soldiers and to the Filipino prisoners? — A. That is the only reason I can give.

Q. They being used to it? — A. Yes, sir.

Q. What was the general conduct of the American officers and soldiers toward the people who were peaceably engaged in work, as to kindness or the reverse?

Sen. Rawlins: The Senator who has propounded this question has always objected strenuously to hearsay testimony, and he is now asking for the witness's opinion.

Sen. Beveridge: As you observe.

Sen. Rawlins: And I would like him to be confined to his own rule.

The Chairman: I understand he is asking what the witness observed himself.

Sen. Beveridge: Yes; what is your observation as to the treatment of the people engaged in peaceable pursuits, as to kindness and consideration, or the reverse, from the American officers and the men?

The Witness: They were never molested if they seemed to be peaceable natives. They would not be molested unless they showed some signs of hostility of some kind, and if they did, if we struck a part of the island where the natives were hostile and they would fire on our soldiers or even cut the telegraph lines, the result would be that their barrios would probably be burned.

Q. After our troops had passed over a district what is the fact as to the people returning to the fields and engaging in the business of tilling the soil, returning to their homes after peace had been established. — A. As far as I could see we would not much more than get through a town until you would see the natives coming back from the hills, carrying little white flags on sticks. As we struck a town we could not see a native hardly, but when we got 200 or 300 or 500 yards beyond the town we could see them coming in with these white flags.

Q. And what is the fact as to their going to work in the fields after peace had been established? — A. They were continually working in the fields, and they would come back.

Q. What did you understand the orders from the officers and the commanding generals to be as to the conduct of American officers and soldiers toward peaceably disposed people engaged in peaceable work; as to kindness or the reverse? — A. We never had any orders to molest any of them who were peaceably inclined, none whatever.

Q. And you say that sick and wounded Filipinos had the same treatment as our own people? — A. That was the First Reserve Hospital in Manila; yes. I never observed them in any other hospital. I spoke of that because I had seen it.

Q. Were you in San Fernando when it was occupied by General Mac-Arthur? — A. Yes, sir.

Q. Were you in the hospital there? — A. No, sir.

Q. You do not know about the treatment they received there, then? — A. No, sir.

Q. As to its being the same as in Manila or elsewhere? — A. No, sir.

Sen. Beveridge: That is all.

Sen. Burrows: I wanted to ask you if at the time of the administration of this water cure any United States officer was in command of the squad? — A. There was an officer present at the time that this water cure was given, and, as I have said, it was about the time that our lieutenants were transferred, and I would not be positive which it was.

Q. Will you give the name of the lieutenant that you think it was? — A. I think it was Lieutenant Aloe.

Q. Of what company and of what regiment? — A. At the time he was first lieutenant of E Company, Twelfth Infantry.

Q. Was this water cure administered by his directions? — A. It must have been, because ——

Q. I do not ask "must have been"; do you know that it was? — A. I do not know that it was.

Q. Do you know that it was done at the command of any officer? — A. I do not.

Sen. Allison: You spoke of this large man that was using his fist on a prisoner? — A. Yes, sir.

Q. How many times do you suppose he used his fist in that way? — A. I think it would be safe to say that he struck him at least forty times right in the pit of the stomach.

Sen. Carmack: What was that; I did not understand it?

Sen. Burrows: That this man who had been filled with water was hit by a big, strong man; that a strong, large fellow came up and struck him in the pit of the stomach.

Sen. Beveridge: That he took a running start to get a better force in the blow.

Sen. Burrows: Did he each time during the infliction of these blows go back and run to get force in his blows? — A. I do not believe I said he ran; he would step back and then strike.

Q. And apparently with great force? — A. Yes; harder than I could strike.

Q. And what officer was present when that was being done? — A. As I said, I believe it was Lieutenant Aloe.

Q. Where is Lieutenant Aloe? — A. I do not know, sir. He was put on staff duty after I left the regiment, and from there I do not know where he went.

The Chairman: What man was it you said did the striking?

The Witness: A man by the name of Frank Koehler.

Sen. Burrows: Of what company? — A. The same as mine, the Twelfth Infantry.

Q. Do you know where he is now? — A. I was told he lived in Cincinnati.

Q. He has been discharged from the service, has he? — A. Yes, sir.

Q. Now give me his full name. — A. Frank Koehler.

Q. Spell it. — A. F-r-a-n-k K-o-e-h-l-e-r.

Q. And you think he is in Cincinnati? — A. I think he is.

The Chairman: Was he a sergeant?

The Witness: No, sir; he was a private.

Sen. Allison: This was done under the direction of these native scouts, or who did this work; was it part of the American soldiery, or was it simply these scouts? — A. It was part of each; it was this man Koehler and two native scouts.

Q. They were the ones that did the business? — A. Yes, sir.

Sen. Rawlins: Was there any effort on the part of any officer there to prevent this being done? — A. No, sir; none that I saw.

Q. You say it must have been ordered by some officers. Why did you say so? — A. I believe the question was asked me if it was ordered, and I said I did not know.

Q. But you started to say it must have been. Those men that were there were under command of officers, were they not? — A. Yes, sir.

Q. And officers were present? — A. I think it was this Lieutenant Aloe that was present, as I stated before.

Sen. Burrows: But the two scouts and this large man were the only ones that participated in the infliction of this water cure? — A. Yes, sir.

Sen. Rawlins: You stated you saw natives coming out of the hills with little white flags of truce. What did they do with them? — A. We never molested them. We let them go about their business. On returning we would find them coming back.

Sen. Beveridge: You said that when you passed by they came back to work?

The Witness: Yes, sir; they came back to work after we passed.

Sen. Rawlins: Certain towns were burned?

The Witness: Yes; some barrios.

Sen. Allison: That is to say, the appearance of our troops induced them to come back. Was that the idea?

The Witness: Some of the natives were afraid of the American soldiers when they would appear in a body, and they (the natives) would run off and hide; but when we got past we would see them coming back with these little white flags, and if we could come back the same way we would find the natives at work.

Sen. Beveridge: In the fields?

The Witness: Yes, sir.

Sen. Rawlins: In other words, when the American troops would approach the natives they would leave the towns? — A. Yes, sir.

Q. And after you got by they would return? — A. Yes, sir.

Q. You stated certain towns were burned? — A. Yes, sir.

Q. How many towns were burned, if you remember? — A. I know of about five myself being burned.

Q. How large were those towns? — A. They would be what we call barrios, villages.

Q. About how many inhabitants did they contain? — A. I could not make much of an estimate on the inhabitants; there were a great many natives lived in one house, and so it would be a guess to try to tell how many there were altogether.

Q. About how many would be in a house? — A. I have seen as high as twenty-four in one small house.

Q. When these villages were burned, what became of the inhabitants?

— A. They would go out and hide for a while, and then, I suppose, build another one.

Sen. Allison: What was the character of these houses?

The Witness: Bamboo.

Sen. Rawlins: Give us your best estimate as to the size of these villages that were burned. — A. There would be probably twenty or twenty-five bamboo huts in one of the villages.

Q. And a large number of natives in each hut?

Sen. Beveridge: He did not say that.

Sen. Rawlins: He said as high as twenty.

Sen. Beveridge: No; he said sometimes he had seen twenty-four.

Sen. Rawlins: I said some as high as twenty, and you say twenty-four.

Sen. Dietrich: How many rooms were there in this hut that you saw twenty-four people living in?

The Witness: Probably four or five rooms; that would be counting the little kitchen they have on behind it.

Sen. Allison: How many stories are these houses? — A. Generally one story.

Q. And they are bamboo huts? — A. Yes, sir; set up on bamboo sticks.

Sen. Rawlins: You stated, as I understood you, in your testimony that the natives up to the time they began applying the water cure were pretty well treated. How was it after they began the infliction of the water cure? — A. I did not see a great number of prisoners taken after that myself, and, as I say, I only saw one actual case of the water cure. I have heard of others. But the other prisoners, as a rule, were taken back to the town called Laoag and confined there and disposed of there according to the ideas of the commanding officer.

Sen. Beveridge: You say that upon your approach — that is, in the first advance — when we would come to a town people would depart? — A. Yes, sir.

Q. After we would leave the town they would return? — A. Yes, sir.

Q. Then, when you came back again you found them at work in the fields? Is that correct? — A. Yes, sir.

Q. Now, then, when you returned back again did or did they not run away as in the first instance? — A. I had in mind the town of Taytay. When we approached that town we approached them under a line of fire, and we drove the natives from the town.

Q. That was on a Sunday? — A. I believe it was.

Q. I remember that very well. But what I am driving at is this: After our column had passed and peace had been established and you returned and found the people at work in their fields, then did they run away again, as in the first instance? — A. No, sir; they stayed right in their town.

Q. They appeared to have lost all fear or misunderstanding of us? — A. It appeared so; yes, sir.

Q. When did you leave there? — A. I left there the latter part of January, 1901.

Q. What were the last prisoners you saw in our custody? Did you see any the last month of your stay there? — A. I was in the hospital at Dagupan, and there was one prisoner brought there that our company had captured. They opened fire on our company at a place called Moncoda, and we captured one man who had been shot a couple of times or three times.

Q. And you saw him? — A. I saw him when they brought him to the hospital. He was taken to our hospital, and then he was taken to another hospital called Lingayen, or something like that.

Q. What treatment was he given? — A. I did not see.

Q. You simply saw that he was taken to the hospital? — A. Yes, sir.

Q. So far as you know then and observed, there was no difference in the treatment of prisoners taken in battle or otherwise, at the end of your service, than there was at the beginning of it; that is to say, our treatment of prisoners — sick, wounded or otherwise — was what as to kindness? — A. They were always fed, and if there was extra work to be done, they did it, as a rule.

Q. Did you observe any cruelty practiced upon the prisoners? — A. The prisoners we had captured?

Q. Yes. — A. No, sir; none that I can think of.

Sen. Patterson: After they commenced the water cure, how many prisoners do you know of being captured? — A. Do you mean by our company or by other companies?

Q. By your command, the command you were with.

The Chairman: What you know yourself.

The Witness: There were very few. I do not think over four or five all told.

Sen. Patterson: By your command? — A. Yes, sir.

Q. And that covered how long a period of time? — A. We left the province in the last part of September.

Q. What province was that? — A. Ilocos Norte.

Q. That is in the island of Luzon? — A. Yes, sir.

Q. You speak of natives running away from towns when you approached. Did you have in mind any special case or did it apply to all towns that you approached? — A. The town I was speaking of at the time was a special town; it is known as Taytay.

Q. And you approached that in a line of fire? — A. Yes, sir.

Sen. Beveridge: You spoke about Taytay and our advance on Taytay. Taytay is a considerable village, is it not? — A. Yes, sir; a city.

Q. It is a city? — A. Yes, sir.

Q. Was there any burning done there? — A. Yes, sir; there was a big church burned.

Q. Who fired that? — A. I think it was fired by shells ——

Q. First, what regiment did you belong to? — *A.* The Twelfth.

Q. You made the charge, then, across the open? — *A.* Yes, sir.

Q. And two of your men were killed? — *A.* Yes, sir.

Q. Early in the morning? — *A.* Yes, sir; Smith and Warner.

Q. Yes, Smith and Warner; and General Lawton came up and ordered that charge? — *A.* Yes, sir.

Q. And before that charge the church was burning, was it not? — *A.* Yes, sir.

Q. When you got into the town, you found it evacuated, did you not? — *A.* Yes, sir.

Q. Is it not a fact that the church there — as was the case of the church at San Fernando — was fired by the insurgents before they left? — *A.* I am going by hearsay.

Sen. Rawlins: This is not proper, Mr. Chairman.

The Witness (continuing): Some of the fellows say the shells fired the church and some of the fellows say that the insurgents themselves set fire to the church before they got out of the town. But the church was burned.

Sen. Beveridge: There is no question about the church being burned. Was there a single house of Taytay fired by our troops? — *A.* No; unless it was that church fired by shells.

Q. Your own opinion about that is what? — *A.* That they set fire to the church themselves before they evacuated the town. It was their stronghold in the town.

Q. What is the fact generally about churches being fired? — *A.* They are generally burned by the insurgents when they get out.

Q. What about the one at San Fernando? — *A.* I don't know who burned it.

Q. It was burning when the American forces entered, was it not? — *A.* Yes, sir.

Q. So that the Americans did not burn it? — *A.* No, sir.

Sen. Beveridge: That is all I wish. . . .

Testimony of William Howard Taft *

Sen. Patterson: Several of the Senators have suggested getting information from you as to the use of the so-called water cure in securing surrenders of guns. . . .

Gov. Taft: I had intended to speak of the charges of torture which were made from time to time, and have been made in letters written

---

* See above, page 35.

from the Philippines by soldiers and others, and which would be made, if they were true, the basis for proper charges against the management of the army.

Sen. Beveridge: Before you enter upon that, you mentioned the deportation to Guam of some irreconcilables, and left the subject at that point.

Gov. Taft: Yes, sir.

Sen. Beveridge: I should like to have you tell the committee the effect upon the people of the deportation to Guam of Pilar and certain other irreconcilables.

Gov. Taft: It was good. It gave the people to understand that we were there to bring about peace; that we were there to assert the sovereignty of the United States. You cannot, in carrying on war, have one purpose in mind and not do the things which will accomplish it, and the deportation to Guam was important. I think there were possibly two orders of General MacArthur, although I am not sure; but there were no more than that. . . .

The Chairman: You were asked about the matter of torture.

Gov. Taft: . . . The kind of warfare that was carried on was chiefly ambushing. The number of insurgents were sometimes large, and sometimes small. They did a great deal of shooting into towns at night. That system of warfare kept the troops on a nervous strain. If you had ever heard an officer in charge of a small post describe his life during that time, you would understand the condition of mind in which he got, his being on edge all the time; when he did not know but that just around him were men who, as soon as he started out, would slip around in another direction and ambush him with rifles which had been buried, and kill him and his men just as they stepped out of the town.

Sen. Patterson: Is guerrilla warfare legitimate warfare?

Gov. Taft: I am not an expert on the laws of war, but I have always understood that it was hardly within the laws of war or legitimate warfare for men to wear the uniform at one time and then slip into a village and appear friendly and then go out again and ambush people.

Sen. Patterson: They have guerrilla warfare in South Africa, and yet when those who are conducting it are captured they are treated, as I understand, under the rules of warfare. They are not regarded as outlaws.

Gov. Taft: There certainly never was a case when an insurgent captured was, with the authority of the commanding officer, treated otherwise than according to the laws of war. But as to what the rules are with respect to guerrilla warfare, you will have to ask an army officer, for I am not competent to tell you.

Sen. Culberson: Without reference to any particular or special method resorted to, is not the only successful way for a people greatly outnumbered in the field to continue war to divide their forces into small bands, so that they can not be overcome by the superior force of numbers?

Gov. Taft: That is quite possible; and so, in this case, it was indispensable to the carrying on of guerrilla warfare that murder and assassination of their own people should be conducted. It could not be carried on otherwise. But I am only stating the facts. Whether it is justified or not is a matter for argument which I prefer not to enter upon.

Sen. Beveridge: The committee is to understand that the persons conducting guerrilla warfare would enter villages of their own people and murder their own people and destroy their property?

Gov. Taft: They would.

I do not say this by way of condemnation of the people who were engaged in it, because our subsequent treatment of certain of the individuals to whom I am about to refer will show that I think they are to be judged by somewhat different standards; but I venture to say there is not a general or a commanding officer of the insurgent forces who in this guerrilla campaign, if the facts were known and proved, could not be convicted of deliberate murder or of being accessory to the deliberate murder of some of his own people who were acting as municipal officers of towns under the American control or furnishing Americans information.

Now, possibly I am wrong in my view of the law of that subject, and that they thought, under the Spanish precedent, it was proper, first, to declare that a man had violated his allegiance to the Philippine Republic; and, second, to send some people to execute him. But my impression is that under the laws of war and under the common law that would be true. Yet we have appointed quite a number of commanders of insurgent forces who came in and gave every genuine evidence, so far as we could see, that they desired to support the American sovereignty and to make government established thereunder a success. We appointed them on the recommendation of military officers who had to do with them. I make this statement to show the feeling we have toward those men.

Now, then, in carrying on guerrilla warfare, it is of course impossible that the forces used shall always be commanded by responsible officers, and frequently the forces which were used in the guerrilla warfare were officered by ignorant, uneducated, and cruel men, for the uneducated native, I am sorry to say, is cruel to animals and has as little regard for human life. Therefore in many instances where soldiers were ambushed, where Signal Service men were ambushed, there were bodies mutilated and evidences of a cruelty that were most likely to cause retaliatory measures.

The Chairman: You mean the bodies of American soldiers were found mutilated?

Gov. Taft: I do. I get this from general officers. General Bell detailed a number of instances of the mutilation of bodies which would naturally arouse the feelings of their comrades.

Sen. Burrows: Did any of these instances of mutilation come under your own observation?

Gov. Taft: No, sir.

Sen. Beveridge: He was not in the field.

Gov. Taft: This, as I have already stated, was hearsay, derived from American officers. Under those circumstances it is not to be wondered at that similar small bodies of American soldiers, under sergeants, even under second lieutenants, with the lack of strength of character incident to lack of experience, should possibly at times have yielded in their outraged feelings against the Filipinos and have resorted to methods which under the circumstances they regarded as more or less justified.

Sen. Culberson: You have stated upon hearsay that the Filipinos have been guilty of instances of cruelty, mentioning some details told you by General Bell?

Gov. Taft: Yes, sir.

Sen. Culberson: Have you heard in a similar way of instances in which American soldiers have been guilty of what might be termed cruelty?

Gov. Taft: Never of the mutilation of bodies.

Sen. Culberson: What have you heard in that connection?

Gov. Taft: I have heard this: I have heard charges of whippings and charges of what has been alluded to as the water cure. They were rife in Manila. And I was about to proceed as to the responsibility and how they came about, and the possible explanations of them. Of course it was no duty of mine. That was a military question.

Sen. Culberson: I will ask you if you have not heard of the case known as the Metcalf instance, where a Filipino prisoner was killed, being shot after he surrendered?

Gov. Taft: Metcalf? No.

Sen. Culberson: It is what is known as the Metcalf case?

Gov. Taft: No, sir; I do not know of the Metcalf case. I never heard of it.

The Chairman: It has been investigated by a committee of the Senate.

Sen. McComas: I understand the investigation has proceeded and been concluded, and the committee unanimously exonerated Metcalf.

Sen. Carmack: But found unanimously that there had been murder.

Gov. Taft: I have not heard of it.

Sen. Culberson: I understand the fact to be that while Metcalf himself was not guilty, other American soldiers did shoot two prisoners.

Gov. Taft: I have not heard of it.

Sen. Culberson: I simply want to learn the truth of the case, if you are advised as to it.

Gov. Taft: What I am trying to do is to state what seemed to us to be the explanation of these cruelties — that cruelties have been inflicted; that people have been shot when they ought not to have been; that there have been . . . individual instances of water cure, that torture which I believe involves pouring water down the throat so that the man swells and gets the impression that he is going to be suffocated and then tells what he knows, which was a frequent treatment under the Spaniards, I am told —

all these things are true. There are some rather amusing instances of Filipinos who came in and said they would not say anything until they were tortured; that they must have an excuse for saying what they proposed to say.

Sen. Patterson: Governor Taft ——

Gov. Taft: If the Senator will let me conclude I will answer his question in a moment. In any event, what I am able to testify to is the efforts made by the military officers in responsible commands, especially General MacArthur, who was in command all the time I was there, while charges of this kind were at all rife, in ordering courts-martial, in ordering investigations, in issuing orders to the troops that such methods would be condemned and must not be adopted. Such orders and public statements by General MacArthur were so numerous that while they evidence the fact that such cases had occurred they also evidence the desire on the part of those who were responsible to prevent their recurrence.

The Chairman: Do you know of any case where men were punished for cruelty or oppression of Filipinos?

Gov. Taft: I suppose there were ——

Sen. Beveridge: I call your attention to one ——

Gov. Taft: I know courts-martial were ordered and some courts-martial were lectured for not punishing more heavily than they did men whom the evidence showed had been guilty of that method of securing evidence.

Sen. Patterson: I do not think the charge of inflicting the water cure has been made against American soldiers as much as against the native troops who have been enlisted in the American army, or as an appurtenance to the American army. For instance, the Macabebes. Many letters have been published making statements of this kind — that Macabebes would be sent out for the purpose of securing the surrender of guns, and the persons would deny that they had any guns. Then the Macabebes would throw them upon the ground, one soldier on one hand and another on the other, secure their feet, pry open their mouths with a stick, and then pour buckets of water down their throats till they swelled up to an abnormal size, and then jump upon their stomachs. It has been stated that invariably under that treatment guns were produced where there were no guns before; this with the knowledge of American officers, the Army getting the advantage of it in securing arms from natives, which they were seeking, without any serious reproof.

Gov. Taft: I have no doubt there were such instances — of course, a great many more than there ought to have been — but if the Senator will excuse me, dependence on private letters from private individuals as to what occurred is dependence on a very broken reed.

Sen. Patterson: I do not know. I saw them published in responsible newspapers, and they were given great publicity.

Gov. Taft: I know. Inasmuch as I have seen some letters with respect to myself and some with respect to a good many others, especially the

Commission, from private individuals who were in favor of the Army and against the Commission, which were wholly unfounded ——

Sen. Patterson: But these purported to be letters from soldiers.

Gov. Taft: I know it. I did not realize the unreliability of such letters until I had experienced what it was. But I was at Manila during all this time. I was there when charges of this kind were being made. I was in daily conference with General MacArthur, and knew the position he took and knew the position that his subordinates took with respect to it. But I was explaining some time since the circumstances of provocation to a violation of duty on the part of officers and sergeants, who by force of circumstances were placed in irresponsible control, to show you that it might have occurred and still have been in the teeth of the instructions of the responsible officers. That is all I can say about it.

I will tell you what General Bell told me in a conversation. It is sufficient to describe it as a mutilation, which is likely to outrage the feelings of any person. A man's bunkie — a bunkie is his chum — comes along and finds a soldier, the man with whom he had associated, mutilated in an outrageous way; a man whom he had seen alive an hour before. You must understand that a soldier has human nature, and that things are done which a commanding officer would not approve and yet can not be prevented because of the outrage of feelings. That is the explanation of a good many things.

The Chairman: You have said that the Filipinos murdered some of their own countrymen. Did the insurgent Filipinos show cruelty toward them in any way or inflict any cruel or unusual punishment?

Gov. Taft: I do not remember an instance of the mutilation of Filipino bodies. Possibly they did not attract so much attention on the part of the persons who reported such things as the mutilation of Americans.

I desire to say, with respect to the treatment of American prisoners by the insurgent officers high in command, that there was usually very little to criticize. When you get to officers lower in command you will find instances of the murder of American prisoners, not many, but enough to cause comment as to the difference in treatment.

Take a man like the one of whom I spoke yesterday, Prado, who was a murderer and a thief, and a ladrone anyhow, and even an American prisoner was not to expect mercy at his hands.

Sen. Beveridge: He did hack with bolos two American prisoners to death?

Gov. Taft: I believe he did.

Sen. Carmack: Right on that point, speaking of the cruelty of the average native in the Philippine Islands, have you read General Mac-Arthur's last report, and do you remember what he said on that question?

Gov. Taft: No; I have not.

Sen. Carmack: He said that the Filipino people are not cruel, but are a kindly, gentle race of people. That is General MacArthur's statement.

Gov. Taft: I should agree with him in a general sense. They are an agricultural people; they are a simple people; but that they regard human life with any particular sacredness I am quite sure is not true, and that they are not tender to animals is true. I think General MacArthur will agree with me in this statement: The uneducated Filipino is a docile person, but left to the natural ferocity which war and hostility of that sort provoke he becomes very cruel. War, of course, provokes some cruelty in everyone. Certainly the experience in China is evidence that civilization itself does not prevent it at times.

Sen. Patterson: When a war is conducted by a superior race against those whom they consider inferior in the scale of civilization, is it not the experience of the world that the superior race will almost involuntarily practice inhuman conduct?

Gov. Taft: There is much greater danger in such a case than in dealing with whites. There is no doubt about that.

After a good deal of study about the matter — and although I have never been prejudiced in favor of the military branch, for when the civil and military branches are exercising concurrent jurisdiction there is some inevitable friction — I desire to say that it is my deliberate judgment that there never was a war conducted, whether against inferior races or not, in which there were more compassion and more restraint and more generosity, assuming that there was a war at all, than there have been in the Philippine Islands. Now, I say that without having been in the war at all, having only been at Manila, where reports were constantly coming in and where I was talking with officers of the Army, and knew what the general orders were and what the general policy was.

The Chairman: You also talked with a great many Filipinos and insurgent leaders, I suppose?

Gov. Taft: I have.

Sen. Culberson: Do you make that statement after reading the order of General Bell's in reference to concentration?

Gov. Taft: The order of General Bell has been published since I left the Philippines. There is something said about reconcentration. I talked with General Bell about it. I told him that I did not think he would find it necessary to have reconcentration there, even in the milder sense in which he used the expression; that when the wealthy people of Batangas, who were suspected of complicity, were arrested and thrown into prison, and there was an embargo put upon the trade of that province, the gentlemen who were really keeping it up, being themselves pinched, would yield. . . .

War has been ended in all these islands except in Batangas and Samar. That which remains is a crime against civilization. It is a crime against the Filipino people to keep up that war under the circumstances, and those engaged in it have worn out the right to any treatment but that which is severe and within the laws of war.

Sen. Patterson: Do you mean by that statement that the army fighting for independence has become so small by captures, by battles, by surrenders, that those who remain fighting for independence are guilty of a crime? Is it a crime because the prospective independence is more remote now than it was two or three years ago?

Gov. Taft: It is a crime because it is subjecting their own people, in whose interests they profess to be carrying on the war, to the greatest privation and suffering.

Sen. Patterson: At the hands of the American Army?

Gov. Taft: The people who are not in those provinces at all. They are keeping them back from earning a living. They are keeping them back from their ordinary vocations. In the very province of Batangas itself the great majority desire peace and are only held there because of the system of terrorism of which I speak. Now, I say that warfare which depends upon terrorism and murder is a crime. That is all I have to say.

Sen. Patterson: Is it because in your opinion the independence of the Philippine Islands has become hopeless that those who are contending for it are guilty of crime?

Gov. Taft: I think independence for the time has become hopeless.

Sen. Patterson: And therefore those who are fighting for it are guilty of a crime?

Gov. Taft: They are guilty of a crime in the method which they seek to attain it.

Sen. Allison: I should like to ask the Governor if he understands that these people are fighting for independence? I supposed they were merely making a guerrilla warfare.

Sen. Patterson: Every statement he has made is to the effect that they are fighting for their independence.

Sen. Allison: That these bands are fighting for independence?

Sen. Patterson: That they are fighting for independence.

Sen. Beveridge: The Governor made the statement yesterday, if the Senator will excuse me ——

The Chairman: Wait a moment.

Sen. Patterson: He said so the other day in response to a direct question.

Sen. Allison: I did not know that.

Sen. Culberson: It seems that you base your opinion that the warfare now being conducted is a crime on the ground that the great bulk of these people desire peace. Now, I will read a sentence from Bell's order:

A general conviction, which the brigade commander shares, appears to exist that the insurrection in this brigade continues because the greater part of the people, especially the wealthy ones, pretend to desire but in reality do not want peace.

Gov. Taft: That statement I should differ with, and I should differ with it as the result of conversation with men from Batangas, which conversations I have had all the time and had just before I left. . . .

Testimony of Leroy E. Hallock *

The Chairman: You were in the Army? — A. Yes, sir.

Q. In what regiment? — A. Twenty-sixth Volunteers.

Q. In what company? — A. Company I.

Q. What rank did you hold? — A. Sergeant.

Q. And you were mustered out as a sergeant? — A. No, sir.

Q. You were mustered out as what? — A. As a private.

Q. And then you lost your rank as sergeant? — A. Yes, sir.

Sen. Allison: When?

The Witness: At Nagasaki, Japan.

Sen. Allison: When?

(The witness did not answer.)

The Chairman: When were you mustered out? — A. On May 13, 1901.

Q. How long were you in the Philippine Islands? — A. I arrived there October 27, 1899, and left there March 6, 1901.

Sen. Culberson: Where do you reside, Mr. Hallock?

The Witness: Boston, Mass.

The Chairman: Did you enlist from Massachusetts? — A. Yes, sir.

Q. At Framingham? — A. At Worcester.

Q. Were you living at Worcester at that time? — A. No, sir.

Q. Where was your regiment stationed during the period you were in the Philippine Islands? — A. The first three months I was stationed at Iloilo. After that the headquarters of the company was Leon, Panay.

Q. Did you see any cases of water cure or torture applied to the natives? — A. Yes, sir.

Q. Where? — A. At Leon.

Q. State the circumstances, please. — A. There were about ten or a dozen natives captured that were thought to be implicated in the murder of one of the members of our company.

Q. O'Hearn? — A. Yes, sir.

Q. It was stated in one of the reports that he was roasted over a slow fire and then hacked to death with bolos. — A. That is the confession of the natives; yes.

Q. And these men were captured who were believed to have had something to do with that? — A. Yes, sir.

Q. Now you may go on and state the circumstances. — A. What led

---

* Biographical details are contained in the testimony.

to the capture of these natives, it was reported that Captain Glenn or some soldiers under his orders gave the water cure to a native and he confessed and told who the others were that took part in the killing of O'Hearn, and these members of our company captured these natives and gave them the water cure, and they confessed it.

Sen. Burrows: Confessed to what? — A. To having a part in the killing of O'Hearn.

Q. Having had a part in it? — A. Yes, sir.

The Chairman: Who inflicted this punishment upon the natives? — A. The members of Company I.

Q. Were they ordered to do so? — A. Yes, sir.

Q. Who ordered them to do so? — A. The first sergeant.

Q. Who was the first sergeant? — A. Januarius Manning.

Q. Do you know him? — A. Yes, sir.

Q. Is he now a resident of Boston? — A. Yes, sir.

Q. You may state any details you wish in regard to the treatment of these natives.

Sen. Allison: You saw this?

The Witness: Yes, sir.

The Chairman: You saw the water cure inflicted? — A. Yes, sir.

Q. Did you take part in it? — A. No, sir.

Sen. Rawlins: Who was in command of this company at that time? — A. Alexander Gregg.

Q. How many troops were at Leon at the time this occurred? — A. About half of the company, I should say.

Q. Was Captain Gregg there at the time? — A. Yes, sir; he was there at the quarters.

Q. How far from the quarters was this torture inflicted? — A. Less than a hundred yards.

Q. Did all the command know about it at the time? — A. Yes, sir.

Q. Captain Gregg knew about it? — A. I don't know how he could help knowing it.

Q. You say that a member of your company had been reported killed? — A. Yes, sir.

Q. That information, I understand you to say, was derived from Captain Glenn? — A. I think a detail of our company was out looking for O'Hearn and they made a detail under Captain Glenn, and they got some native and gave him the water cure and he confessed and gave the others away and told who took part in it.

Q. That was, as you understand it, the result of the application of this torture; as a result of that torture some native, to relieve himself, stated he had taken part in the killing of this soldier? — A. Yes, sir.

Sen. Allison: I object to Senator Rawlins putting words in the mouth of the witness — "to relieve himself." He said nothing of the kind.

Sen. Rawlins: I am asking if that was not what was reported to you;

that, as a result of this torture, this native stated he had participated in this killing? — A. Yes, sir.

Q. And named about a dozen other natives? — A. Yes, sir.

Q. And these twelve who were also reported by Captain Glenn to have been named by this native after the water cure had been given to him, where did they live? — A. In the vicinity of five or six miles from our quarters.

Q. Five or six miles from the army? — A. Yes, sir.

Q. And upon that information they were arrested? — A. Yes, sir.

Q. And brought to Leon? — A. Yes, sir.

Q. And they were taken out and the water torture applied to each of them? — A. Yes, sir.

Q. You may state whether it was given to them more than once. — A. It was given to them on two different days; it was given to them on August 21, 1900, and on August 23, 1900, to the best of my recollection.

Q. And what was the purpose of subjecting them to the torture? — A. To see if they had participated in the murder of O'Hearn.

Q. The first day they did not get all the information they desired — was that it? — A. Yes, sir.

Q. And so the torture was repeated the following day? — A. Yes, sir.

Q. And on the following day, as I understand you, these persons who were subjected to this torture confessed that they participated in the killing of the soldier? — A. On the 21st and 23rd of August.

The Chairman: Was this 1900?

The Witness: Yes, sir.

Sen. Rawlins: What was the effect upon these natives of giving this water cure? — A. They would swell up — their stomach would swell up pretty large — and I have seen blood come from their mouth after they had been given a good deal of it.

Q. And on the second day, do you know what information they gave; how was it obtained? — A. No, sir; only that they confessed to having had a part in it.

The Chairman: Did they confess to having killed O'Hearn?

The Witness: To having taken a part in the murder of O'Hearn.

The Chairman: Did they confess to having roasted him over a slow fire?

Sen. Rawlins: Let me complete this examination before I am interrupted.

Q. Was the communication from these prisoners subjected to this torture given through an interpreter? — A. Yes, sir.

Q. A native interpreter? — A. Yes, sir.

Q. You could not understand what they said, I suppose? — A. I could understand some of it.

Q. Can you give anything that any one of these men subjected to this torture said; what their language was? — A. No, sir.

Q. You cannot? — *A.* No, sir.

Q. Did the company detailed to subject these men to this torture get any information the first day from these twelve men, or any of them? — *A.* The first day they gave them the water treatment?

Q. Yes. — *A.* Yes, sir.

Q. Do you know what information they got the first day? — *A.* It was in regard to the killing of O'Hearn. There were twelve of them that were given this water treatment, and I do not think they got through with all of them on the first day, and they finished it on the second day, the 23rd of August.

Sen. Allison: That is, they did not repeat it on those that had taken it the day before? — *A.* Yes, sir; some of them.

Q. On some of them they repeated it? — *A.* Yes, sir.

Sen. Rawlins: What was done with these twelve men after they had been subjected to the water cure? — *A.* They were confined there in the guardhouse. Some of them escaped and some of them were killed trying to escape.

Q. How many of them were shot to your knowledge? — *A.* I should say five or six.

Q. You know of five or six of them having been shot? — *A.* Yes, sir.

Q. How soon after the infliction of the water torture? — *A.* I could not state the exact time. It was before we left there.

Sen. Beveridge: Shot while trying to escape?

The Witness: Yes, sir.

Sen. Rawlins: About how long? — *A.* I should say some of them were shot within four or five months.

Q. Where were those men confined? — *A.* At the guardhouse, in quarters at Leon.

Q. Can you describe that guardhouse? — *A.* It was a room about twenty or twenty-five feet by twenty-five feet, with iron bars at the windows; there was one window and two doors entering the room. The doors were kept locked by means of a padlock, and there were iron bars at the window.

Q. How many soldiers stood guard? — *A.* At the guardhouse?

Q. Yes. — *A.* This guardhouse was at the guard quarters and the sergeant or corporal who was in command of the guard was stationed at the door all the time, and then there was the number one sentry who stood right in front of the quarters, and at night he stood at the door. So there were one or two there all the time, besides the door being locked.

Q. And how near were the soldiers stationed to the guardhouse? — *A.* The soldiers' quarters were right above on the next floor, upstairs.

Q. How many soldiers were there? — *A.* It varies. I should say from thirty to fifty all the time.

Q. How many prisoners were kept in this guardhouse — natives, I mean? — A. Some of the time there were ten or a dozen and sometimes as high as eighteen, I should say.

Q. Do you remember the occasion when any of these particular natives who had been subjected to the torture tried to escape? — A. I could not give the date, but I remember times they did.

Q. Did they succeed in getting out of the building? — A. It was not when they were in the building they tried to escape; it was while they were working down at the river, taking a bath.

Q. Who had them in charge at that time? — A. Sentries.

Q. How many altogether were shot at that time?

Sen. Beveridge: He stated that twice.

Sen. Rawlins: No; he has not.

Sen. Beveridge: Five or six, he said.

Sen. Rawlins: No; I asked him how many altogether. He stated five or six of these men who had been tortured were shot.

Sen. Beveridge: Five or six were shot while attempting to escape; although I have no objection to his repeating it.

Sen. Rawlins: Will you answer the question? — A. I do not understand the question.

Q. These attempted, you say, to escape; how many of those were killed? — A. I do not know what time you mean.

Q. As I understood you, on some occasion after this torture was inflicted some of these native prisoners while out from the guardhouse attempted to escape, and some of them were killed. I want to know, if you know, how many were killed at that time. — A. There was one occasion, one night, somewhere about five or six o'clock, that they were taken down to the river for a bath. I think there were five or six of them. They tried to get away while down there and one of them was shot and three or four escaped. Then on another occasion they were out working and there were four shot at that time while trying to escape.

Q. Did all these prisoners escape that were confined? — A. No, sir.

Q. How many of them mere killed altogether? — A. I cannot give the exact number. Five or six.

Q. Were all killed who did not escape? — A. I think so. There may have been one that was given his freedom, I won't say for sure. It seems to me there was one who was let go.

Q. With the exception of one all escaped or were killed? — A. Yes, sir.

Q. Are you sure as to whether that one was given his freedom or not? — A. Yes, sir.

Q. While you were there were there any villages burned? — A. Yes, sir.

Q. How many? — A. I was only present at the time one was burned; but I have known of as many as half a dozen being burned.

Q. How large were these villages? — A. The one that I witnessed being burned I should say was three or four thousand people; that that many people lived there.

Q. What was the name of it? — A. I don't know the name of it.

Q. How large were the others that you know of having been burned? — A. There was a town about eight miles from Leon which was burned. I think there were 8,000 or 10,000 people there.

The Chairman: Was that Igbarras?

The Witness: No, sir. The name of that town was Tubungan; that is about half way from Leon to Igbarras.

Sen. Rawlins: What others were there that you know of; you have named two, I think, one of 3,000 and one of 8,000?

Sen. Beveridge: Do you know of these towns being burned simply by hearsay? — A. I witnessed one of them.

Q. But the others; do you know of their being burned simply by hearsay? — A. I know of their being burned by the members of the company talking about them.

Q. Can you name the member of the company who told you about that now? — A. I could not name anyone that told me, but I can name several that were present.

Q. Can you name anyone who told you? — A. No, sir.

Sen. Beveridge: I object to any testimony on this subject that is hearsay.

Sen. Rawlins: I will ask the witness this. You observed the flames in the distance, did you? — A. The smoke; not the flames.

Sen. Beveridge: Is this direct examination?

Sen. Rawlins: This is cross-examination.

Q. And you saw the smoke of the villages that you did not see being burned? — A. I saw smoke from this town of Tubungan when that was burned.

Q. Have you been over the ground where these towns were, that you learned were burned? Have you been over that ground since they were burned? — A. Yes, sir.

Q. And what have you observed there at those towns; were they left or were they burned? — A. They appeared to be deserted; everything was burned, houses and shacks, with the exception, perhaps, of a few on the outside of the town, on the roads or trails that would not be burned, that were close to the town.

Q. I will ask you — you have been around in that vicinity and you had occasion from time to time to visit around — while you were stationed at Leon and Panay what if any towns were left unburned? — A. The town of Tigbaüan, the town of Oton, the town of Alimodian, the town of San Miguel, the town of Arevalo, and a good many smaller barrios.

Q. And how many towns were burned; that is, towns you know by having learned that the towns were burned and afterwards having been over the ground and seen that they were burned? — A. There was only one that I was a witness to.

Q. But you know the others by reputation, and you say that you had occasion to visit them afterwards, as I understand it, and saw that they had been burned? — A. Tubungan is the only large town that I know of. If we were out on a march over the mountains if we found any evidence of insurgents being there we burned the small barrios as we went along.

Sen. Beveridge: Did I understand you to say after having been there that you personally know of these six towns you mentioned having been burned?

The Chairman: Those were the six towns not burned that he mentioned.

Sen. Beveridge: I understand; but Senator Rawlins, after he named a town that he knew of being burned, attempted to show that other towns were burned by asking him whether he had not seen smoke?

The Chairman: I understood the witness to say he only knew of one town of that kind.

Sen. Beveridge: That is the point. Senator Rawlins was proceeding upon the assumption that he had visited all these other towns.

Sen. Rawlins: No; I proceeded upon no such assumption.

Sen. Beveridge: That is what your questions show, and I wanted to clear it up.

Sen. Rawlins: What became of these people who inhabited these towns that were burned? — A. I think they went into other towns. They didn't build up the towns at all.

Q. They did not attempt to rebuild the towns? — A. Not to my knowledge.

Q. Do you know whether or not they were permitted to rebuild these towns that were destroyed? — A. I could not say.

Q. Do you know of any attempt on the part of the natives to rebuild any town that was destroyed? — A. No, sir.

Q. Did you know of any natives around Leon who were begging for food? — A. Yes, sir. They have a market day there in those towns once a week, and on that day a good many beggars would be around.

Q. You may state to what extent the burning went in the case of these towns that were burned — whether it extended to food and household articles and things of that description. — A. Yes, sir.

Q. Did it so extend? — A. The one that I witnessed being burned, they did not have time to get anything out to speak of; they might have had time to get what valuables they had out, but they did not have time to move their furniture or food.

Sen. Allison: You only witnessed the burning of one town? — A. Yes, sir.

Q. And that was done rapidly? — A. Yes, sir.

Sen. Rawlins: This burning you have described and the infliction of the water torture — you may state whether or not it was a matter of common repute among the soldiers with whom you came in contact that those things were practiced.

Sen. Beveridge: I object. We have had that question up two or three times.

The Chairman: I think the witness is entitled to say whether the thing was a matter of common repute.

The Witness: It was reported that if the soldiers wanted to get any information out of the natives they gave them the water cure, and in any town where there was any evidence of being insurgents the town was burned.

Sen. Rawlins: Then, as I understand it, that was a matter of common repute; the inflicting of this water torture and the burning of these towns was a matter of common repute?

Sen. Allison: If you understand it, you do not understand it from the witness.

Sen. Rawlins: I asked the witness whether or not it was a matter of common repute, and he said it was reported among the soldiers that whenever they wanted to get information they applied the water torture, and when they obtained the information and they found that a town contained insurgents they burned the town. Let it rest at that. . . .

Q. Have you no other source of information except the confessions of these men who were subjected to this torture? — A. What the natives confessed to is the only information we had.

Q. What the natives confessed to is the only information you had. Did they confess to that before or after the infliction of the torture? — A. After. After we had found his bones — the bones of O'Hearn.

Sen. Allison: Burned bones?

Sen. Rawlins: The Senator will allow me to interpose his own objection. Where did the Senator get the information that the bones were burned?

Sen. Allison: Nowhere; I was only wanting to ascertain that fact.

Sen. Beveridge: It is a fair inference that the bones were burned when these prisoners confessed that they had burned the man.

Sen. Patterson: I think the Senator from Indiana will admit that they confessed they burned the man to escape the water torture after they had been dosed with it two or three times.

Sen. Allison: I will withdraw any remark that is offensive.

Sen. Dietrich: I would like to ask a question.

Sen. Rawlins: Please wait until I get through my examination. You found the bones of what you understood to be this missing member of your company? — A. Yes, sir.

Q. Where were they found, or do you know — were you present? — A. I was not present when the bones were found.

Q. You do not know, then, of your own knowledge, in what condition the bones were when found? — A. Only by hearsay.

Q. Do you know whether those remains were brought to Leon? — A. The bones were brought to Leon.

Q. Did you see them after they came there? — A. Yes, sir.

Q. Was there anything left except the mere skeleton? — A. Only pieces of bone, the head and different parts of the skeleton.

Q. What was their condition? — A. They were all in small pieces; the head was the largest piece, the piece that seemed to be the most intact.

Sen. Culberson: How did you know that skeleton was the skeleton of the deceased soldier?

The Witness: The surgeon who was stationed at the quarters said that he was very sure it was O'Hearn's body by a front tooth being missing.

Sen. Rawlins: The only means of identification was the absence of one front tooth; is that it? — A. Yes, sir; and the testimony which the natives gave that there was where they buried the bones.

Q. As I understand it, you had obtained the remains before the torture — or afterwards? — A. This native that was given the water cure first by Captain Glenn, as I heard, testified where the bones were, and they took the bones up and got the rest of the natives who testified that they had taken part.

Q. They had discovered the remains before they inflicted the torture on these twelve men?

Sen. Beveridge: He did not say anything of the kind. This witness is attempting to testify very clearly.

Sen. Rawlins: I am asking that very question.

Sen. Beveridge: No, you are stating that he did. The witness is doing the best he can. He had just before that said that they found the bones where the man who had had the water cure told them they were to be found.

Sen. Rawlins: I am not insisting upon the form of the question. What I want to know is, whether or not the remains had been discovered before the torture was inflicted upon these twelve men; that is what I want to know. — A. I am positive the bones were brought in the same night that the men were brought into the quarters.

Q. Then it was before the infliction of the tortures? — A. Upon these twelve men, yes.

Q. That is what I wanted to arrive at. Therefore, these twelve men who were subjected to the torture did not give the information which led to the discovery of these remains, or these bones? — A. The native to whom Captain Glenn gave the water cure, as testified a while ago, told who the other ones were that took part in it.

Sen. Beveridge: So that the discovery of the bones was the result of the water cure first administered to this one man.

Sen. Rawlins: That you have no information about it except by hearsay, as I understand it; that is, what the others told you? — A. What the members of the company talked about and told to each other.

Q. All you know about it is what the others told you? — A. I was not a witness to it.

Q. How many men of your company had been killed during the entire time you were stationed at Leon in Panay — you were there all the time? A. Yes, sir; on the island of Panay.

Q. How many men were killed? — A. Two men.

Q. Two men altogether? — A. Yes, sir.

Q. How many natives were killed during the same time by American soldiers? — A. I could not state the number.

Q. About how many? — A. It would be very hard for me to tell.

Q. Give us a general idea, if you can. — A. Well, if we got into a skirmish we could not tell how many men were killed or wounded.

Q. Were there a good many killed? — A. There were more killed than there were Americans.

Q. How many do you know of yourself having been killed? — A. Do you mean altogether in the fights we had there?

Q. Yes. — A. That the regiment participated in?

Q. That your company participated in — yes; the regiment. — A. In the neighborhood of 200 or 300, I should say, for a guess.

Q. How many fights did you yourself participate in? — A. Three, I think, sir.

Q. And in those three fights how many natives were killed? — A. In the neighborhood of 200, I should say.

Q. How many Americans were killed in those three fights? — A. I should say 20.

Sen. Beveridge: What means have you of knowing how many Filipinos were killed?

The Witness: The only means I have is the official report.

Sen. Beveridge: The rumor?

Sen. Culberson: He said official report.

Sen. Beveridge: The official reports? — A. Yes, sir. I only say this; that I guess that number.

Q. Then you are not attempting to quote official reports; you are making your estimate? — A. Yes, sir.

Sen. Rawlins: How many wounded, Mr. Hallock, in those fights? — A. I could not say.

Q. You do not know that? — A. No, sir.

Q. Apart from the information that was derived from natives as a result of torture do you know how this soldier met with his death? — A. The only information we had was what we got from the natives; what the natives confessed.

Q. The circumstances therefore of his death, what led to it, or how it occurred, all you know about it is what you have stated, that obtained from the natives as a result of application of torture? — A. Yes, sir.

Sen. Patterson: I would like to ask a few questions.

The Chairman: I would like to ask a few questions first, having been waiting patiently.

Sen. Patterson: I have no objection, if I can ask some afterwards.

The Chairman: Did you witness any other cases of water cure? — A. No, sir.

Q. These were the only cases that you saw? — A. Yes, sir.

Q. Did the natives confess that O'Hearn was burned before he was murdered? — A. They confessed — perhaps I had better tell you the story of his capture and everything.

Q. Yes; tell the whole story. — A. O'Hearn, in company with two other soldiers from our company, was sent to Iloilo, after the mail, I think, and when they arrived back within about five or six miles of the company, or where the company was stationed, they were ambushed by about 100 insurgents, and two of them were captured. O'Hearn made a break to get away. This was on June 30, 1900. He made a break to get to the quarters, or at least we thought he did, and fell in, as we supposed, with friendly natives. They captured him, and on the next day, July 1, he was tied to a tree at 7 o'clock in the morning, and was tortured by cutting with bolos and by slow fire until 5 o'clock at night. So the natives confessed.

Q. The natives confessed to that? — A. Yes, sir.

Q. When they applied the water cure to these natives in order to get their confession, did you know that he had been tortured before being killed? — A. No, sir; we did not know anything about it.

Q. Then the infliction of the torture was entirely a voluntary confession?

Sen. Culberson: He has not said it was voluntary.

The Witness: The confession was gotten from the natives by means of the water cure.

The Chairman: But did they ask them whether he was burned or whether he was murdered? — A. They asked him through the interpreter how they killed him.

Q. And then they confessed to the statement which you have just made? — A. Yes, sir.

Q. These men were subjected to the water cure in order to extort this confession. Did they die under the water cure? — A. No, sir.

Q. Were any of them executed subsequently for it? — A. Before given the water cure?

Q. I mean after they confessed, were any of them taken out and shot? — A. No, sir.

Q. They were simply confined in prison? — A. Yes, sir.

Q. What was the general attitude of the soldiers toward the natives;

I mean toward the friendly natives among whom you lived? How did they treat them in ordinary life? — A. They treated them very well if they thought they were friends.

Sen. Patterson: Mr. Hallock, do you know what demand they made of the first Filipino they tortured before they tortured him? — A. No, sir.

The Chairman: Did you see the torture of that man, that first one, whom Glenn tortured?

The Witness: No, sir.

Sen. Beveridge: Of course this word "torture" is used here referring to what you refer to as the water cure. I do not know whether the soldiers themselves refer to it as a torture.

Sen. Culberson: It is, in fact, a torture.

Sen. Patterson: There is no misunderstanding about what it means.

Sen. Beveridge: But I wanted to make the word "torture" clear. No soldier uses the word torture in speaking of the water cure.

Sen. Patterson: When I use the word torture I mean the water cure.

Sen. Beveridge: That is your construction of water cure?

Sen. Patterson: Some people call murder homicide.

Sen. Patterson: Did they commence the torture of this man, the first man, for some definite purpose? — A. I don't know. . . .

Q. Do you know whether this man denied any knowledge of the missing soldier before they applied the water torture to him? — A. I could not say, sir.

Q. Were you present when the water torture was applied to the other twelve? — A. I was present in most cases.

Q. Do you know whether, before it was applied, they had denied any knowledge of the affair? — A. I think they did deny it.

Q. Were they given to understand what they were to confess to, to avoid the water torture? — A. Yes, sir.

Sen. Beveridge: Do you understand that question?

Sen. Patterson: I will keep on asking it, so that there will be no trouble.

Sen. Beveridge: I do not know whether there will be any trouble or not.

Sen. Patterson: If you wait you will see.

Sen. Beveridge: I understand your question and its purpose very well.

Sen. Patterson: No; you do not.

Sen. Beveridge: Senator Lodge asked that same question in a direct way, and now you put this question in a way, as we all very well understand, to imply that what to confess was suggested to them.

Sen. Patterson: Wait until I get through.

The Chairman: What is the question?

The stenographer repeated the question, as follows: "Q. Were they given to understand what they were to confess to, to avoid the water torture?"

Sen. Patterson: If you will wait I will ask another question that will settle all the controversy.

Sen. Beveridge: But when you ask a question like that I propose to exercise my duty as a member of this committee to object to it.

Sen. Patterson: I understand you will. What was it they were given to understand they were to confess to? — A. They were given the water cure and then asked questions through this interpreter what they knew about the killing of O'Hearn.

Sen. Beveridge: Ah!

Sen. Culberson: That is a very proper exclamation, of course.

Sen. Patterson: Before the water cure was applied to them were they given to understand about the death of a soldier — that is, the soldier that was missing? — A. Before they were given the water cure?

Q. Yes. — A. The only way I know that they could know it would be by talking amongst themselves.

Q. What was the water cure applied to them for? — A. What was the water cure applied to them for?

Q. Yes. — A. To see what information they had in regard to the death of O'Hearn.

Q. Had they been told of the death of O'Hearn? — A. Not to my knowledge.

Q. Then, of course, they could not deny having any knowledge of the death of O'Hearn unless they had been told about it, could they?

The Chairman: Is it not proper to say, "Did they deny it?"

Sen. Patterson: Yes.

The Witness: Please repeat that question.

Q. They could not very well deny having knowledge of the death of O'Hearn unless they were told of his death, could they — unless they had actually participated in his killing?

Sen. Beveridge: The witness has already testified, in answer to the questions put, what they did know about the death of O'Hearn.

Sen. Patterson: I think these interruptions are intolerable.

Sen. Beveridge: The Senator is a lawyer and he knows very well that the question he just now put would submit him to a reprimand from the judge in a court, and I propose to object.

Sen. Patterson: If the attorney on the opposite side of a case was to persist in interruptions such as the Senator from Indiana indulges in he would be fined for contempt, and if he still persisted in it he would be sent to jail.

Sen. Burrows: Either sent to jail or given the water cure.

Sen. Patterson: He would go to jail before he would take the water cure.

(The question was repeated by the stenographer.)

Sen. Patterson: Do you understand the question?

The Witness: Do you mean that they could not deny having any knowledge of it?

Sen. Patterson: They could not very well have known that they were charged with participating in the killing of O'Hearn unless they were told so, could they? — A. I don't see how they could.

Q. If they had not denied having knowledge of the killing of O'Hearn they would not have applied the water torture, would they? — A. They applied the water cure to see what they did know about it.

Q. And if they had not denied knowing anything about it, would they have applied the water torture? — A. No, sir.

Q. If they had persisted in knowing nothing about the killing of O'Hearn, do you know how many times the water torture would have been applied? — A. I do not.

Q. They were relieved from further torture when they stated that they knew about the killing of O'Hearn; is that when they were relieved from the water torture? — A. Yes, sir.

Q. You say that after the first Filipino was tortured or had the water cure, whichever term you desire to use, they then went out and brought in some human bones. Is that right? — A. As I understood it, they were told where the bones were and the others that were complicated in it, and they went and got the bones and the other natives.

Q. The means of identification, as stated before, was simply the loss of a tooth, a missing tooth? — A. The loss of a tooth and what the natives told, that they confessed where they buried him.

Q. I understand that; but independent of what the natives said it was simply the loss of a tooth? — A. Yes, sir.

Q. These natives that underwent this torture were kept in the prison about five or six months? — A. Before they were given the water cure?

Q. No, after they were given the water cure. — A. I could not state exactly the time; I should say from three to seven or eight months.

Q. Were they ever brought to trial? — A. I do not think they were, sir.

Q. There was never any court-martial over the affair at all that you have any knowledge of? — A. There were some officers came up from headquarters, from Iloilo, and they had a hearing over at the officers' quarters at one time.

Q. Had a what? — A. Had a hearing about it.

Q. When was that? — A. I could not state the time, it was some time after the water cure was given to them.

Q. Then, what did you mean when, in response to a question, you said these Filipinos had never been brought to a trial? — A. They never had, to my knowledge.

Q. You say, then, the Filipinos were never brought to a trial, but you say something of these officers coming up from Iloilo and some proceedings. What was that? — A. I could not say. It was reported that it was something with reference to these prisoners.

Q. Sir? — A. It was reported that they were having some kind of a hearing about these prisoners.

Q. Simply the officers by themselves? — A. Yes, sir.

Q. Do you know why it was, if these natives confessed to the killing and the torture of O'Hearn, and the officers of the company or the regiment believed they had the correct men, that they were not tried and executed for the murder? — A. I could not say.

Sen. Culberson: You have testified, I believe, that five or six of these men were killed in attempting to escape? — A. Yes, sir.

Q. Do you know whether or not their effort to escape was encouraged by the American officers and soldiers? — A. I do not know, sir.

Q. What I wanted to find out was whether it was a bona fide effort on their part to escape or whether they were ever encouraged to make the effort for the purpose of affording an opportunity to shoot them. How was that? — A. All that I know is that it was reported that they were killed while trying to escape.

Sen. Dietrich: How were these prisoners treated while in this guardhouse? — Were they well treated — did they have plenty to eat? — A. Most of them got fat.

Q. Was this guardhouse the same guardhouse American soldiers were confined in when they had disobeyed rules? — A. No, sir; they never quartered the American soldiers in the same guardhouse with the Filipino prisoners.

Q. What was the standing of these natives? Were they men of influence and prominence, or were they just looked upon as being very common people? — A. A common run of people.

Sen. Patterson: You speak of two or three hundred Filipinos being killed and twenty or twenty-five Americans being killed in several conflicts you have referred to. Were any prisoners taken in any of those conflicts you have referred to? — A. Yes, sir.

Q. How many, about? — A. I should say, for an estimate, twenty or thirty.

Q. Do you know what became of them? — A. No, sir; I do not.

Q. How many were wounded; were there any wounded after these conflicts that were taken care of by the American soldiers? — A. Yes, sir.

Q. About how many? — A. There is only one case that comes to my mind now. He was taken to the hospital at Iloilo and treated.

Q. How many did you say? — A. One, to my knowledge.

Q. And do you know of any others? — A. No, sir.

Q. In these attacks or fights that you speak of, the Americans won, did they? — A. Yes, sir.

Q. They had possession of the field? — A. Yes, sir.

Q. Do you have knowledge of any more than one wounded in these conflicts that you were connected with falling into the hands of the Americans? — A. No, sir.

Q. Was there any opportunity for the Filipinos themselves to carry off their wounded in these conflicts? — A. They had the same opportunities that the Americans had.

Q. The Americans did, to do what? — A. To carry off their wounded.

Q. I understand the Americans charged, did they, as soon as there was an attack? — A. Yes, sir.

Q. The Filipinos fled, did they? — A. Yes, sir.

Q. What opportunity was there for the Filipinos to carry off wounded while they were fleeing and being pursued by the Americans? — A. They would carry them off in their arms.

Q. Did you see anything of that kind? — A. No, sir.

Q. Did you learn of anything of that kind in those conflicts? — A. It was a general report that they always carried off their dead if they could — and their wounded.

Q. That was the general report. I mean, did you have any knowledge of anything of this kind in these conflicts?

(No answer.)

Sen. Beveridge: Mr. Hallock, speaking about these prisoners and wounded that Senator Patterson has been asking you about, this one man that you personally know about was taken to our hospital, did you say? — A. Yes, sir.

Q. And what physicians or surgeons attended him there — ours? — A. I could not say what physicians.

Q. Was it in the same hospital where our wounded were taken? — A. I think it was, sir.

Q. Was it the general understanding that Filipino wounded received the same treatment that our wounded did after they were brought in through our lines; or was there any general understanding that you know of about the subject? — A. I could not say about that.

Q. You merely know about the one case that fell under your observation? — A. Yes, sir.

Q. This was about two years ago, as I remember your testimony; it was in 1900? — A. It was in 1900 that this man was wounded.

Q. This whole occurrence that you have been testifying about? — A. It was in 1901.

Q. The application of the water cure was in 1900? — A. Yes, sir.

Q. The application of the water cure was about two years ago. It is not important as to dates; I am simply fixing the general lapse of time. How long had you been in the Philippine service at that time? — A. Before the water cure was given?

Q. Yes. — A. I arrived there the 27th of October, 1899, and the water cure was given in August, 1900.

Q. Then, your entire service in the Philippines was how long? — A. About seventeen months, I think.

Q. During that time where were you most of the time? — A. At Leon.

Q. Is that in Panay? — A. Yes, sir.

Q. While General Hughes was in command there? — A. Yes, sir.

Q. Now, aside from the application of the water cure to these men under the circumstances you have told of, what was the general conduct of American officers and soldiers toward the people, as to kindness or otherwise?

Sen. Patterson: He has said that where they were friendly it was good.

Sen. Beveridge (continuing): Where they were friendly? — A. I should say they treated them very well.

Q. And you observed during your period of service there prisoners in addition to these thirty that were brought in in these three conflicts? — A. Yes, sir.

Q. And when those prisoners had been captured what was their treatment by American officers and soldiers as to kindness and care, and as to the food they were given and places they were put? — A. They were put in the guardhouse and made to do some little work. They always had plenty of rice to eat, and hardtack they gave them sometimes, and coffee.

Q. That was substantially the same rations as our own men received, except as to rice, was it not? — A. Yes, sir.

Q. Did they prefer the rice to our kind of food? Is that the usual food of the natives? — A. That is the food they used; yes.

Q. With reference to the identification of these bones, what sized man was this man O'Hearn? Was he a man of your size or my size? — A. Not quite so tall; he weighed about 150 pounds, I should say.

Q. The surgeon examined these remains, you say? — A. Yes, sir.

Q. You may state what his opinion was, first, as to whether it was the skeleton of an American. — A. He was very positive that it was the bones of Private O'Hearn.

Q. Our men are very much larger in physique than the Filipinos? — A. Yes.

Q. So it could not have been the skeleton of a Filipino. What were your general orders from officers and General Hughes as to care and consideration for peaceable natives?

Sen. Rawlins: I object to that, upon the ground that the written orders, if they are obtainable, are the best evidence.

Sen. Beveridge: What is your understanding, Mr. Hallock, as to what your officers and the commanding general, General Hughes, expected of soldiers in their treatment and intercourse with the friendly natives? — A. To use them well.

Q. And you followed those orders? — A. I did; yes, sir.

Q. And of course your comrades the same? — A. Yes, sir.

Testimony of Arthur MacArthur *

Sen. Patterson: What is the proportion of the killed to the wounded? . . .

Sen. Rawlins: The summary of the enemy's loss [is] 800 killed and 30 wounded; while the summary of our loss is, killed, 40; wounded, 72.

Sen. Patterson: That shows there are about 25 killed to 1 wounded.

Gen. MacArthur: It shows that is what we have tabulated as reports, Senator; it does not show all the facts, because we did not get hold of their wounded.

Sen. Proctor: They carried off their wounded, I suppose?

Gen. MacArthur: Yes. I was going to explain how that occurred, especially in the early operations, where the tactical operation was normal; that is, where we fought in line and observed the usual method of tactical action. In the first instance the insurrection had an abundance of men but a limited number of arms. I have a memorandum on that subject I can introduce at the proper time.

Sen. Beveridge: So that the reason the proportion of the wounded to the killed is so small is because the wounded were removed and you have no data from which to give figures?

Gen. MacArthur: I was going to show how the insurgent army was organized to accomplish that purpose. They have such an excess of men that their fighting line was accompanied by many men without arms. Some carried ammunition. One of the great problems for solution in a modern war is to supply the firing line with ammunition, and the insurgents did that admirably, because they had men bearing ammunition who had no guns, and it was their duty to feed the firing line with ammunition and to remove the wounded. In the great battles around Manila, which approximated very much to the conditions of a modern battle, there were something like 18,000 men, perhaps, employed on both sides. The casualties were numerous; the fighting was precisely as it was in one of the minor battles of our Civil War. But by reason of this reserve of unarmed men who handled ammunition, whose duty it was to pick up a gun — now, we got very few guns in the early part of the war.

Ordinarily we should have picked up 1,000 or 1,500 guns on the battlefields around Manila. I doubt if we got 10 guns, because of the precious value of those guns to the insurrection and the careful preparation they had made to prevent their falling into our hands. The moment a man was wounded they would seize him and get him off the field, and a man would seize his gun. We got very few wounded men around Manila. I was amazed myself. I could not account for it until I made some investigation and found out how they were organized to prevent

* See above, page 54.

precisely that thing. In front of my division we buried approximately 400 men, and I looked around for the wounded and found none. That was in open battle, in open field, line against line, man against man, without any mixture ——

Sen. Patterson: If that theory is true; if that accounts for not finding wounded, and the proportion of killed and wounded of the Filipinos would be normal, then we would have this state of affairs: Filipinos, killed, 801; wounded, 2,403; making a total of killed and wounded of 3,204, against 112 Americans killed and wounded.

Gen. MacArthur: If that is what the mathematics of the situation call for I presume it is true.

Now, I am speaking a little offhand in presenting this. I have not prepared on that basis, but I have reached a conclusion from my own observations that the proportion of wounded is not as large. I can tell you what I saw one afternoon at the little town of Malabon.

Sen. Patterson: You were in the battles around Manila in February?

Gen. MacArthur: Yes.

Sen. Patterson: And a conservative estimate of the killed and wounded of the Filipinos is 3,000, and about 250 Americans?

Gen. MacArthur: Yes.

Sen. Patterson: Those are the official reports?

Gen. MacArthur: I think that is as near an approximation as possible if those are the official figures.

Sen. Beveridge: In battle the object is to kill and wound as many of the enemy as possible, and to put them out of action?

Gen. MacArthur: Yes.

Sen. Beveridge: And the more you kill and wound the quicker the victory?

Gen. MacArthur: Yes. Target practice with great guns and small arms is the secret of success in war. The more money you give for target shooting the more certain you are of destroying your adversary when you come in contact with him, and that has been exemplified in our modern war. There was the battle of Manila Bay. Not a man killed in the American fleet! Why? Because our fleet destroyed the adversary before he could do them any harm. That was not an accident; that was the result of years of target practice.

Sen. Patterson: But after years of practice there is no greater fatality in shooting at Filipinos than there would be in shooting at the soldiers of any other nationality. Because an army is composed of Filipinos is no reason why there should be greater proportion of killed to wounded than among the soldiers of any other nation.

Gen. MacArthur: That may appear to you in that light, Senator; it does not to me. I have seen the Filipinos and know how inefficient they are as marksmen. . . . The Boer is the best individual marksman in the world.

Sen. Patterson: I am not talking about the proportion of killed and wounded of the two armies, but the disproportion in one army. For instance, we find, if these mathematics are correct, that in the year referred to by Senator Rawlins there would have been 3,204 Filipinos killed and wounded, while there were, killed, 801; wounded, 38; and the American loss was only 112. Is there anything in the fact that soldiers are Filipinos that there should be such a tremendous disproportion?

Gen. MacArthur: I have tried to explain that. It is conclusive to my own mind. I regard it as a very fortunate circumstance that our American soldiers escaped as they did. If the increased death rate of the American soldier had established a better equilibrium it might have been satisfactory to some arguments, but it would have been a very mournful thing to the United States.

The Chairman: On the disproportion between killed and wounded, in any battle, is it not almost impossible for the victorious party to estimate the number of wounded in the defeated party? That is, they can estimate the killed because the killed are largely left on the field, but they have no means of estimating the wounded. And that is something that is reached by later statistics when you get the reports of both sides, is it not?

Gen. MacArthur: In many instances I think you reach an approximation. With civilized nations men lie on the field with absolute certainty of protection. The Filipinos later on became familiar with our methods and they did not take much pains to carry away the men when only two or three were wounded. In these big battles around Manila they did not know what was going to happen to them. The Spaniards had misrepresented us in such a way that they felt that they were in very dangerous hands when they fell into the American line on the battlefield.

Sen. Patterson: Where you have a uniform disproportion in the killed and wounded of two contending armies, anywhere from fifteen to one; that is, there would be fifteen killed and wounded upon one side or twenty killed and wounded upon one side, while there would be one killed and wounded on the other, in that proportion, does not that become pretty nearly slaughter instead of war?

Gen. MacArthur: No, no; not when your adversary stands up and fights. . . .

Testimony of Robert P. Hughes [*]

Sen. Patterson: Was there usually the same disparity in killed and wounded in conflicts between the American and Philippine forces that existed in the attack of the 5th of February?

Gen. Hughes: Well, Mr. Senator, I can not say positively, but my impression is that it grew greater as the struggle progressed.

[*] See above, page 27.

Sen. Patterson: A greater disparity?

Gen. Hughes: The best fight, so far as my knowledge goes, that the Filipinos ever made was made on the 5th of February.

Sen. Patterson: There was then a disparity of at least ten to one, according to the statements?

Gen. Hughes: I have not looked it up.

Sen. Patterson: There were ten Filipinos killed or wounded where there was one American, and you say that disparity increased.

Gen. Hughes: I think you make a mistake in reading General Otis's report as you read it to me. He states the "loss." The loss included prisoners, wounded, and killed. I think he says he had filled his prisons, and I know that I received hundreds of prisoners on that day.

Sen. Patterson: If he buried on the field 700, according to the usual proportions, it would have resulted in more than 2,500 being killed or wounded, would it not?

Gen. Hughes: The percentage of wounded to killed does not hold good with those people over there. I always felt as if we were hitting a woman in fighting those people. They did not know the first earthly thing about how to fight.

Sen. Patterson: Then the percentage, the difference between their killed and wounded and ours ——

Gen. Hughes: I was going on to say that you can occupy those people in front and send a command — really your attacking force — around by flank and fire on them, and I have known them to be caught that way time and time again. They never seemed to learn.

Sen. Patterson: In any event, four or five to one would be a large percentage of wounded to killed, would it not?

Gen. Hughes: Oh, no; I think if you will go into the records of our Civil War you will find that it is ten to one in many instances.

Sen. Patterson: That is what I say; four or five to one is really a small percentage.

Gen. Hughes: You said "large."

Sen. Patterson: I ought to have said a small percentage of wounded to killed.

Gen. Hughes: Yes, sir.

Sen. Patterson: If you buried on the field 700, without counting those who may not have been buried or whom you may not have found or who had been carried off, according to experiences in our Civil War, the total loss in killed or wounded would have been much greater than 2,500?

Gen. Hughes: If that holds good. The close-quarter engagement that these fellows gave in their trenches at Manila was very different from the ordinary general action.

I will give you an instance. In one of our operations around Richmond the losses amounted to 40 percent on our side. In my own immediate command I think the killed exceeded the wounded. But there was not a shot fired into it until it was within a hundred yards of the line of the enemy. In this instance over there they waited the attack, and of course the killed would be very much heavier than it was ordinarily.

Sen. Patterson: If there were 700 buried on the field, which would not include those who may have been carried off or those who crawled away and died or those who died at hospitals, to say that there was a loss of 2,500 or 3,000 would, according to our experiences and the experiences of modern warfare, be a conservative estimate, would it not?

Gen. Hughes: In ordinary cases it would, and I have no doubt it was so intended at that time.

Sen. Patterson: You think that was the best fight the Filipinos put up?

Gen. Hughes: So far as I know, that was the best fight they ever put up.

Sen. Patterson: And the disparity between the killed and wounded of the Americans and the Filipinos continued to increase as time went on?

Gen. Hughes: Yes. I think they had at that time gotten in pretty much all the men whom the Spaniards discharged; that is, from the native organizations. They were discharged by the Spaniards and had probably been taken up; in fact, I know a great many of them went right into their ranks. These men were taught to shoot. They had been educated by the Spaniards to shoot. As those men were killed off and they had to take the ordinary tao [man], they could not hit a stack of barns.

Sen. Patterson: That would indicate either one of two things — either that the war has been pretty much of a slaughter or else the Filipinos were brave to a fault.

Gen. Hughes: To a what?

Sen. Patterson: Brave to a fault. If the battles result in the killing and wounding of, say, ten Filipinos to one American, it would indicate it, would it not, either that it was pretty much of a slaughter or else that the Filipinos were brave and cared nothing for death — would stand to be shot down or otherwise killed, presenting a front to the American Army?

Gen. Hughes: I do not think you are correct in that.

Sen. Patterson: How do you account, then, for the immense disparity in killed and wounded between the two forces?

Gen. Hughes: The difference is that our men can shoot. As I said before, the ordinary Filipino could not hit a stack of barns.

Sen. Patterson: Nevertheless, ordinarily, when a man finds his comrades dropping around him and he cannot do any execution upon the attacking force, he will turn tail and run, and you are not liable to have such a tremendous disparity in the killed and wounded between the two forces.

Gen. Hughes: I have known instances where it seemed to be absolute indifference.

Sen. Patterson: Do you find much of that?

Gen. Hughes: No; the usual tactics, among the Visayans at least, after the first licking they got and breaking up, was to select their position and pick off odd men or get in two or three volleys from some concealed position where they were protected and then run.

Sen. Patterson: But that method of warfare would protect their men from being killed and wounded?

Gen. Hughes: Certainly.

Sen. Patterson: But here is this terrible disparity of which you speak?

Gen. Hughes: But occasionally they would make the mistake of allowing themselves to be caught in a hole somewhere or in a place from which it was difficult to escape.

Sen. Patterson: When they were in a hole, or in a place where it was difficult to escape, what would be the result; would you kill them?

Gen. Hughes: Not at all.

Sen. Patterson: Or would they stand and fight?

Gen. Hughes: They would sometimes make a desperate effort to run. Sometimes they would attack. I have had cases reported to me by the officers in charge, although I never saw them, where a single boloman, who, hid in the grass, was stumbled on by one of our skirmishers, kept on cutting and hacking with the bolo until, I think, some six men got around. He hurt some three of them.

Sen. Patterson: I suppose there are cases of that kind.

Gen. Hughes: You know what a bolo is, Mr. Senator?

Sen. Patterson: Yes.

Gen. Hughes: There is a specimen here.

Sen. Patterson: You showed me one the other day. I saw it the first day you brought it here.

Gen. Hughes: Some of their men will use that until they are killed. This man of whom I speak was not killed. He was clubbed on the head, and of course that knocked him senseless, and they took him a prisoner. That shows how desperate occasionally they will be. But those are rare occasions.

Sen. Patterson: I cannot account for the great disparity in the number of killed and wounded, ten to one, increasing as the war went on, except upon the theory either that they were stoically brave as a class and would stand and die, or else that there had been simple slaughter.

Gen. Hughes: There has been nothing of the kind, unless you take it to be slaughter where armed enemies will continue to fight and refuse to surrender when you have them in a bad hole.

Sen. Patterson: That is stoicism; it is bravery.

Gen. Hughes: It is not bravery.

Sen. Patterson: What is it?

Gen. Hughes: I think it is more likely to be the obstinacy of their leader. Their leader is the man ——

Sen. Dubois: Indifference to death, he said a while ago. . . .

The Chairman: I should like to ask the General a question. Speaking of slaughtering or killing the Filipinos, is there any shooting down in cold blood by our men?

Gen. Hughes: Not to my knowledge. My instructions given with caution — because you cannot bind by an absolute rule a man who meets an enemy — was [sic] not to kill unnecessarily; that killing the tao, the ordinary man, accomplished nothing, but that if they could kill the leaders they would accomplish something; that the tao, when shot down, could be replaced by two more without any trouble whatever, but if they could pick out the leaders and kill them they were accomplishing something. Those were the instructions.

The Chairman: But, in the case of prisoners or anything of that sort, after they had ceased to fight ——

Gen. Hughes: To my knowledge there never was a case of that kind, and if there had been, the man responsible would have been tried for it as soon as it could have been done.

The Chairman: In this connection there are a great many rumors and statements of cruelties practiced on the natives after they had ceased to fight as prisoners. Was there any systematic cruelty or oppression?

Gen. Hughes: There never was any so far as I know. The prisoners taken were all brought to the military prison. The only one we had in the department was at Iloilo. That was under my personal care. It was inspected by me personally not less than once a week, if I were in the city, and very often twice a week, and each time I visited it I went through it, looked after the care that was being taken of the sick, the condition of their food, the condition of their quarters, receiving all the complaints, either written or verbal.

The Chairman: What were the orders of the department or of the commanding general and your orders in the district in regard to the treatment of peaceful Filipinos?

Gen. Hughes: The orders of the division commander were to observe strictly the laws of war. My instructions, so far as the peaceably disposed were concerned, were to make friends with them, as after they got acquainted with us we usually could get along with them, but the trouble was that the armed enemies would not allow the peaceably disposed people to get acquainted with us if they could help it.

The Chairman: If cases of cruelty or oppression toward a prisoner or toward a peaceably disposed native occurred, were the men tried and punished?

Gen. Hughes: They certainly would have been. The point is this: I cannot say there were no such cases, because that would be one of the things that would meet with immediate action on my part, and if they occurred they would not let me know it if they could help it, and there may have been occasional cases of it without my knowledge, but I never knew of any case in all my two years and a half in the Department of the Visayas.

Testimony of William Howard Taft *

Sen. Culberson: In your judgment is there any part of the Philippine Islands in which a regiment of native troops might be organized, armed with the best American equipment, and placed in control of native officers? Would it be safe to organize such a regiment in any part of the Philippine Islands?

Gov. Taft: I do not think, to begin with, that you could get native officers probably who could organize a regiment as it ought to be. I think it probably could be done ——

Sen. Culberson: In what part of the islands?

Gov. Taft: In the north part of Luzon, but I certainly would not advise it.

Sen. Culberson: Why not?

Gov. Taft: I think the regiment would not be efficient. It could not be trusted, for instance, not to oppress its own people.

Sen. Culberson: In what other instances could it not be trusted, if any?

Gov. Taft: So far as loyalty is concerned I can only give you this statement with respect to native soldiers, that the percentage of desertions from the native soldiers who have been enlisted is considerably less than the percentage of desertions from the American Army.

Sen. Culberson: Could it be trusted in any governmental controversy between the natives of the islands and the United States government?

Gov. Taft: That has never been tried, and I should think, in a country which had been in war as this has been, to put in command of a Filipino a thousand men with a thousand rifles would not be wise. I have not any hesitation in saying that.

Sen. Culberson: I was simply asking your opinion about it.

Gov. Taft: That is my opinion. I have much more confidence in the Filipino and his loyalty than have a good many of the military officers.

Sen. Burrows: That is, than the military officers have of them?

Gov. Taft: Yes, sir. I think the mixture of Filipino officers and American officers as we mix them in the constabulary would be very good. The Filipino likes his cloth. He feels proud of being a member of a military organization or a civil constabulary organization, and while I might give it as my judgment that such a regiment would not prove dangerous, I should not like to have it done on my advice alone, certainly. . . .

Sen. Burrows: I want to understand that. It is very important. Do you mean to say that in any of the pacified provinces the attachment of the Filipino to the United States government is so slender that it would not be safe to trust a thousand of them with arms under the command of their own officers?

* See above, page 35.

121

Gov. Taft: I think that the presence of such a regiment under the control of Filipinos might give rise to plotting to secure the services of the commanders in leading their troops into either ladronism or insurrectoism.

Sen. Burrows: And that condition exists in all the pacified provinces, you think?

Gov. Taft: I think it would be dangerous.

Sen. Burrows: How would it be if they were under command of American officers?

Gov. Taft: I have not the slightest doubt that under the command of American officers they would be entirely loyal.

Sen. Carmack: I wish to call your attention to a reported speech made by General Wright in advocating the so-called treason and sedition laws, in which he spoke of the inflammable character of the people in the pacified provinces and their inclination to be led away by enthusiasts and demagogues appealing to their love of independence. Do you think putting arms into the hands of the people might give an opportunity to those enthusiasts and demagogues to stir up the people and get them to join the insurgents?

Gov. Taft: As I have said, with nine-tenths of the people absolutely ignorant and credulous to a degree that the committee would hardly believe, it is possible by misrepresentations to move whole villages. It has been done in Sorsogon. It was done in Pangasinan by the most absurd stories. Whole villages have been led to migrate to another village to take service, so to speak, under some religious fakir — I use that term advisedly — who professed to be able to cure them miraculously or to bring some benefit to them, or to enable them to avoid some unfounded danger.

Now, with people of that ignorance, certainly, if General Wright referred to that, he was justified by the facts. The possibility of educated men among the Filipinos misleading their people, I think I have already referred to a number of times.

Sen. Carmack: Then, is it not the condition there that the people are liable at any time to be led into some insurrectionary movement by a turbulent demagogue?

Gov. Taft: That is quite possible, and that, if you will permit me to say so in passing, is one of the chief reasons why the Filipino people are utterly unfit for self-government. . . .

Sen. Culberson: You stated in reply to the chairman, I understand, that recently it has been arranged that 10,000 troops should be taken out of the islands.

Gov. Taft: Yes, sir.

Sen. Culberson: That will leave how many?

Gov. Taft: About 30,000.

Sen. Culberson: Do you believe it is now necessary to retain in the islands as many as 30,000 troops? . . .

Gov. Taft: I am not a military man, but I can state generally what my judgment is without stating the number. My judgment is that there ought to be through the islands as a moral restraint against disorder and violence a considerable number of soldiers, possibly a battalion, possibly two companies, at convenient points either in each province or at some convenient point with reference to three or four provinces.

They ought to have nothing to do with the policing, but simply be there for the purpose of being called upon in case of emergency. Now, I assume that the estimate which Captain Allen makes of 15,000 men is reached on the basis of such a policy.

Sen. Culberson: A battalion to every province?

Gov. Taft: Yes, sir.

Sen. Culberson: Amounting to fifty-eight battalions, as I understand it?

Gov. Taft: I do not know that it would require a battalion in each province, but a considerable post, perhaps not one for each province, but so situated with respect to two or three provinces that it would operate as a moral restraint in those provinces. . . .

Sen. Culberson: . . . [U]nder your instructions, was not the Commission under the control of the Secretary of War and were not all your acts subject to the approval of the Secretary of War?

Gov. Taft: Yes, sir; under the Secretary of War, who is a civilian. I am speaking now of the authorities resident in the islands.

I have studied, of course, the instructions issued by President McKinley with a great deal of care, and have watched their operation in the development of the government of those islands. . . . I think they constitute one of the greatest state papers ever issued in operating as they were intended to operate and in bringing about a state of affairs that they intended to bring about; and their operation was this: There was insurrection in the country. How far that insurrection attracted the sympathy of all the people is of course a mere matter of opinion, upon which there will always be a substantial difference. That there were two parties, however — those who favored the exclusion of American sovereignty altogether, and a substantial party who favored the government which we are now establishing — is undoubtedly true, and that there was a large body of ignorant people who were entirely indifferent, provided peace could be established and they could be protected from oppression and violence and assault, and who had very few political ideas at all, is also true.

Sen. Beveridge: This third division is the great body of all?

Gov. Taft: Yes; ignorant people.

Now, the problem there was on the one hand to suppress the insurrection, and that had to be done with the Army. On the other hand, it was to teach the people that our purpose was not to continue a military government, but by object lessons to show them what civil government was by legislation and by putting it into force.

Now, here was a dual government. There was the military arm on the one hand and there was the civil arm on the other, and the effect of those instructions — you can see it operate every day — was to bring the Filipino — and I do not except anybody in that statement; I do not even except the insurrectos — to bring the people into more friendly relations with the civil government than with the military government.

The conduct of a dual form of government of that sort was of course difficult. The instructions were framed so that they have worked. But the coming into the minds of the people [of] a consciousness of the existence of power in the civil government and its effect on them, and the gradually [sic] placing [of] more and more power in the civil government, which the instructions contemplated, have had a marvelous effect in showing the people what our purpose was. . . .

. . . [T]he theory of the Commission in its formation of civil government has been this: First, that the indispensable aid to the ultimate success of a popular government there, with qualified suffrage, is the extension of education through the islands; but that of course cannot have great effect short of a generation or two generations, because the people affected by education are those who are now children, though there are some ten thousand adults studying English in the night schools. But the main effect of education must be on those who are coming into manhood or will not come into manhood possibly for ten or fifteen years.

In the meantime the reliance of the Commission is on the small educated portion of the community. With this as a nucleus and with the aid of American control we think a stable government can be erected. A majority of the provincial board in each case is American, and I say without hesitation — of course it is an expression of opinion — that lacking the American initiative, lacking the American knowledge of how to carry on a government, any government there must be a complete failure until by actual observation and practice, under the guidance of a people who know how to carry on a government, who understand the institutions of civil liberty, there may be trained a Filipino element who may then be able to carry on the government without so much guidance and so much initiative as now are absolutely necessary to the carrying on of a decent government at all. . . .

The Federal party was projected in November. Its organization continued into December and January, and it spread, I may say, like wildfire.

Sen. Allison: January of last year?

Gov. Taft: Yes, sir. Now, it [has been] suggested . . . that the reason why the party spread with such rapidity was because of a plank in its platform which was for statehood. I have been trying to find that platform. Possibly some gentleman present may have it. I cannot find it among my papers. . . .

My recollection of the platform is that it is divided into two parts. The first part concerned what was at hand — the present purpose of the party — and the second part contained what may not be characterized as aspirations of the party, but something equivalent to that. In the first part they ask for amnesty to all political offenders, for the organization of a partially popular government, and some other things that do not now occur to me. In the second part is the statement of their hope that they may be made part of the States when fitted for self-government, and some other things.

Possibly in the first part, too, is the plank that they shall have two or three delegates representing them before the executive and legislative departments in Washington.

Now, the real reason for the spread of the Federal party was the urgent desire for peace on the part of substantially all classes except those people who were in the mountains. I make that statement without the slightest qualification. . . .

Another party formed in Manila after the successful organization and spreading of the Federal party was called the Partido Conservador. They were all in favor of peace; all insisted that peace was essential before anything else was done. They propose, in the future, to ask for a separation of the islands from the United States and a protectorate, possibly disposing of the protectorate after that is feasible. That party was made up largely of the Spanish mestizos, with a sympathy with Spain rather, and while it had representatives in Manila, so far as I know it never secured any agencies or any recruits from any other parts of the islands. . . .

Then there is a party which is now called the Party of the Peace, which is considerably larger than the Conservador party, though it does not seem to be organized much out of Manila. It is composed of those who were regarded as *intransigentes* — that is, irreconcilables. In their number are some of the junta who have come to Manila and who have been interesting themselves in the things that are proceeding there. They have appointed a number of delegates to go to Malvar and Lukban to see if they cannot induce a cessation of hostilities there. I think I have stated now all the parties that there are.

The only party of any organization at all throughout the islands is the Federal party. In the appointment of natives the fact that a man was a member of the Federal party was always a good recommendation for him for appointment, for the reason that we regarded the Federal party as one of the great elements in bringing about pacification, and if a man was in the Federal party it was fairly good evidence that he was interested in the government which we were establishing, and would do as well as he could. . . .

Sen. Patterson: What was the size of the army in the first instance?

Gov. Taft: I cannot give you the figures. I do not know that anybody can exactly, but it certainly went above 10,000 men. I think there were more than that. Possibly Senator Beveridge can say, because he was there at the time and I was not.

Sen. Beveridge: Are you speaking of its size originally? Originally it was supposed, at the outbreak of the hostilities, that they had something in the neighborhood of 30,000 men. Luna alone had 10,000 in San Fernando.

Gov. Taft: . . . When that army was scattered the question was, What were the insurgents to do — whether they were to surrender or to make guerrilla warfare, or attempt to gather their forces and make a continued fight, as they had been making?

Upon that issue I have understood that Aguinaldo and Luna differed. Luna desired to continue the warfare as it had been conducted, in an open fight. Aguinaldo was for a guerrilla campaign. These two men were opposed to each other, at any rate, and Aguinaldo directed Luna's killing. I should not say that if I had not direct evidence on the subject from General Funston, who says that Aguinaldo said the question was whether Luna should kill him or he should kill Luna, and he took steps to secure the death of Luna. The killing was at the headquarters of Aguinaldo, and Luna was shot by guards.

After that there was no question about the campaign, and the Filipinos went into a guerrilla campaign, which consisted of dividing up into small forces, who should have fastnesses in the mountains, and who depended for their support upon contributions of food and money from the people. The guerrilla campaign rested necessarily on a system of terrorism.

It could not have existed otherwise. My impression is that under the Spanish methods of conducting war there it was thought proper to condemn a man in his absence and then direct his assassination. Certainly that was the policy which the insurgents pursued, not against Americans, but against their own people. When, therefore, one of their own people was serving the American government as a municipal officer and doing good service in that way, and failing to give information to the insurgents, he was warned, and in the end, if he continued, it usually resulted in his death.

Now, I think anyone who studies the situation impartially, with a knowledge of all the circumstances, will say that without that system of terrorism the guerrilla campaign would have ended very quickly, because the people wanted peace, as they now want it, and as they always, so far as I know, since I have been there, have wanted it.

But it continued. It was impossible to identify the guerrillas, who would dress like amigos at one time and then sneak out of the town where they had assumed that character, and become part of the insurgent force. Information was constantly given to the insurgent forces as to the movements of the American troops, and the campaign had that difficulty, which cannot be exaggerated by those gentlemen who were present to see what it amounted to. . . .

Now, when you consider the difficulties of the quartermaster department and the commissary department in furnishing, in a country infested with guerrilla bands and in a country practically without roads, the quartermaster supplies and the commissary supplies for 500 different posts, the escorts that were necessary, and combine with that the duty of chasing the guerrilla bands from point to point in the most impassable mountains, you can see what a tremendous task the army had, and as you look back it is most remarkable that it succeeded as it did; and the insurgents were chased by the Americans with an activity and a skill and an ability that was of great surprise to them, in view of Spanish methods of carrying on warfare. The insurgents were finally, by the energy, the activity, the skill, and the bravery of the American troops, made very tired of guerrilla warfare. I say they were very tired of it, for I have talked with the insurgents who were engaged in it. They could not rest more than two nights in a place, and as a consequence the guerrilla chiefs were, after this active campaign, put into a situation where they would have liked to have a life of more leisure than that which was given.

Now, that was the condition about the time of the election.

Sen. Hale: You mean in November?

Gov. Taft: The Presidential election in which Mr. McKinley was reelected. The insurgents hoped that Mr. Bryan would be elected, as that meant a change of policy and the giving up of the islands to them and an opportunity on the part of those who were in arms to assume control.

When Mr. McKinley was reelected, they thought that the policy of the indefinite retention of the islands was settled. I think all felt that — both the Filipinos not in arms who desired American sovereignty and those who were in arms.

The operations of the Army, therefore, were the main basis. Then followed the election. Then followed a greater activity in the Army, because the dry season was coming on. Then followed more rigor in the treatment of insurgents who were captured. The leaders who refused to take the oath of allegiance were sent to Guam. The men who were captured in the field were sent to prison. Before that time the men who were captured were generally turned loose. . . .

Testimony of Arthur L. Wagner

Colonel Arthur Lockwood Wagner was a career officer. Born in Ottawa, Illinois in 1853, he was graduated from the United States Military Academy in 1875, and went on active duty immediately. His career was divided between serving with troops in the Indian Wars and teaching military science. In 1898 he had the rank of lieutenant colonel and he was assistant adjutant general. At the time of the Spanish-American War, he was chief of the War Department's division of public information, and his name was familiar in commissioned ranks because he had written a number of books on tactics and military history. He was quickly detached for service in Cuba, and upon the surrender of Santiago, he went to Puerto Rico for brief duty. After the Insurrection began, he was sent to the Philippines. Late in 1901 following various assignments he became adjutant general of the Department of Northern Philippines, combining the old Departments of Northern Luzon and Southern Luzon.

Sen. Culberson: You have stated what the orders were previously with reference to burning. What were the orders issued by the department commanders subsequent to that as to burnings?

Col. Wagner: There were not any written orders, as I recollect; it was understood, however, that any houses that were used as rendezvous for those bands of ladrones, used as cuartels, as we term it, were to be destroyed wherever found. Any houses from which our troops were fired upon of course would be destroyed. That is according to the rules of war, always.

Sen. Culberson: Is the other character of burning contrary to the rules of war?

Col. Wagner: Not at all, sir; it is certainly in accordance with them.

Sen. Culberson: You seemed to make some distinction; that was the reason I asked the question.

Col. Wagner: The burning of buildings from which troops were fired upon is specifically set forth in almost every treatise, I imagine, that has ever been written on the rules of war.

Sen. Culberson: What are the rules of war with reference to burning the houses of noncombatants, measured by the general order issued by President Lincoln, No. 100, in 1863? What rule would prevail as to the burning of the homes and residences of noncombatants?

Col. Wagner: In case such people had given information to the enemy or committed any hostile acts against any portion of our forces in territory occupied by our forces it would be a perfectly legitimate proceeding to burn their houses or even to take their lives.

Sen. Culberson: I am asking you with reference to noncombatants.

Col. Wagner: In case the noncombatants were friendly or guilty of no hostile acts there would be no authority for burning those houses unless they were used for shelter or for military purposes by people who were engaged in hostile acts against us.

Sen. Culberson: Well, in that case the noncombatants would be classed as enemies, would they not?

Col. Wagner: Not at all, sir. A noncombatant might own a house which is seized by the leader of a hostile party against the wishes of the owner; but this leader makes use of this house and property, we will say, for his protection, for his shelter, and as a place from which to operate against our forces. In such case we would be perfectly justified in burning this house, notwithstanding the fact that it was used without the consent of the owner or, in fact, against his wishes.

Sen. Culberson: A former captain of the Twenty-sixth Infantry, United States Volunteers, testified yesterday, Colonel, that he burned a town or barrio, taking the houses indiscriminately; that is to say, he did not discriminate between houses that were used by the insurgents there as abiding places, or places of refuge or places where provisions were stored, but that indiscriminately he burned all the houses, including the residences of the town, with the exception of one or two, which the American troops desired to use themselves. Would you say that that was within the rule provided by Order No. 100?

Col. Wagner: Under the circumstances, yes, sir. It is not always possible to discriminate between those who are active enemies and those who are not. It is not always possible to discriminate between these people or between the houses owned by them. We know that a certain community has been conducting itself very badly, that many people in this community have been acting as guerrillas, appearing in arms to fight, and afterwards, when pursued, assuming the guise of innocent and inoffensive people, or have been guilty of assassination, or cutting telegraph wires, destroying bridges, etc. In such a case, when we know that this town is used as a rendezvous, a place from which these people operate, it would be justifiable to destroy the town, although we might burn the property of inoffensive people by so doing.

Sen. Culberson: Do I understand you, then, to say that if American troops in the Philippine Islands would have information that two or three houses in a town had harbored insurgents, or been allowed to be used by insurgents for hostile purposes, and the American troops were unable to discover which particular several houses had been so used, that they would be authorized to burn the entire town?

Col. Wagner: No, sir; that would be a very extreme measure to take for the degree of the offense on the part of the inhabitants. You assume, I understand by your question, that only two or three people had been guilty of these acts.

Sen. Culberson: I wanted to know where you are going to draw the line, and I wanted you to be kind enough to draw the line for me somewhere.

Col. Wagner: Yes, sir; I will endeavor to do so. If it were known that several people who had been committing depredations were harbored in a town and on application to the authorities of the town the surrender of those people was refused, it would be justifiable to notify such town authorities that if they continued to harbor these people and did not surrender them or cause their depredations to cease a certain number of buildings in the town would be destroyed as a retaliatory measure, because the mere fact of harboring these people, the mere fact of giving them shelter without reporting them to the authorities, makes the people of the town participants in the hostile act.

Sen. Culberson: This preliminary step which you have indicated in your answer must precede the burning?

Col. Wagner: An officer must use judgment; he must be satisfied that the conduct of the entire community has been such as to deserve it before he would undertake to destroy all the houses in a barrio. So far as I know, indiscriminate burning of barrios has never been approved and never allowed.

Sen. Beveridge: When a town or barrio has been notoriously known as a rendezvous, place of departure and return of ladrones, what then would be a justifiable course to pursue?

Col. Wagner: If the town were notoriously a nest of ladrones, if it was impossible to get the rest of the people to yield them up, it would be justifiable and proper to destroy the town, even though we destroyed the property of some innocent people. The Almighty destroyed Sodom, notwithstanding the fact that there were a few just people in that community — less than ten.

Sen. Beveridge: How strange; I was thinking of that instance of Sodom and Gomorrah.

Sen. Culberson: I am not asking with reference to accidental burning; of course I understand that in the case of burning a town that harbors insurgents, if by reason of the close proximity of that building to the others it is accidentally and unavoidably destroyed, that party must suffer; but I am speaking with reference to the deliberate act of burning the houses of noncombatants, as seems to have been done in some cases in the Philippines, which have been testified to before this committee. That is the case I am trying to get your judgment upon.

Col. Wagner: The destruction of the property of noncombatants, when the property is known to belong to noncombatants and there is no military necessity for destroying it, is inexcusable. The destruction of property of noncombatants may be necessary, though, for two reasons. It may be impossible to separate the property of innocent people in their towns from property of the guilty. The whole community there must suffer, if the crimes of the community have been sufficient to warrant it. Again, as I stated before, I think, the property of a noncombatant must be destroyed if an enemy is making use of that to our prejudice and hurt in military operations.

Sen. Culberson: Now, coming to so-called tortures in the Philippines, either by hanging by the neck, or by the thumbs, or by the feet, or by the water cure, I will ask you if you have any personal knowledge on the subject?

Col. Wagner: No personal knowledge. I have seen communications on the subject; I recall that in the month of June, 1900, a rumor came to headquarters that some cruelty had been exercised toward natives, for the purpose of extorting information. I think that related to the case of two volunteer officers of the Twenty-seventh Infantry, who were not in our department, but in the Department of Northern Luzon. These officers were both tried, but that was out of our department, and I mention it simply as a means of giving an idea of the reason for issuing an order which was then issued, prohibiting any acts of cruelty for the purpose of extorting information. This order was issued, I think, on the 5th of June, 1900, by the commanding general, General Bates, who was then in command of the Department of Southern Luzon, and who, as soon as he heard of these acts outside of his own department, directed me to issue the order.

Sen. Culberson: Prohibiting it within his jurisdiction?

Col. Wagner: Yes; of course he could not prohibit anything outside.

Sen. Culberson: I understand.

Col. Wagner: Then there were some complaints from different sources — general newspaper clippings or letters written to the War Department. There was one of them from a negro by the name, I think, of Peter Pearl, who styled himself an attaché of the Twenty-ninth Volunteers, making complaints that officers had administered the water cure and specifying officers of the Twenty-first Infantry and Twenty-ninth Infantry. This communication was referred to the commanding officers of those regiments for investigation, and it was found that there was nothing in the complaint at all.

Sen. Culberson: About when was that complaint made?

Col. Wagner: The complaint was received at our headquarters in 1901; I do not remember the month. I do not know when the complaint was made; the complaint had been sent in to Washington, and came all the way out to the Philippines.

Sen. Culberson: Now, you can state any other information that you may have with reference to these so-called tortures having been inflicted on Filipinos by American troops.

Sen. Beveridge: Personal knowledge.

Col. Wagner: From my personal knowledge I know of none, absolutely none.

Sen. Culberson: We have not been confining other witnesses to their personal knowledge.

Sen. Beveridge: I understood you to ask him as to his personal knowledge.

Sen. Culberson: I had gotten away from that and was asking him about any information he had.

Sen. Beveridge: In view of the large mass of testimony on that subject in which we have direct evidence I supposed you were not asking for hearsay.

Sen. Culberson: The Colonel is adjutant general of northern Luzon, and he may have some official information about it. That is what I want to get.

Sen. Beveridge: Go ahead.

Col. Wagner: There was a letter written by a soldier of the Forty-sixth Volunteers to friends at home in which he claimed that the Filipinos were shot down like rabbits. This letter was printed. A newspaper clipping containing the letter was sent from the War Department to the Philippines for investigation. It came to our headquarters; it was referred to the commanding officer of the Forty-sixth Infantry, who was ordered to investigate the matter carefully.

The result of the investigation showed that the story was made up out of whole cloth, and the writer of the letter confessed he had written it with a view, to use his own words, "of jollying the old folks." I might mention a complaint against Lieut. Preston Brown, of the Second Infantry, for shooting a prisoner of war. A court was ordered for his trial; he was duly tried and convicted. Another complaint was in the form of charges and specifications preferred by Major Gardener, who was then governor of the province of Tayabas, against a young officer for striking a Filipino with his gun because the Filipino did not take off his hat to him, for gambling with natives, and for kicking a Chinaman. An investigation of the matter showed that this young man, who was then in the hospital, was mentally unsound. . . .

Testimony of Seiward J. Norton *

Sen. Beveridge: As the witness has been called at your instance, will you proceed with the examination, Senator Culberson?

Sen. Culberson: Where do you reside? — A. In Los Angeles, Cal., at present.

* Biographical details are contained in the testimony.

Q. Did you serve in the army in the Philippines? — *A.* Yes, sir.

Q. In what regiment, and how long? — *A.* I enlisted the 12th of July, 1899, and was sent to Presidio, and from there was sent to the Philippines and was assigned to the Eighteenth Infantry, Company L, and joined my company on the 23rd of September, 1899. I was discharged from the army by special order the 16th of October last. The order was issued August 19, I believe.

Q. What part of the Philippines did you serve in? — *A.* On the island of Panay; that is all. . . .

Q. According to your information, Mr. Norton, was not the water cure resorted to by the soldiers in the Philippines for the purpose of securing information? — *A.* Yes, the practice is prevalent there in that organization, the scouts, and around Iloilo. I never saw it in the northern part of the island.

Q. Who commanded these scouts? — *A.* Lieutenant Conger.

Q. Are those known as the Gordon Scouts? — *A.* Those are the Gordon Scouts.

Q. Where was General Hughes's headquarters at the time this water cure was administered? — *A.* At Iloilo.

Q. How far was that from the place where it was administered? — *A.* Well, I imagine about ten miles; about three miles from Iloilo to Jaro, and then it is about seven miles from there to San Miguel.

Q. Did you witness the burning of any towns by the United States soldiers over there? — *A.* Oh, yes.

Q. Just state what towns you saw burned. — *A.* Well, we were out on this expedition this time; we started one morning at three o'clock and rode around the country to the north of Jaro to San Miguel and came back down this road. It was not the town of San Miguel, but houses built along the road side by side — barrios — and we burned that old string of houses there, it is my impression, to San Miguel. Brown was my scout leader, and I was his squad. I was the only one in the squad present. Brown was acting corporal in the scouts and was ordered to go out with his squad and burn houses there, and he obeyed the order.

Q. How many houses did you burn at that time and place? — *A.* I could not say how many houses we burned. We burned a great many of them and doubtless a great many we left we did not burn. The troop was traveling right along, and we did not make any observation after we lighted a house.

Q. Why was that barrio burned? — *A.* I think to intimidate the natives. I know after we got through our burning, coming back to San Miguel, we came across the bodies of two American horses, two carcasses of horses that had been ridden by the soldiers that were fired upon.

Sen. Beveridge: Oh, they had been firing from these barrios?

The Witness: They must have been.

Sen. Culberson: He. stated that the soldiers were fired upon before that.

Sen. Beveridge: From these barrios?

The Witness: I do not know whether it was these barrios or not. The barrios were on this side ——

Sen. Beveridge: I do not want to interrupt, but is it your inference that those barrios were burned because our people had been fired upon from them?

The Witness: That is it.

Sen. Culberson: What other barrios and towns were burned besides these you have mentioned, within your knowledge? — A. We burned a great many barrios which I did not know the names of. We burned a good deal of the country as we were fired upon. It was the practice, in fact, if a column was marching along and was fired upon to burn the buildings in that neighborhood. That impressed the natives with the fact that they could not fire upon us with impunity, although they did not often do very great damage.

Q. Can you state about how many towns you saw burned? — A. Oh, no.

Q. Can you state the population of all the towns which you saw burned? — A. I could not imagine what it might be.

Q. Were the people in the houses warned to get out before setting fire to them? — A. Oh, yes.

Q. You allowed the inmates time to get out and then their houses were burned? — A. Yes, sir.

Q. You have stated that with the exception of isolated cases the treatment of Filipinos by the American soldiers was humane? — A. Yes, sir; very much so.

Q. And considerate? — A. So humane and considerate that it was deemed a weakness on the part of the natives.

Sen. Beveridge: You mean the natives deemed it a weakness on the part of the Americans?

The Witness (continued): The Americans' leniency was deemed a weakness by the natives. . . .

4 THE FILIPINOS:
THEIR CAPACITY
FOR NATION-BUILDING

Testimony of Arthur MacArthur *

Gen. MacArthur: It was my privilege to join the Eighth Corps at San Francisco in June, 1898, and on the 27th of that month I sailed for Manila in command of the third detachment of the corps, consisting of five ships and approximately 5,000 men. Aside from the high spirits and feelings of self-confidence which actuated all concerned, the distinctive characteristic of the command was absolute ignorance of the Philippine Archipelago in respect of geography, climate, people, and the general aspects of nature.

There was little or no literature aboard from which instructive information could be obtained. One writer to whom we had access advised all travelers to carry coffins, as few returned alive from Manila. Another and more optimistic writer cited an Eastern epigram to the effect that for romance and adventure the entire Eastern world relied upon Manila. These two facts constituted about all we could learn by investigation.

As a general proposition, when the command entered Manila Bay everybody was in a totally ignorant but especially sensitive and receptive state of mind. It was apparent, however, that we had entered a new world of various and great resources, teeming with a dense population that was in a paroxysmal state of excitement.

Under the influence of the far-Eastern sun the heated imagination had a boundless scope for indulgence of the boldest assumptions. Discrimination and sound judgment were taxed to the limit in order to reach anything like a conservative conception of the situation, which was filled with paradoxical suggestions and apparently hopeless conclusions. Visible indications manifested themselves which were incongruous with each other and irreconcilable with facts regarded of reliable record and which were generally accepted as the bases of important deductions in the premises. In my own behalf I determined not to theorize; but while carrying out the plain mandates of military duty to allow surrounding circumstances to exert their normal pressure, and thus permit my mind,

* See above, page 54.

if it should become sufficiently permeated, to record such conclusions as its own involuntary actions should suggest. . . .

During my three years' contact with the people of that archipelago I became very much attached to them. I appreciated them, I think, perhaps, as much as any other American that has been there. My belief in the possibilities of their development is almost unqualified. I therefore submit this idea without any reservation at all.

When the Filipino people realize the grandeur of their future destiny by reason of association with the great Republic, and come to understand that they are a chosen people to carry not only American commerce but also republican institutions and the principles of personal liberty throughout Asia, they may be relied upon to rally to the inspiring thoughts thus suggested and follow and support the American flag in whatever contests the future may have in store for it as the symbol of human liberty throughout the world.

Although the idea of developing our material interests in the East is indescribably attractive to the speculative investigator, the considerations which arise from the psychological inquiry are vastly more interesting and instructive, as far as I am personally concerned. And in opening this branch of my remarks I will say this is what I call my ethnological premises. It goes back; it is perhaps more academical than anything I have yet said.

Many thousand years ago our Aryan ancestors raised cattle, made a language, multiplied in numbers, and overflowed. By due process of expansion to the west they occupied Europe, developed arts and sciences, and created a great civilization, which, separating into innumerable currents, inundated and fertilized the globe with blood and ideas, the primary bases of all human progress, incidentally crossing the Atlantic and thereby reclaiming, populating, and civilizing a hemisphere. The broad actuating laws which underlie all these wonderful phenomena are still operating with relentless vigor and have recently forced one of the currents of this magnificent Aryan people across the Pacific — that is to say, back almost to the cradle of its race — thus initiating a stage of progressive social evolution which may reasonably be expected to result in substantial contributions in behalf of the unity of the race and the brotherhood of man.

From the beginning of civilization man has tried to mitigate and escape as far as possible from the consequences of his own barbarous environment. In pursuance of these laudable efforts, the human race, from time immemorial, has been propagating its higher ideals by a succession of intellectual waves, one of which is now passing, through our mediumship, beyond the Pacific, and carrying therewith everything that is implied by the beautiful flag which is a symbol of our nationality.

We are now living in a heroic age of human history, from the opening aspect of which many of our own people recoil with misgiving, as though we were of choice and de novo entering upon a questionable enterprise, the remote consequences of which must inevitably prove disastrous to all concerned.

At the time I returned to Manila to assume the supreme command it seemed to me that we had been committed to a position by process of spontaneous evolution. In other words, that our permanent occupation of the islands was simply one of the necessary consequences in logical sequence of our great prosperity, and to doubt the wisdom of which was simply to doubt the stability of our own institutions and in effect to declare that a self-governing nation was incapable of successfully resisting strains arising naturally from its own productive energy. It seemed to me that our conception of right, justice, freedom, and personal liberty was the precious fruit of centuries of strife; that we had inherited much in these respects from our ancestors, and in our own behalf have added much to the happiness of the world, and as beneficiaries of the past and as the instruments of future progressive social development we must regard ourselves simply as the custodians of imperishable ideas held in trust for the general benefit of mankind. In other words, I felt that we had attained a moral and intellectual height from which we were bound to proclaim to all as the occasion arose the true message of humanity as embodied in the principles of our own institutions.

There is one very noticeable feature in the American occupation of that archipelago. It arises from contrast with the inspiring motives that have actuated and controlled the action of other branches of the Aryan race, which have worked their way back, coming in the opposite direction. We are planting in those islands imperishable ideas. All other governments that have gone to the East have simply planted trading establishments; they have not materially affected the conditions of the people. They have perfected organizations which have systematized living conditions, but have not planted an idea that would be self-sustaining. There is not a single establishment, in my judgment, in Asia today that would survive five years if the original power which planted it was withdrawn therefrom.

The contrasting idea with our occupation is this: In planting our ideas we plant something that cannot be destroyed. To my mind the archipelago is a fertile soil upon which to plant republicanism. Once planted it can never be eradicated. What the evolution may be through political necessities and expansions is not involved in that branch of the inquiry. Beneficent republican American institutions once planted in the Philippines will last forever, and therefrom will radiate an influence the appreciation of which it is hard to estimate. But that fact in itself is beyond any possibility of dispute. We are planting the best traditions, the best characteristics of Americanism in such a way that they never can be removed from that soil. That in itself seems to me a most inspiring thought. It encouraged me during all my efforts in those islands, even when conditions seemed most disappointing, when the people themselves, not appreciating precisely what the remote consequences of our efforts were going to be, mistrusted us; but that fact was always before me — that going down deep into that fertile soil were the imperishable ideas of Americanism.

Sen. Patterson: Do you mean that the imperishable idea of which you speak is the right of self-government?

Gen. MacArthur: Precisely so; self-government regulated by law as we understand it in this Republic.

Sen. Patterson: Of course you do not mean self-government regulated by some foreign and superior power?

Gen. MacArthur: Well, that is a matter of evolution, Senator. We are putting these institutions there so that they will evolve themselves just as they have here and everywhere else where freedom has flourished.

Sen. Culberson: In South Africa, for instance.

Gen. MacArthur: Here is a group of eight or ten million in a mass of seven or eight hundred million. I have tried to show how the spirit of the nineteenth century got into that little group. That it is there I think is beyond any question, and that it will make it easy for us to organize our institutions there I do not think there is any doubt. But beyond and above that is the magnetic and radiant power that is going to go out of those islands when they once thoroughly understand what we are doing for them and what we intend to do, and that condition is approximating very rapidly.

The value of a true moral or political principle may be tried with absolute certainty upon any people under the sun. Therein I differ a little from some other investigators. I believe those people can be organized, and very rapidly. It is the prerogative of self-government that it adapts itself to every circumstance which can arise. Its institutions, although sometimes defective, are always appropriate and strong, for they exactly represent the living conditions of human life.

The establishment of perfect justice, of perfect liberty, of perfect civil equality, is the very simple secret which will most effectually bring happiness in the East, as it has to these highly favored shores of the Western world. Whatever there is of merit in our institutions will readily plant itself and come forth honorably in new generations among our brethren of the eastern sun, who are now being permeated with the spirit of the American Constitution, which is of such scope and universal application to the affairs of man that under its beneficent folds injustice or oppression are [sic] impossible.

In connection with that idea I would like to report an experience arising from an interview with one of the most eminent men in the Eastern world, who is the general manager of one of the largest financial institutions anywhere. He called on me, and the conversation took a very wide range. Finally he concluded somewhat in this wise. He said:

"You people in America do not appreciate your own industrial strength. I have spent a year in the United States recently. I have been amazed at everything I saw in connection with industrial production. Your progress is so rapid, both in the production of wealth and in increase of population, that you would be a menace to the whole world if your institutions were not beneficent. As far as I am concerned," he said, "I have no apprehension; I believe that wherever the American flag goes mankind will be benefited thereby."

The general conclusion that I draw from the whole preceding discussion is that we are unmistakably the instruments by which great events are being accomplished which may possibly influence the future history of the world to a greater extent than any event since the discovery of America. Inspiration and hope go with our flag. A magnificent and mighty destiny awaits us in the East.

Those were my views when I entered the city of Manila to take the supreme command, and in the light of such views my purpose was to conduct operations in the field relentlessly — with a drastic hand — having always in view the limitations of the laws of war; and, on the other hand, in the civil administration to conciliate, to instruct, to strengthen the efforts of those people toward the organization of their civil government and to attach them to us by a sense of self-interest and gratitude. . . .

. . . [I]n my judgment, from an intimate knowledge of military operations of the islands, from the operations against the Spanish in Manila, until I left the islands on the 4th of July, 1901, I doubt if any war — either international or civil, any war on earth — has been conducted with as much humanity, with as much careful consideration, with as much self-restraint, in view of the character of our adversary, as have been the American operations in the Philippine Archipelago. . . .

The Chairman: What do you think their feelings are toward us?

Gen. MacArthur: They like our institutions. They have some mistrust of us individually, because our deportment is so entirely different from anything they have been familiar with. The Filipino is naturally an exceedingly polite person. The poorest laborer is imbued with that idea of Spanish deportment. The American idea of deportment is not exactly the same thing. So that the first intercourse between the Filipino and the American is apt to lead to misunderstanding.

Sen. Beveridge: Ours is brusque and direct.

Gen. MacArthur: Ours is brusque and direct, a thing that they do not understand at first, but which they begin to understand later on, because that brusqueness is accompanied with friendliness and a neighborly disposition, which. finds expression between the soldiers and natives, in our people helping them whenever they are in distress. A Filipino family in trouble has the sure support of the nearest American soldier.

Sen. Beveridge: When your arms passed on and insurrection no longer existed in any particular locality or district, what is the fact about the people returning to their fields and homes and transacting the business and labors of everyday life in peace and freedom?

Gen. MacArthur: They returned in large numbers.

Sen. Beveridge: And went to work?

Gen. MacArthur: In fact, whenever I invited them to come back they always did.

Sen. Beveridge: And went to work?

Gen. MacArthur: Yes. That was noticeably so in the towns northeast of Manila immediately after the first outbreak. They of course had been misinformed and were apprehensive, and when we entered the town they all fled; but on our invitation they always returned.

Sen. Beveridge: What is the fact about their having fled and about the insurrection itself having been aided and maintained by false reports of its leaders concerning us — our methods and purposes?

Gen. MacArthur: That obtained to a very great extent; not only the Filipinos, but the Spaniards had ——

Sen. Carmack: What was the character of those false reports?

Gen. MacArthur (continuing): Talked of our peculiarities and stated many things that were not true, and the people were very apprehensive until they came in contact with us.

Sen. Beveridge: And then they found this to be untrue and returned to their homes and industries?

Gen. MacArthur: Yes. . . .

The Filipino people certainly have rudimentary republican ideas and aspirations, and are therefore in an essentially plastic condition, which, under the tuitionary control of the United States, in my opinion, would admit of rapid molding of the body public into a consistent, self-supporting commonwealth. On the other hand, while the existence of elementary republicanism is apparent to the sympathetic investigator, it is equally apparent that even the most advanced thinkers among the Filipinos have no conception whatever of the practical mechanical methods whereby the results they are all anxious to attain can be successfully accomplished.

American withdrawal from the islands, therefore, would, in my opinion, result in permanent failure of republicanism in the East, and the devastation of the archipelago by internecine and fratricidal war, which would continue indefinitely until suppressed by some external force. That such force would be applied there can be no doubt.

The incalculable and indescribable value of the archipelago, strategi-

cally and commercially, has attracted the attention of constructive states-
men throughout the world. Many nations are looking in that direction
with longing eyes. The islands in case of our withdrawal would unquestionably become the theater of gigantic political and warlike operations.
The inevitable collision which would result from such an American
policy could not be confined. It would resound on all the shores of the
Pacific and affect the commerce of the world. It would bring the powers
of the world face to face and prematurely initiate a struggle for supremacy
in the East from the consequence of which America could only protect
herself by participation in the general conflict which would result directly
from her own efforts to escape from the pressure of circumstances which
are carrying her to a magnificent destiny. We would thus not only sac-
rifice the Filipino people, but would bring upon ourselves staggering
responsibilities, in respect of which the present problems in the Philippines would appear as mere child's play.

In the belief that history never goes backward, a broad generalization
is reached to the effect that enlightened self-interest, sound economy,
and pure morals agree in their judgments, and corroborate each other,
and suggest that we must retain the archipelago as a tuitionary annex; that
there we must plant our institutions; there we must contest for commercial power, and perhaps combat for political supremacy.

To overcome the inherent difficulties of the situation will, of course,
require the most profound efforts of constructive statesmanship, but
the event of introducing our civilization, our institutions, and our commerce into Asia is fraught with such gigantic consequences that it is calculated to fix the attention of the most careless observer and to warm
the fancy of the most indifferent.

That is the general basis upon which I reach the conclusion that chaos
would result in the Philippine Islands if we left them.

Sen. Carmack: The question was raised here some time ago with reference to the introduction of a witness and it was said that opinions were
not competent as evidence and ought not to be introduced as evidence
before this committee. Now, I have been very much interested myself in
General MacArthur's views, but it seems to me that if that rule is to be
made it ought to be adhered to. If argument is to be made before the
committee and received in these hearings as testimony it ought to be open
to the other side, to people who have different views, to present other
arguments in the way of testimony.

Sen. Dietrich: I should think it would be allowable to have the conclusions of men who have been on the ground and speak from facts.

Sen. Carmack: That has absolutely nothing to do with a great deal of
the testimony we have had before the committee. A great deal of General
MacArthur's argument has been based not upon any personal observation or experience of his own, but simply upon the geographical position

of the islands with reference to other countries of the East and to general conditions which a man does not need to go to the Philippines to form an opinion about. He has spoken of the importance of the islands from a military and strategic point of view, and from a commercial point of view. Now, I would just like to know from the committee whether or not it would be competent to introduce some other witness who has not been to the Philippine Islands but who could give an opinion as a military man, as a student of strategy and of conditions affecting the military strength and weakness of a nation; and then a man who has made a study of commercial conditions with respect to the Philippine Islands; whether or not it would be competent to bring such witnesses before the committee in order to make statements on the contrary side.

Now, the fact that a man has been in the Philippine Islands ought to qualify him as a witness to anything that may have occurred under his observation, to anything that has been a matter of experience with him; but it does not make it any more competent for such a man to lay a philosophical dissertation before the committee, or a prepared study in regard to questions of strategy, or trade, or commerce, that have nothing to do with his personal observations in the islands, than anybody else, and if such argument is competent before this committee, to bring witnesses here simply because they have been in the Philippines, to present elaborate arguments in favor of permanent holding of the Philippines in order to establish our power in the Orient and to strengthen ourselves from a military point of view; I say, if a man can do that simply because he has been to the Philippines; then a man who has never been to the Philippine Islands ought to be allowed to present views to the contrary, if he is otherwise a qualified witness, a man who has made a study of military affairs.

So far as I am concerned I want to protest right now against presenting elaborate arguments before this committee for no other purpose except to sustain a certain policy, not testimony at all in the ordinary sense of the word, but simply an elaborate argument in favor of a certain policy, and an argument that is not based upon personal observation or upon personal experience in the Philippine Islands. . . .

Sen. Allison (acting chairman): Your view is to enter a protest against the answer of General MacArthur, as not pertinent to the inquiry in which we are engaged?

Sen. Carmack: No; I do not say that it is not pertinent.

Sen. Allison: Or if pertinent, then we must go beyond and ask our opinions elsewhere?

Sen. Carmack: That is my opinion.

Sen. Patterson: When you find a man competent?

Sen. Carmack: Yes.

The scope of these hearings has never been defined except the committee can admit anything or exclude anything it pleases. Before other committees we frequently do have arguments and opinions presented, similar, perhaps, to the statement of General MacArthur, delivered, as his was, in a very thoughtful and scholarly manner, and I am not complaining in the least that his testimony is not proper before this committee; but if it is I say a great deal of it is not based at all upon his personal observations in the Philippine Islands. It is based on his knowledge as a student of conditions.

Now, if other men of character and standing have made a study of conditions there, although they have not been on the ground, it seems to me it would be entirely proper for this committee to hear them. Suppose there was another man, a military man, who believed that the holding of the Philippine Islands would be a weakness to the United States. Suppose there is a man who believes, as Admiral Sampson declared, that it would greatly increase our dangers of a foreign war, and that it would be a sort of weakness instead of strength. A man may not have been to the Philippine Islands and still may be as competent to speak as General MacArthur or anybody else who has been there.

Sen. Patterson: Referring to the answer that you have just read, if I understand you, you regard the Philippine Islands as of the utmost importance to the United States, both from a commercial and a strategical standpoint. Indeed, that is the most potential thought that you have advanced in connection with the retention of those islands.

Gen. MacArthur: No; not to my mind.

Sen. Patterson: Let us have the most potential.

Gen. MacArthur: My mind is more definitely fixed on the evolution of republicanism in the East as an incident of our occupation than it is on the strategical and commercial importance, although both are of such a character that they corroborate each other and dovetail into each other.

Sen. Patterson: Then I do understand you to convey the idea that the principal end to be attained by the retention of the Philippine Islands is the initiation of and propagation of republican principles in the East?

Gen. MacArthur: The investigation of that branch of the subject has been much more interesting to me than that of the material branch.

Sen. Patterson: Then the chief object to be attained, according to your notion, by the retention of the Philippines, is the education of the Asiatics in the principles of self-government and the doctrine of personal liberty?

Gen. MacArthur: That I should say would be one of the chief objects. I would not like to record myself absolutely on that point ——

Sen. Patterson: Then, next to that, strategic and commercial benefit?

Gen. MacArthur: They all combine in such a way as to form a unit, and without giving prominence as to importance I would simply say that in my own investigation the psychological side of the question appeals to me strongly.

Sen. Patterson: It is your idea, then, that if a cult with your views should conclude that the ownership of Japan would give to the United States a more advantageous position in the East for the purpose of propagating these educational ideas, that we should go and capture them and subjugate them that we might get that seat of learning?

Gen. MacArthur: By no means, Senator. But if Japan should come into our hands in the clean manner, with the clean conscience, with the pure morals, and the definite purposes that we have in the Philippine Islands, I should say, keep it by all means.

Sen. Patterson: Very well. Do I understand your claim of right and duty to retain the Philippine Islands is based upon the proposition that they have come to us upon the basis of pure morals, honorable dealing, and unassailable national integrity?

Gen. MacArthur: That proposition is not questioned by anybody in the world, excepting a few people in the United States.

Sen. Patterson: Will you kindly answer the question? Whether or not a statement is questioned or not is not answering it. I am asking whether it is your view.

Gen. MacArthur: It is, most decidedly.

Sen. Patterson: Whether it is or not will be a matter of discussion, but not here or with you.

Now, General, in the preparation of the answer which you read this morning did you proceed upon this theory, that there are two schools of thought in the United States, one that is governed by what we might call scruples of conscience as to the justice of the course of the American government in dealing with the Filipinos and the Philippine Islands, and that it is essential to impress upon the public mind for the purpose of combating, whatever their views may be, the idea that nothing but anarchy could result should the American troops withdraw, and, having established that, then the commercial and strategical elements of this question would ultimately prevail in the American mind? Was that the theory upon which you have framed the answer you have read?

Gen. MacArthur: I will have to ask the stenographer to read that question.

Sen. Allison: I would like to hear that question again.

(The stenographer repeated the question of Senator Patterson.)

Gen. MacArthur: My theory, embodied in that answer, embraces all the ideas of good morals, conscience, and material interests, and the remote political consequences to the country. As to the scruples of conscience, I do not understand what the question implies. So far as my own conscience is concerned I have examined that pretty carefully, and my views express my conscientious belief that our presence there is going to be an unmitigated benefaction to the Filipino people, and that the consequence of holding the islands will produce vast material benefit to the whole country that will act and react, and we will be benefited, and the Filipino people will be benefited, and that is what I meant by the original proposition ——

Sen. Patterson: Do you mean the Filipino people that are left alive?

Gen. MacArthur: I mean the Filipino people.

Sen. Patterson: You mean those that are left alive?

Gen. MacArthur: I mean the 10,000,000 people living in the archipelago.

Sen. Patterson: You mean those left alive after they have been subjugated?

Gen. MacArthur: I do not admit that there has been any unusual destruction of life in the Philippine Islands. The destruction is simply the incident of war, and of course it embraces a very small percentage of the total population, which is dense and consists of many millions.

Sen. Patterson: Thirty-three and one-half percent of one province.

Gen. MacArthur: If you prefer to believe that, all right; I do not accept that as true.

Sen. Patterson: We have as good a right to believe that from an American officer who has been the civil governor of the province, and who is there in the province, as we have to accept your statement, have we not?

Gen. MacArthur: You can believe what you wish, and I will believe what I wish; that is all.

Sen. Burrows: You must remember that the loss of life was from disease, as the governor of the province stated, and not from war.

Sen. Patterson: Disease, starvation, and war — all the result of the war. . . .

Testimony of Ewell S. Otis *

Sen. Patterson: What is the character of the bulk of the Philippine people; taking the people as a body, how would you classify them?

Gen. Otis: There is everything in the Philippines, from a high state of civilization to the most degraded barbarity; you will find everything there.

Sen. Patterson: But I mean among the Tagalos and the Visayans, not the Moros; how would you class the general run of those people?

Gen. Otis: A great mass of the people are ignorant and very superstitious.

* See above, page 31.

Sen. Patterson: What else would you say about them — anything good?

Gen. Otis: Anything good?

Sen. Patterson: Yes; any good traits?

Gen. Otis: Yes; they like to remain at home and till the soil and would be quiet if they were let alone.

Sen. Carmack: Peaceably disposed, but easily wrought up.

Sen. Allison: Controlled by leaders or by men ——

Gen. Otis: Yes.

Sen. Patterson: Then the people, so far as their public conduct is concerned, would depend largely upon attitude and the desires of the leaders?

Gen. Otis: Yes.

Sen. Patterson: That is the case in a good many countries, is it not? For instance, Mexico and the South American republics?

Gen. Otis: Yes; it is the case in Mexico.

Sen. Patterson: Where there is that population, or something similar to it?

Gen. Otis: There is some sort of peonage among them that exists, you might say.

Sen. Patterson: Take the general run of them; are they reasonably honest people?

Gen. Otis: I should not care to trust them; I do not think so. Why should they be?

Sen. Patterson: I am not asking you why. Good people, who have, perhaps, as great a knowledge of them as you have, think they are.

Gen. Otis: I mean to say that they have been under Spanish domination for a great many years, of course, and they have concealed their intentions. They have concealed their actions, to a certain extent. Any people who have been under such domination for three or four hundred years, under a government of that kind, will develop secrecy.

Sen. Patterson: How are they in reference to the payment of their debts, big or little?

Gen. Otis: Oh, they are honest about that. You can trust a Filipino, as far as that is concerned, but they are generally about a year or two behind. . . .

Sen. Patterson: . . . General, you state that the great bulk of Filipino people are farmers, are connected with the land and tilling the soil?

Gen. Otis: Yes, sir; in small holdings, which, in many cases, are owned by large proprietors.

Sen. Patterson: They have families?

Gen. Otis: Yes.

Sen. Patterson: There is an ordinary degree of family loyalty and affection existing in those families, is there not?

Gen. Otis: That is very strong.

Sen. Patterson: They have been subjected to governmental rule for a great many years, have they not?

Gen. Otis: To domination.

Sen. Patterson: I do not care what you call it.

Gen. Otis: Now, If I might be allowed to speak, the communities in the Philippines have developed from the tribal, the family relation entirely. You will find that each of those little barrios that are connected with the municipality, although it may be eight or ten miles removed from the city itself, consists of a little band or tribe, which formerly consisted of a family and which is controlled to a great extent by what you might call the chief of the tribe. This is the way all the suburbs grew up around Manila.

Sen. Patterson: There are hundreds and hundreds of municipalities in the islands, are there not?

Gen. Otis: There are hundreds of them; yes.

Sen. Patterson: And they have their municipal officials, have they not?

Gen. Otis: Yes.

Sen. Patterson: They have a system of laws, have they not?

Gen. Otis: They have a system of regulations prescribed by the Spanish government.

Sen. Patterson: Very well, they have a system of laws or regulations, I care not what you call them. Until they arose they lived practically as law-abiding communities, did they not?

Sen. Beveridge: That relates to a condition before he was there.

The Chairman: What was the question?

Sen. Patterson: Until they arose in rebellion against Spain.

Gen. Otis: No. The chiefs of the provinces were Spanish officers. There were what we called nineteen free provinces, and they were under the control of certain officers of the Spanish army and with a superior control emanating from Manila. It was military control through the entire islands.

Sen. Patterson: General, I am told that until about ten or eleven years ago there were few if any troops in the Philippine Islands?

Gen. Otis: And they mostly native troops.

Sen. Patterson: That is your understanding, is it not?

Gen. Otis: Certainly; they had certain corps of engineers and so on. They probably had about 5,000 European troops there altogether.

Sen. Patterson: Now, General, we learn that they rose against the friars. Is that not some evidence that they are not altogether slaves to the religion?

Gen. Otis: The church questions are many, and go back into the entire history ——

Sen. Patterson: I am not asking you to do that. They expelled the friars or the great bulk of them, did they not?

Gen. Otis: They expelled the friars who had large holdings. That is, they expelled four of the communities; the other four, who held no property whatever, they did not expel; and they have always been acceptable to them. It was only the orders who held the large amount of property, that is all who were expelled.

Sen. Patterson: We have it from the history of that country that these friars were guilty of treating them in a grossly improper way. I believe the testimony taken before the Philippine Commission disclosed that many of the friars were extremely immoral; that they levied heavy tribute upon the people of the Philippine Islands for the purpose of many of the ceremonies of the church, such as marriage and the like. These people, by reason of those things committed at the hands of the priests of their church, arose against them and drove them out. That is true, is it not — drove the bulk of them out. Now, I want to ask you ——

Gen. Otis: Those belonging to those four orders.

Sen. Patterson: Now, I want to know whether, in your judgment, that was an evidence of unfitness for self-government, or whether it was an evidence of independence of church rule, when the church rule, or those who were to enforce the rules of the church, were guilty of wrong and oppression.

Gen. Otis: No. One great trouble arose between the clergy proper and the friar orders. The Filipino clergy were not allowed to perform certain sacraments in the church. The friars were allowed to perform those sacraments to the exclusion of the Filipino clergy; whereas, in no country of Europe can they perform those sacraments except by special permission. They performed them there in the Philippines.

If the Filipino people had continued in the same state of ignorance in which they were for a great many years there probably would have been no trouble so far as the friars were concerned, but all the education they have, all their acquirements, have been given them by the friar orders. Their men were most excellently educated. From those representative men they acquired their sentiments. In my mind they have been greatly abused by the friar orders.

Sen. Patterson: Do you find honest, intelligent, capable Filipino gentlemen throughout the islands?

Gen. Otis: No; I could not say that. I had a great deal of trouble in filling some of the offices. I only appointed upon the recommendation of Filipinos whom I could trust, and in a number of instances they were deceived. We were deceived in persons we appointed to judicial positions, especially in the city of Manila itself. One we had to remove. That has prevailed in the north to a certain extent. I had to remove certain officials in the customhouses who were guilty of peculations, but I believe that with care we can find a great many broad people who will make excellent officials.

Sen. Patterson: You were dealing with the people, at the time you were there, under exceptional, and very exceptional, conditions, were you not?

Gen. Otis: Yes.

Sen. Patterson: There was a rebellion first against Spanish and then against American government there. For whatever reason, dissatisfaction was, at first, at least, very widely diffused throughout the people of the islands. You naturally, when you went to treat with those people, regarded most of them with grave doubt and suspicion, did you not?

Gen. Otis: No; I had the assistance of a great many Filipinos, and without their assistance I never could have succeeded there.

Sen. Patterson: Do you say, then, that you did not, in dealing with the Filipinos under those exceptional conditions, naturally regard at first, until they were tested and tried, most of the Filipinos that you dealt with with doubt and suspicion?

Gen. Otis: Not as much as I should have done, because I was deceived a great many times, and I exercised more caution after I had been there a few weeks.

Sen. Patterson: You have been deceived a great many times also in your life in one direction or another, have you not?

Gen. Otis: I am not going to confess that; no. . . .

Sen. Dubois: Now, General, you have stated that white labor is out of the question, and that the Filipino labor is inadequate and insufficient, and that there must be some other labor, either Chinese or coolies or Japanese.

Gen. Otis: Asiatic labor; yes.

Sen. Dubois: Now, we intend to exploit those islands; that is our object. To do that we must have a good deal of labor if our capital goes over there. Now, when they raise their sugar, do you mean to say that that sugar will not come in competition with our sugar? Do you mean that the laborers raising that sugar in the Philippine Islands will not be in competition with our laborers here who are raising sugar?

Gen. Otis: It depends entirely on whether you keep up the present tariff provisions; if we have free and unlimited trade it might come in competition with our sugar interests in this country.

Sen. Dubois: Suppose we erected the highest protection walls we could and excluded all of their products entirely from this country, would not those products go to other countries?

Gen. Otis: Yes, certainly; just as they have.

Sen. Dubois: Would not they come in competition, then, with ours?

Gen. Otis: Oh, well ——

Sen. Dubois: Would they not in the other markets of the world?

Gen. Otis: I have not considered the question to that great extent.

Sen. Dubois: But you made a flat answer that even if this was so it would not come in competition with our labor.

Gen. Otis: Our labor in the Philippines, as I understand it.

Sen. Dubois: Oh.

Sen. Beveridge: What I had in mind was this ——

Gen. Otis: White labor in the Philippines?

Sen. Beveridge: Of course I was not through, but I am very glad to have Senator Dubois or any other Senator interrupt me.

Sen. Dubois: I beg your pardon. I thought you were through.

Testimony of William Howard Taft *

Sen. Carmack: As a general proposition, will it not be necessary to pay large salaries generally in the Philippine Islands in order to get first-class men to leave the United States and go to the Philippine Islands?

Gov. Taft: Yes, sir; it undoubtedly will.

Sen. Carmack: Low salaries would only be tempting to a low order of men; I mean men of inferior order of ability.

Gov. Taft: Yes, sir; it forms a temptation to men whose moral stamina is not very stiff and resisting to temptation to piece out their salaries with illegal collections and that kind of thing.

Sen. Carmack: In other words, it puts the offices in the hands of mere adventurers?

Gov. Taft: Yes, sir. Under the Spanish rule the salaries of the Spanish officials were so low that you can hardly credit the low salaries that were paid to them, and you cannot understand it either unless you add to it the fact that in almost every instance the compensation of the official was largely made up by illegal assessments and "squeezes," as they are called in the Orient.

Sen. Carmack: The opportunity for that and the temptation will always be great there, will it not?

Gov. Taft: Yes, sir. I think if you will consult our first report you will see the dangers that we may reasonably anticipate in a government out there; and upon those dangers we found the urgent necessity for the maintenance of the strictest kind of civil service reform system.

It is quite true that Americans, removed 10,000 miles away from home influences, from the natural restraints that come from being among neighbors and being with people whose opinion they value, may be more easily led to yield to temptation than at home. That is the difficulty of the organization of government. That is the necessity for the prompt arrest and the prompt prosecution of Americans who are faithless to their trusts there, with much more vigor indeed than that need be used against natives.

* See above, page 35.

That is one reason; and then another reason is that we regard it as of the utmost importance that the Americans should maintain a high standard, with a view of showing to the Filipinos the possibility of an honest administration of government — something that they have never known under Spanish rule, and that they never knew under their own rule for the eight months during which they had a government under Aguinaldo.

It is almost impossible to impress on the average Filipino of intelligence and education the idea that an office is to be managed for anything but the personal emolument of the person holding it, and it is only by example, in our judgment, that that can be eradicated from their minds. . . .

Sen. Carmack: I wish to recur for a moment to a line of inquiry on which I had started Saturday when the adjournment came. At the close of your statement on Saturday you spoke of the indolence of the people in the Philippines as a reason for disposing of lands in large bodies instead of selling small farms to actual settlers. Would not this constitutional indolence of the people be as serious an obstacle to the development of the country in the one case as in the other; that is, if the development depends on native labor?

Gov. Taft: I think not, but I do not think that your statement in that respect is quite an accurate review of my remarks. What I was meeting was the suggestion that all the land might be disposed of to actual settlers. Of course the example before us of this country at once presents itself, where a very large part of the public domain (I think I am not in error) was disposed of to actual settlers. If the same condition prevailed in the Philippines, the suggestion would have much more weight than it really does, in view of the lack of enterprise of the individual Filipino and the indolence to which I have referred. . . .

Sen. Carmack: I wish to ask you whether you think it will be necessary to throw open the doors to Chinese immigration in order to secure a supply of efficient and helpful labor for the development of the country?

Gov. Taft: I am profoundly hopeful that it will not be. Pressure has been brought to bear upon the Commission to recommend such a policy. In certain parts of the archipelago the admission of Chinese labor without permission to trade, keeping him a laborer, and requiring those who bring him in to take him out again, may possibly aid, and would doubtless aid, in the development of islands like Mindanao, where the population is scarce, but in Luzon, in Panay, in Negros, in the thickly populated islands, I am now hopeful that we can gradually give the people a motive for labor and that they can be so encouraged that their labor will be more efficient than it now is.

Of course we must take into consideration that the time now is after four years of war. That always, I think (possibly not in the case of the

South after the war, but generally), induces habits of indolence, because during a war there is a suspension of industry, and industry is a matter of habit which can be lost or gained, I presume. There is that disadvantage which the present Filipino laborer has.

Then I think when the contractors for labor understand the Filipino character better and arrange the hours and methods of labor to suit the views of the laborer when it will not interfere with their efficiency, they may be able to secure better results.

I say so because I think the differing results secured by different army officers who have been engaged in employing labor and by different civilians who have been employed in engaging labor show that there is a good deal in the management, and that when more is learned and more experience is had better results may be secured. That there are enough Filipino laborers, if they will labor, is undoubted. . . .

Sen. Carmack: Is it not true that one of the great obstacles to the pacification of the islands has been, and is, the fear of bringing Chinese labor to the country, and the fear of sudden and excessive exploitation, and the belief that the United States want the islands purely for purposes of such exploitation?

Gov. Taft: Certainly there has been, if one can judge by the proclamations of the insurgents and by the statements of insurgent leaders, a very considerable attempt to make the public believe that that is the purpose of the Americans; and from that fact you may infer that a great many people have thought so. Now, with respect to the effect of Chinese importation, possibly that goes with it.

Sen. Carmack: What is that?

Gov. Taft: With respect to the effect of allowing the importation of Chinese, that may go with it as part of the charges of future exploitation. General MacArthur's view of the proposed importation of Chinese labor was expressed in a telegram — I think a telegram — to the Secretary of War, in which he made it somewhat more immediately serious, I thought, than anything that we saw or that I have seen there would justify.

The Chairman: The Chinese are not coming in as a matter of fact? They are prohibited now?

Gov. Taft: They have been since I have been there, with some few immaterial exceptions.

Sen. Patterson: Are Chinese prohibited from coming in by law or by order of the military?

Gov. Taft: By order. That is law.

Sen. Patterson: Whose order?

Gov. Taft: By order of General Otis.

Sen. Patterson: Not by any act of the Commission?

Gov. Taft: No, sir. By virtue of the instructions all of the general orders of the military governor continue as law until amended by the Commission. That is the case, for instance, with the civil marriage, which we had up the other day, and so with respect to many other subjects.

Sen. Carmack: General MacArthur says: "In this connection it may not be improper to state that one of the greatest difficulties attending military efforts to tranquillize the people of the archipelago arises from their dread of sudden and excessive exploitation, which they fear would defraud them of their natural patrimony and at the same time relegate them to a status of social and political inferiority."

Again, he says: "If a spirit of Philippine speculation should seize the public mind in the United States and be emphasized by means of grants, concessions, and special franchises for the purpose of quick exploitation, the political situation and permanent interests of all concerned might be seriously jeopardized."

Gov. Taft: That is the danger of too sudden exploitation.

The Chairman: Has the Commission ever proposed to admit Chinese?

Gov. Taft: No, sir.

Sen. Carmack: I know that.

Gov. Taft: No action has ever been taken by the Commission on the subject.

Sen. Carmack: You spoke of the insurgents making efforts to create a certain impression. I will ask you if the people there could not find abundant opportunities for such dread in the general tone of the speeches and newspaper articles in the United States advocating the retention of the Philippines? Have not those articles and speeches dwelt a great deal more upon the profits we are going to make by the exploitation of the country than they have upon the benefits the Filipinos are to derive from our government? Do you not think that is true?

Gov. Taft: I am not an expert on what has been going on in the American political arena since I have been in the Philippines, for the reason that when papers come to you thirty days late there is a great deal that you skip, and after a time you really do not keep up with the course of public opinion here.

Sen. Carmack: I will suppose a case then.

Gov. Taft: We have been criticized severely — we are criticized in every way — and I think I can refer you to an article in an American newspaper in Manila, on the ground that we are always legislating for the Filipino and that the American comes second in our attention.

Sen. Carmack: The Americans over there are getting very impatient?

Gov. Taft: And then on this side we are charged with oppressing the Filipino. So we are between the devil and the deep sea.

Sen. Carmack: How much longer do you think you can live under those circumstances?

Gov. Taft: We have to struggle to get along.

Sen. Carmack: I was going to suppose a case to you. Let us suppose that these speeches and articles ——

Gov. Taft: I wish to say this seriously, if I may. I think our position in the Philippines toward the Filipino people, and the anxiety we have expressed and I hope have shown in the legislation we have passed, to aid the Filipino people have given a great many of them a confidence that we are trying to do the best we can for them.

Sen. Carmack: I was not speaking of the action of the Commission.

Gov. Taft: The fear of exploitation is undoubtedly one that has been impressed by the insurgents and by others who did not sympathize with us, as part of that great body of representations, some reasonable, with some foundation, and others utterly unreasonable, which have been carried before the ignorant of the Filipino people with a view of raising their prejudice against us.

Now, what you say about exploitation is not unreasonable because of the expressions that Americans themselves use frequently. On the other hand, let me give you an example, and I think it is relevant, as showing some of the ignorance of the ignorant people of the Philippines.

A Filipino gentleman told me himself of an experience he had in Batangas; and Batangas possibly is a province in which education has been rather more extended than in other parts of the islands. He said he was driving in a carromata from where his estate or his wife's estate was to Manila. He talks Tagalog; it is his native tongue. He said he "always talked with the common people whom he meets. Batangas is a great province for horses or for ponies, for they are all ponies there."

The driver turned to him and said, "When the American government is established here and the *Americanos* are in control, how far shall I be allowed to go out of one mile square, for I understand that is the regular policy of the American government to keep us in a certain area. Secondly, what kind of a cart, wagon, or carromata shall I have to help pull, because I understand the Americans are buying up all the horses in the Philippines with a view to killing them, so that the Filipinos shall be made the beasts of burden."

Now, that came in this way. Horses have doubled in value. The Spaniards, when we first came there, taking advantage of the fact that in Japan and in China the jinrikisha was used, in which men are the method of propulsion, issued caricatures showing Uncle Sam in a carromata with a Filipino between the shafts, and just as soon as the Spaniards went out of the islands the same caricature was used in proclamations of the insurgents.

Now the belief of that, unreasonable as it is, is to be classed with the belief in exploitation, not that one is unreasonable and the other more reasonable, but it shows how that kind of thing can be brought to the people.

Sen. Carmack: It shows how an idea with a foundation may be exaggerated?

Gov. Taft: Yes, sir. . . .

Sen. Carmack: What I was going to ask you a while ago was this: Suppose the speeches and articles and the published statements to which I referred, which you say you have not closely read, coming from leading representatives of the so-called expansion policy in the United States, express utter contempt for the character of the whole Filipino people, morally, mentally, industrially, and otherwise, declaring in substance that they are utterly unfit to have any share in the government of their country or to play any important part in its industrial development; suppose that distinguished United States Senators have spoken to this effect and have said that the people of the country were intellectually on a level with carabao bulls; and suppose that an ex-member of the Philippine Commission had said the only question for us to consider is whether we can make money and profit out of the islands, and if we cannot those people may cut each other's throats for all we care, is it not likely that such expressions as those have helped to create the impression of which General MacArthur speaks, and thereby placed obstacles in the way of pacification?

Gov. Taft: Any article which would have the effect of arousing the Filipino public against the Americans usually finds its way into the Philippine Islands.

Sen. Carmack: Speeches of that character have been circulated over there?

Gov. Taft: I have no doubt they have been. I cannot remember individual instances, but I know that when the visiting Congressmen were there, there was one member of the delegation who expressed very emphatically an unfavorable view of the character of the Filipino people, and that was made the subject of very considerable discussion in the Filipino press.

Sen. Carmack: With a bad effect?

Gov. Taft: Yes, with a bad effect. The Filipino people or the educated ones among them are in many respects a sensitive people and they naturally resent an impeachment of their intelligence, and they do not like to be characterized as savages.

Sen. Carmack: Or bulls?

Gov. Taft: Or bulls. The course of the Commission has been one of sympathetic effort to help them and not to hurt their feelings. I said to the delegation of 3,000 people, representing the Federal party, that came up to Malacanang to say goodby to me, and I say it here, that I am exceedingly fond of quite a number of Filipino gentlemen with whom I have come in somewhat intimate relations, and that I like the whole people, without being blind to their serious defects, many of which are due to the environment, social and political, which has been presented by their history of three hundred years, but that I hope, with a different environment, socially and politically, many of those defects can be eradicated.

The educated Filipinos are not blind to the defects of their people, and often in the course of conversation with prominent men they are severer in condemnation of their own people and in contemptuous reference to some of their defects than any member of the Commission or anybody engaged in sympathy with our work. That arises, of course, from particular instances which at the time impressed them with those defects of the uneducated.

The Chairman: I wish to ask you in this connection what is the effect of speeches and articles and pamphlets, which have appeared in this country encouraging the Filipinos to resist the authority of the United States. What effect have they had?

Gov. Taft: Of course they have been a great obstacle to the success of our efforts there.

Sen. Carmack: The point I wish to make is that we are not the only sinners.

Gov. Taft: That general subject I had expected to come in a little later on. We have gotten off a little from what I had expected to take up.

Sen. Carmack: I wish to finish with two or three more questions, with the permission of the committee, and then I will not recur to this subject again.

Sen. Rawlins: Those who have expressed friendly feelings toward the Filipinos have not been the ones who have incited them to insurrection against this government? . . .

Gov. Taft: It is a little hard to discriminate between people. Those who in this country have attacked the policy of the United States as infamous and murderous have certainly not helped us in what we are attempting to do in the islands. It seems to me there is the middle course. . . .

I think there were some other gentlemen who came there who possibly were not so guarded in their expressions. Certainly no objection could be taken to what Senator Bacon said with reference to its effect on the situation. He expressed great friendship for the Filipino people, and I am sure he has it.

Sen. Rawlins: To illustrate, speeches giving the character of the Filipino people, as we understand it, which is not unfriendly, recognizing their aspirations, as we understand them, not encouraging them to resist the United States by force of arms, but appealing to the people of the United States to accord them justice and gratify their aspirations under proper conditions — do you concede that any such line of advocacy and policy tends to incite those people to insurrection?

Gov. Taft: Not put just in that way.

Sen. Rawlins: That is the way I put it. Of course I do not put it in any other way. I should like you to answer the question.

Gov. Taft: I could select some speeches that perhaps you would think come under that description which I would not think would come under it, but if you will permit me, I would rather not be drawn into a discussion of this subject until I can treat it altogether, if I may. . . .

Sen. Patterson: Take Senator Hoar's speech the other night, full of sympathy for the Filipinos, and expressing the opinion that they were entitled to their independence. Along that line I wish to ask you, Governor ——

The Chairman: It seems to me it is not fair to ask the governor about a speech made by a Senator in the Senate.

Sen. Patterson: I should like to be given the privilege of framing my question. If anybody should circulate that speech in the Philippines, would he not be subject to arrest and imprisonment?

Sen. Allison: I object to that question.

The Chairman: I object to such a question, relating to a specific speech made in the Senate.

Sen. Hale: When we come to consider the effect of the statutes and the force of them and the Governor gives us his opinion of sedition and the necessity for such laws, and the question of their application, I take it a question of that kind may be asked. But I would say ——

Sen. Allison: Is it proper to ask the Governor to give an opinion about a speech made on the floor of the Senate?

The Chairman: Yes; what Senator Hoar said on the floor. I think that is a question with respect to which we have not a right to expect an answer from the Governor.

Sen. Hale: The Governor might decline, of course.

Sen. Patterson: It will serve, by illustration, to show the real meaning and effect of the laws that have been mentioned.

The Chairman: I do not think it is right to oblige or attempt to oblige Governor Taft to pass on speeches delivered in the Senate by members of the Senate. I think it would put him in a very false and unfair position.

Sen. Hale: Undoubtedly; but that will be up when we come to consider the statute.

Sen. Patterson: I suppose the opinion of the Chairman will prevail.

Gov. Taft: What I ask now is that I be not drawn into that subject, where one remark may be twisted to mean something else, but that I may be allowed to make a complete statement in my own way with respect to the conditions there, to justify those statutes and explain their operation.

Sen. Hale: I think that is right: I do not think we ought to press the Governor on that now. . . .

Gov. Taft: On the general question of the honesty of the Filipino, you will find some very exaggerated and extreme statements in which I do not concur — for instance, that they are all dishonest and that they are all treacherous. That thievery prevails to an embarrassing extent among the Filipino servants would seem to follow from the everyday arrests that you hear of. That there are Filipinos who make very faithful and very honest servants is true. So it is a little hard to make a general statement on the subject.

The charge of treachery against them is unjust, I think, in this respect: They are an oriental people, and the oriental believes in saying to the person with whom he is talking what that person would like to hear. That is the tendency of the race. You graft onto that the Spanish tendency to superlatives — and the orientals themselves have some such tendencies without the Spanish mixture — and a Filipino will talk to you in language so that, if you do not weigh it in the light of that trait, you are quite certain to misunderstand him, and be misled by what he says. He, on the other hand — and it is fair to take his standpoint in judging whether he is deceitful or not — supposes that the person to whom he is speaking understands the medium in which you are to interpret what he says, and that has given rise, it seems to me, to charges of deceitfulness where they probably ought not to be made.

Then, too, the position of men in municipal governments serving under the American sovereignty who have been detected in assisting insurgents by information and contributions has been made the basis for a charge of treachery against the race. Those men were in a situation which explains their so-called treachery without making it necessary to indict and arraign a whole people. If they did not furnish the information, or if they did not make the contributions, they were subject to assassination by the agents of the insurgent soldiers, and many of them were assassinated. If they did and were detected by the Americans, they were imprisoned, and they preferred to run the risk of imprisonment. I do not think under such circumstances two-faced conduct ought to be made the basis for an arraignment of the entire race.

Now with those qualifications I do not think that the Filipino differs from others who have tendency to err and to misrepresent. All the human race is subject to those weaknesses.

Sen. Patterson: Do you not find the worst development in Manila and in and about the large cities?

Gov. Taft: I suppose it is true in every country that the most vicious gather in the large cities, and it is certainly true in the Philippines.

Sen. Patterson: So that the visitor going to the Philippines and keeping in the cities is not apt to get a proper appreciation of the Tagal or Filipino character as a whole?

Gov. Taft: The same defects in his observation occur there as in any other country.

Sen. Patterson: This document states — and that is the only reason I call your attention to it — speaking of the Tagals, as follows: "Those in and around Manila are a degeneration of the race from foreign admixture."

Gov. Taft: No; I would not say that. You will find the admixture of the races throughout the islands. The mestizos are not by any means confined to Manila.

Sen. Carmack: What is the number of mestizos in the archipelago?

Gov. Taft: You cannot tell. I think there is an admixture of probably Japanese in Ilocano and of the Chinese in Pampangan. There are a great many Chinese mestizos in Iloilo. There is no means of knowing what is the distribution. . . .

Testimony of David P. Barrows *

The Chairman: Mr. Barrows, you have been in the Philippine Islands?
Mr. Barrows: Yes, sir; I have been there since October, 1900.

Sen. Hale: Will you let Mr. Barrows state where he is from?

Mr. Barrows: California. I am a native of Illinois, but California has been my home all my life.

The Chairman: What position have you occupied in the Philippine Islands?

Mr. Barrows: I went out to assist in organizing schools in the islands, and I continued in school work under the direction of Dr. Atkinson until October of last year, when I was placed in charge of this new bureau organized by the Commission for the investigation of conditions and the recommendation of legislation for the pagan and Mohammedan tribes of the archipelago, the non-Christian tribes. . . .

The dominant element have wealth, they live in handsome houses, and they have very great social influence.

My observation, speaking about the historical condition, is that they are directly descended, or at least their social prestige is a direct inheritance, from the conditions which the Spaniards found there three hundred years ago.

Sen. Hale: What are the rest?

Mr. Barrows: The rest are a population who have no education, who have no wealth, and who are controlled economically and socially by the upper class, or, as it is called, the *gente ilustrada* — the illustrious class.

* Biographical details are contained in the testimony.

I thought it necessary to preface any remarks I might make with this explanation.

Sen. Hale: I think we understand now your statement as to these two classes. Now, state your observations as to those two classes, their conditions, and their sympathies, and all that, so far as you know.

Sen. Rawlins: In those provinces which you visited, as the result of your own observations.

Mr. Barrows: The *gente ilustrada*, this upper class, is very ambitious. That is one of its first qualities, I think, that strikes one. They are keenly ambitious — ambitious for education, ambitious for participation in the political affairs of the islands. They are willing to make large sacrifices in order to secure what we must all, I think, regard as a legitimate field for their aspirations. They are exceedingly hospitable; they are an exceedingly pleasing people; they will entertain you, not only royally, but with sincere hospitality. They are among the most charming people I have ever met. I think they will compare favorably with the similar class in Japan, at least in the matter of intellectual qualities.

Sen. Hale: What is your observation about their feeling with reference to our invasion there?

Mr. Barrows: I think the feeling of this class, which is really the only class we have to consider, has undergone several changes since American occupation.

Going back a little from my own experience, from the fall of 1898, through the period of active fighting, it was for the most part one of bitter hatred, and was ——

Sen. Hale: In this class?

Mr. Barrows: Yes, sir. There is an element among them, and that element comprises some of the most brilliant minds among them, the best educated among them, who were very early friendly to us or at least were desirous of giving us a trial. But I think the feeling among the great majority of them was one of very great hostility to us through the year 1899 and through a large part of the year 1900.

This was due, in my opinion, to a misunderstanding. They did not know us and we did not know them. There is really no person in the world, so far as I know, who knew both us and them. The foreign element in the Philippine Islands did not know us and really had no correct comprehension of our purposes. There were foreigners, certainly, who knew us, but who did not know the Filipino. The consequence was, for two years the Americans and this controlling class in the Philippine Islands labored under very great misapprehension of each other. This would apply to the Spanish element in the Philippines. One has only to consult the last report of the Philippine Commission to observe the calumnies of the Spanish people in the Philippines addressed to the Filipino and treating of the Americans. . . .

Sen. Hale: Will you give instances, not introducing any new matter? State about the time when you think you perceived a change and in what that change has consisted, and why you think it has changed and what evidence you have of it.

Mr. Barrows: The real outward and visible change became apparent, I think, in the winter of 1900–1901. The first widespread evidence of it that I witnessed myself was the celebration of Washington's birthday by the Federal party in Manila at that time. That was about the time of the organization of the Federal party. The people assembled there in very large numbers. There must have been thousands of them upon the Luneta, and they listened with interest and enthusiasm to the addresses of Governor Wright and various Filipinos, and with great sympathy, apparently, with the purposes for which they called them together, which was peace.

Sen. Hale: I am not going to ask about any new matter. I wish you would go through and stick to your point about the upper class and tell us what evidences you have of the change in the feeling of the upper class.

Mr. Barrows: I have talked with members of the upper class in a good many different towns in the provinces of Luzon of which I have spoken. In almost every case they have been members of the Federal party and have accepted its program. In some cases they have voluntarily discussed the conditions under which government is now organizing there, and have expressed themselves as being satisfied and as being hopeful for a large measure of political activity for the Filipinos. . . .

Sen. Hale: Now go on and complete what you have to say about the upper class and then come back and take up the other class, and then when you get through we will cross-examine you.

Mr. Barrows: This upper class possesses an influence over the lower class which I think we have been slow to appreciate. In the beginning of my remarks I was about to speak of the class who were under a bonded indebtedness, who were in a semifree condition when the Spaniards arrived there. That class still exists and in my own observation it is very considerable.

Sen. Beveridge: Do you mean when the Spaniards arrived in the islands?

Mr. Barrows: When the Spaniards arrived in the islands there was a semifree class and a class of outright slaves. This semifree class, as I say, is large at the present time. I do not know how the condition of this class arose, but it is evident that a man of the *gente ilustrada* can claim the services on special occasions of large numbers of hombres, as they are called, or the *gente baja*.

Sen. Hale: You are speaking of the present condition?

Mr. Barrows: The present condition.

Sen. Hale: How large is this class?

Mr. Barrows: The class in a semifree condition?

Sen. Hale: Yes.

Mr. Barrows: I have no method of estimating its numbers.

Sen. Hale: The witness has stated that the upper class he refers to will be in the proportion of about a dozen families in a town of eight or ten or twelve thousand people, and now he is talking of another class which is called the semifree class. I want you to describe them and tell us what the proportions are and what you have observed about them as to their feeling toward us.

Sen. Carmack: I should like to know in this connection how he differentiates this semifree class from the other class. What is the badge of their semiservitude?

Mr. Barrows: There is in their position no apparent hardship that I have observed.

Sen. Beveridge: But their services may be claimed?

Mr. Barrows: Their services can be called upon under a variety of circumstances, and while in answer to the question I am unable to say how numerous they are, I met with that class of people in every town with which I have become at all connected.

Sen. Carmack: What fixes the right of a man in the upper class to demand the services of one particular man in the lower class and not the services of another man?

Mr. Barrows: In many cases I know it to be debt. In other cases I am unable to account for it unless it is a historic ——

Sen. Beveridge: Custom?

Mr. Barrows: Custom.

Sen. Carmack: How does that custom fix itself upon one man and not another?

Mr. Barrows: When the Spaniards arrived there it was inheritable; a man inherited that condition, and I am inclined to think that the same fact prevails today — that a person may inherit a condition of obligation.

Sen. Carmack: A sort of feudal villenage? Is it attached to land in any way?

Mr. Barrows: I think not.

Sen. Beveridge: More like the clans?

Mr. Barrows: I think it is possibly economic.

Sen. Hale: It is individual?

Mr. Barrows: It is possibly something like the peonage of Mexico.

Sen. Beveridge: Still the fact exists?

Mr. Barrows: The fact I am certain of.

Sen. Hale: It exists to some extent?

Mr. Barrows: To some extent.

Sen. Hale: How do these people feel?

Mr. Barrows: They do not express a great amount of feeling. What I wish to bring out is that they do as the *gente ilustrada* tell them or influence them to do, both in matters of public concern and in private matters, matters of small range of interest.

Sen. Hale: Have they been drawn upon in any way to take place or office under the government?

Mr. Barrows: To a limited extent. In the organization of the municipalities, where there are positions known as the *consejales* or councillors, you will find people whom you will ascertain to have come up from the ranks of the *gente baja*. I think there is the hopeful thing in connection with the matter, that there is a movement from the *gente baja* into the higher class. I have in mind one Filipino general of the lower class of society who is now a man of very great influence, and who fought us determinedly, and who since the surrender has been a very staunch friend of ours: I refer to General Geronimo, who was in command of the Filipino forces when General Lawton was killed at San Mateo.

Sen. Carmack: It is a class not without ambition?

Mr. Barrows: Not without ambition. We see the ambition of this class in the parents bringing their children to school, desiring education for them, desiring to improve their condition. There is a strong desire among them for social betterment.

Sen. Carmack: Is there any feeling of hatred between them and the other class?

Mr. Barrows: As a whole I should say decidedly not.

Sen. Carmack: Do the relations between them seem to be kindly?

Mr. Barrows: Yes, sir; kindly.

Sen. Beveridge: Is the ambition of which you speak a class ambition or individual ambition?

Mr. Barrows: I should say that ambition was the prevailing characteristic of the Filipino. You find it in all classes. In some cases it takes the form of a desire to better himself in a material way. There is considerable mobility of labor in the Philippines. For instance, the Ilocano population of the northwest coast can now be found in a great many places throughout Luzon engaged in service of one kind and another. They have moved from their homes at considerable sacrifices for the sake of bettering themselves materially.

Sen. Beveridge: So there has begun to be a weaving in of the people among each other which did not prevail before?

Mr. Barrows: There has, I think.

Sen. Hale: Now, you have described two very limited classes. Now, what is your observation about the mass of population in the provinces that you have studied?

Mr. Barrows: The great mass of people are included under the term *gente baja*. They are not cultivated, educated, nor well-to-do. Some of them are agriculturists and own their own little farms. Many of them, of course, are fishermen. Others of them pursue other pursuits — domestic service, cattle raising to a limited extent. I think they all, however, would be included, all except this upper, cultivated, well-to-do class, or grouped in the class *gente baja*. In this class of *gente baja* there does exist a class who are only partially free.

Sen. Hale: I am directing your attention to the great number who neither belong to the upper class, the very few, or the half-free class, and I wish you would state to the committee the reasons for your belief as to what their feeling is, as you have observed it, with reference to our advance in the islands — how much you have been with them, how much you have talked with them. They are not an educated class, I take it.

Mr. Barrows: They are not the class with whom one ordinarily comes in contact in going into a town. Quite naturally, you would go to the official class first, and then your acquaintance reaches out to those who can speak Spanish and those who would naturally come to present themselves.

Sen. Hale: Have you had sufficient means of observation so that you think you can state what is the present feeling of the people?

Mr. Barrows: Of the great mass?

Sen. Hale: Yes; with reference to our invasion.

Mr. Barrows: They have followed, I think, the feeling of the more influential class, and their present attitude is one where they are desirous of peace (so that they can pursue their normal activities) and of compliance.

Sen. Rawlins: The question of Senator Hale was, "How do you know that?"

Sen. Hale: I want you to give your observations and the extent of your observations — why you have come to this conclusion.

Mr. Barrows: I base my conclusions, so far as that is concerned upon the fact that in any province, say of northern Luzon, where the influential class has become reconciled to the American authorities and where the insurrectionary leaders who have been out leading forces have surrendered, and almost in every case thereafter worked in harmony with governmental forces, in those provinces there has immediately occurred a subsidence of revolt and violence and armed activity.

Sen. Hale: And resistance?

Mr. Barrows: And resistance.

Sen. Carmack: In other words, whenever their leaders have ceased to be in active hostility, the people have no longer been in open and active hostility?

Mr. Barrows: Yes, sir; that is the case precisely.

Sen. Carmack: That would not necessarily argue a change in the sentiments of the people, would it?

Mr. Barrows: No, sir; no intelligent change.

Sen. Carmack: Any people would require leadership for organized hostility.

Mr. Barrows: The great mass which forms the population of the Philippines has simply followed closely the directions and the feelings of its leaders.

Sen. Carmack: You think they have sympathized with the feelings of their leaders? Is it true throughout the islands that they have simply accepted the views and adopted the feelings and sympathized with the feelings of their leaders? Has that been the conduct of the masses of the people?

Mr. Barrows: I should say so, Senator.

Sen. Hale: You do not find, when the leaders of authority and influence as well as the military leaders have come in and submitted and given signs of their acquiescence, that other leaders come in in their places and still keep the people hostile? You think the people follow their leaders?

Mr. Barrows: That has been the result, I think, in every province of Luzon where surrenders have been brought about.

Sen. Culberson: The leading military officers, or some of them at all events, in the United States say that this feeling of reconciliation upon the part of the upper or wealthy class is merely apparent and feigned; that really the true sentiment is yet one of hostility. If that be the case ———

Sen. Beveridge: Of course ———

Sen. Culberson: Let me ask the question.

Sen. Beveridge: I have not interrupted you.

Sen. Culberson: You were about to, I thought.

Sen. Beveridge: Do not anticipate my interruption.

Sen. Culberson: I will if I think you are going to interrupt me.

Sen. Beveridge: If you can see what I am revolving in my mind, go ahead.

Sen. Culberson: Mr. Chairman, I do not want to say what I am rather inclined to say. Mr. Barrows, if that is true, if it is mere feigned reconciliation, then the lower classes are merely following, as you stated, I believe, the upper class. Now, I will ask if you agree with these military officers as to whether this feeling is feigned or real?

Sen. Beveridge: I think it is proper that the witness should know that no testimony of that kind has yet been given to the committee.

Mr. Barrows: It is very difficult, of course, for an American to penetrate the mind of a Filipino or of any one of the Malay races, so different from ours, but in my own view, and this is the view of almost every civilian worker in the islands, I think, there has been a very great hopefulness produced by the change of attitude which has taken place within the past twelve months. I would still be inclined to think that if we should alienate the controlling elements in the islands, thoroughly alienate them, they could arouse large districts there to insurrection. But at the present time the tendency is not toward any alienation. It is toward a warmer feeling and a feeling of more confidence.

Testimony of A. Lester Hazlett *

The Chairman: I have some papers here from the War Department. They send a copy of a report from Mr. Lester Hazlett, who was sent out by the Woman's Christian Temperance Union, as to investigations, as to moral conditions, and also some investigations caused by his report at Jolo; and an additional report as to Macabebe scouts. I will print these as part of the record.

A VIEW OF THE MORAL CONDITIONS EXISTING IN THE PHILIPPINES
By A. Lester Hazlett, A.M., Ph.D.

In accordance with the recommendation of Major General MacArthur (that a commission or committee be sent to the Philippine Islands to investigate the foundation for charges made against the military administration), and by the authority of the Woman's Christian Temperance Union of Columbus, Wis., I have made what I believe to be a most thorough examination into the moral condition of the city of Manila, together with a tour of the islands. And whereas it has been charged that "the military authorities have been guilty of licensing prostitution," that "houses of ill-fame have been authorized under the express direction and supervision of the American War Department," that they "require prostitutes to pay for a permit to land in the islands," and also "that the anticanteen law is openly violated," I have the honor to submit the following report of conditions as I have found them:

It must be understood that in no sense was I a government commissioner, neither was I appointed by the War Department. As a citizen, jealous of the good name of his country and anxious to know the truth of certain statements that have appeared from time to time in the press regarding government connivance with vice, I gladly accepted the opportunity to visit the archipelago, being properly credentialed by the W.C.T.U. of Columbus, Wis., and in accordance with the recommendations of General MacArthur as made by him while military governor of the Philippines.

The War Department very kindly extended to me the courtesy of transportation, and aside from this every dollar of expense, including the price of meals on board transport, was defrayed by myself. I make this statement simply in order that it may be understood that I was in no sense a government employee. This being the case, together with the fact

* Biographical details are contained in the testimony.

that I am a clergyman, and thus a civilian, it seemed to those most interested in my mission that the report rendered by me on my return would be perfectly impartial in character. . . .

I did not find Manila to be in the strictest sense a model city, but can truthfully say that in my judgment it is the peer of any American city of equal population in the matter of cleanliness and order, and I believe its moral tone to be such as to fairly challenge comparison with our best cities of 400,000 population. The police docket shows that the moral condition of the city is better than ever before since American occupation. The arrests for drunkenness have steadily decreased in number. Chief Curry, of the city police, told me that he has never known an officer to be resisted in making an arrest. This certainly speaks well for law and order. I looked over the police entries at the central station for December 3, 1901, and found forty as the total number of arrests for the day, in a city approximately 400,000, and nearly all of these were for petty offenses.

There is a total of 111 saloons in Manila, counting the restaurants, that have license to sell liquor. . . .

Probably in no other country in the world do white men become so degraded and demoralized, through associating with the natives, as in the Philippines, and nowhere else do they sink so quickly to the level of the native. I speak now of the lowest class of the Filipinos. Large numbers of Americans here are either married to, or else keep as mistresses, native women of the lowest class, who are mostly drawn from canteen keepers, camp followers, and prostitutes. A respectable native or mestizo woman would not live with an American and would hardly marry one, unless there was some great advantage to be gained, which is seldom the case. The women who consent to live with Americans are, as a rule, ignorant, lazy, and filthy in their habits, generally afflicted with some loathsome cutaneous disease, and it is hard to comprehend that an educated American, decently brought up, can live among dirty, frowzy natives, who have not one redeeming quality.

The querida system prevails to a large degree in the islands, and marriage in many instances has been made impossible in legal form by the exorbitant charge made by the padre for the performance of the marriage service. Unable to pay the fee, men and women simply consent to live together. However, as a rule, they are faithful to each other.

Often the question is asked: "Are the natives a moral people? Are they virtuous?" I would answer, Yes, as a whole. While in some localities girls can be purchased for immoral purposes, there are many places, like Tanay, on the Laguna de Bay, where no such thing is possible, and where the reverse of this obtains, the natives have been debauched by their conquerors.

All over the East concubinage is common between foreigners and native women, and especially is this true in Japan and China, where large numbers of unmarried white males keep native mistresses. This is not so largely practiced by the Filipino people, though there is much of it.

In Japan neither concubinage nor prostitution causes a woman to lose caste or necessarily implies disgrace, it being well known that the large proportion of Japanese women who have been concubines or prostitutes marry respectable Japanese, whereas to become a prostitute in the Philippines is to lose caste at once, and an inmate of a house of ill-fame cannot return to her people.

Prostitution in Japan has, from time immemorial, been a staté institution, and at the present time is practically so. Poverty is the general cause of prostitution in Japan, and it is still considered honorable for a daughter to enter a brothel for a certain specified time to repay a loan, advanced to discharge a parent's debts. The arrangements made between the inmate and the brothel keeper is in the form of a contract, and is equally binding upon both parties, and is strictly and fairly enforced by the local authorities.

Prostitution is not licensed in the Philippines, nor has it ever been since the islands came under our authority. It has been claimed by some that the liquor license which many of the houses have obtained are equivalent to a license to prostitution. This, however, can hardly be substantiated, as there are 11 houses that have not even a liquor license. There are 46 houses of ill-fame known to the police, and they are all in the San Paloc district. Twelve of them have a first-class liquor license, 23 have second-class liquor license, 11 native houses having no liquor license. The complete list of inmates were [sic] as follows, November 4, 1901:

Americans	14
Europeans	2
Spanish	1
Russians	12
Japanese	124
Roumanians	3
Hungarians	1
Australians	1
Italians	2
Turkish	1
Filipinos	72
Total	233

. . . A general movement had been started, before I left Manila, to break up the querida system; many arrests had already been made. It cannot be said that the city authorities encourage prostitution. Women who are discovered to be prostitutes are not permitted to land. Many do land, however, under false representation, some coming presumably as nurses, and others impersonating schoolteachers. Many discovered to be prostitutes have been deported from the islands.

That there should exist a district devoted to this nefarious traffic in virtue is a blot upon the fairness of the well-kept city, and a reproach to our civilization. I recognize the fact that here, as elsewhere, this is a very difficult problem to solve. To impose fines, as will be done in the near future, for violation of the proposed antiprostitution law, will not be prohibitive, no matter how high the fine may be. I sincerely pray that the good people will lose no opportunity, by press or otherwise, to strike at this hideous evil. . . .

While the military government did not and the civil government does not provide for the maintenance of this infamy, there is a good deal of wrong to be righted, and we should earnestly seek for a good and efficient method for the total expurgation of the dreadful evil. . . . My observation led me to believe that extraordinary efforts are being made to lessen the amount and horrors of the most awful diseases. I am persuaded that the results have not been all that was expected, and although the authorities have done what they could, the results of this terrible evil, in the matter of disease of body, is very great, to say nothing of that of the mind. . . .

To arrive at a safe conclusion in regard to the "canteen" question as related to the Philippine Islands is not an easy matter. I have sought to arrive at a just conclusion by getting the views of the most efficient, sober, and useful officers and men of the Army, at the same time keeping my eyes open to conditions as I found them, from Luzon on the north to San Boango on the south.

I believe, after a careful study of this great question, with unbiased judgment, I can truthfully say that to revoke the anticanteen law would be to take a step backward. Never was the health and morale of the Army better than it is today. The records of medical corps and those of hospitals give ample proof of this. One of the arguments used by those who plead for the beer canteen is that the proceeds of such a canteen, being turned into the mess fund, gives the soldiers a more varied ration. And it is because of this that many of the enlisted men long for its reestablishment. I have proven beyond question that the same result can be obtained without the beer.

I am a firm believer in nothing but a canteen or exchange in which no liquor brewed or distilled shall be sold. Colonel Beck, at Binan, has such an exchange under his directions. Various soft drinks, with ice cream and other luxuries, are sold. As a result, a very neat sum is realized, which is each month added to the mess fund at Pasig. Captain Bishop maintains a similar canteen or exchange, the profits of which aggregate one hundred dollars per month. This is a good net return, when we consider that there are but seventy men here at any time, while often it is much less. Captain Bishop is not adverse to the use of liquor, but he assured me that the beer canteen was in no wise essential to the comfort of his men; he wanted a sober troop. . . .

There should be a soldier's clubroom at every post, with provision for innocent games, abundance of reading matter, with the enforcement of the rule against gambling. It is argued that if the men have access to the canteen, where beer is sold, they will spend their evenings quietly, and, while they will drink moderately, they will retire when quarters are sounded comparatively, if not entirely, sober; whereas if they spend the evening in a saloon outside the post, they may fail to hear the bugle sound to quarters, and then, because "they are in for it, anyway," as they express it, "make a night of it." This may be true or not; it seems to me to be the duty of good government to protect the youth, and the temptations of the canteen for those who have never drank are very great, and it is the welfare of the American boy that should receive our attention.

Those that enlist in the army as drunkards will not be apt to reform; those who are accustomed to drink will obtain it in some way as long as it is manufactured. The most terrible of all intoxicants used by our soldiers is the native vino, the excessive drinking of which causes insanity, several cases of which came under my notice. This drink, together with "tuba," is extensively used by the natives. One manufacturer of vino in Manila said that if his business was closed he would lose more than $100,000 in six months.

At Jolo I find the unique condition of absolute prohibition. . . . At the abolition of the canteen the last place where liquor could be bought was closed. The territory surrounding the city being a Government reserve, the sale of intoxicants is forbidden, and as natives are searched before being admitted to the city, every old toper is perforce a teetotaler. As a result of the enforced abstinence the troops have most excellent health.

I went to the islands an ardent anti-expansionist; I return a firm believer in the policy of the Administration. I frankly confess that I had a wrong idea of conditions in the archipelago. I believed the people ready for self-government; now I know that while some of them are, the great mass of the people are not capable of it; but they will be, and that, perhaps, before a generation shall have passed. The Filipino is fully as bright as the Japanese. They learn quickly, and are extremely anxious to acquire. God has given us a wonderful opportunity, for which I am sure He will hold us strictly accountable. To refuse to accept this heaven-bestowed privilege to elevate to a like plane with ourselves a people ready to learn and anxious to secure all that is requisite for the building of a nation is to prove unworthy of so high an honor.

I went to Manila with the thought that Admiral Dewey should have sailed away after the destruction of the Spanish fleet, but am now convinced that future generations of Americans, and Filipinos as well, will arise to bless and honor him because he did not. . . .

EPILOGUE

The hearings were adjourned on June 28, 1902. Their immediate impact was blunted by the passage a few days later of the Philippine Government Act — and the issuance of a Presidential Proclamation on July 4 formally ending the Philippine Insurrection and providing an amnesty for the rebels. The Act ratified all the actions undertaken up to that time by the President and the Philippine Commission. It made the inhabitants of the islands citizens of the Philippine Islands entitled to the protection of the United States. It extended to the Filipinos the provisions of the Bill of Rights, but only as the instructions to the Commission in 1900 had defined them: the traditional Anglo-Saxon guarantees excepting trial by jury and the right to bear arms. The Act also provided for a biennial, elective assembly and for an upper house consisting of members of the Commission. The judicial system created by the Commission was to be continued, although appeals to the United States Supreme Court would now be allowed in certain instances. In sum, the Act may be said to have satisfied, after a fashion, the aims of both the imperialists and the anti-imperialists.

The fact that the hearing had been closed to the public prevented their frequently sensational substance from becoming the stuff of newspaper headlines. And as the Philippine Islands moved in successive stages toward the full independence they received in 1946, the memory of the Insurrection grew dimmer. In the face of another conqueror, Japan, the United States became, by one of those strange about-faces of history, the redeemer of the islands, and Arthur MacArthur's son, Douglas, became a revered figure among Filipinos.

Today, however, these hearings are as apposite as they were almost three-quarters of a century ago. They show the inherent awkwardness — to which most imperialists were blind — in seeking to impose the cultural outlook of the conqueror upon the conquered. They show vividly the effects of American racial prejudice in making this cultural contact ferociously and unnecessarily violent. They show in lessons only partially learned at the time the severe limitations even of advanced military technology in cooling the molten nationalism then beginning to flow in nonindustrial lands. They show how a nation's good intentions fall short of fulfillment when the character of the means for implementing them are made to seem unimportant. They show, in an impressive flash of irony, that even as independence was being denied the Filipinos, the

171

Senate Committee, in calling to account the nation's uniformed giants, was serving and strengthening the republican principle that the military arm of government must be subservient to the civilian authority.

Finally, the hearings reveal the deep conflict in the American mind between respect for republicanism and lust for imperium. Nevertheless, Americans who feel dismay will note, and possibly with satisfaction, that the imperialistic mood lasted only briefly. By the time that Aguinaldo died in 1964 he had become by adoption an *American* hero, having once, unknowingly, kept bright when it was in danger of eclipse, the American ideal of liberty for all.